# Developing Electric Power

Thirty Years
of World Bank Experience

A World Bank Publication

# Developing Electric Power

Thirty Years
of World Bank Experience

*Hugh Collier*

*Published for The World Bank*
The Johns Hopkins University Press
*Baltimore and London*

The Johns Hopkins University Press
Baltimore, Maryland 21218, U.S.A.

*Editor*    Jane H. Carroll
*Binding design*    Joyce C. Eisen

**Library of Congress Cataloging in Publication Data**

Collier, Hugh, 1920–
   Developing electric power.

   Includes index.
   1. Electric power—Developing countries.   2. World
Bank.   I. Title.
TK153.C557   1984          338.4′736362          83-22655
ISBN 0-8018-3222-5

# *Contents*

Preface                                                                    *vii*

Introduction                                                                 *3*

1. A General Perspective                                                     *7*

The World Bank as a Project Lender    *7*
The Project Cycle    *9*
The Evolution of Electric Power Systems    *12*
The Choice of Projects for Lending    *14*
Bank Activities Other than Lending    *17*
Volume and Distribution of Lending for Power    *18*
The Trend of Power Lending    *20*
Bank Disbursements and Investment in Developing Countries    *22*


2. Financial Policies and Results                                           *24*

Evolution of the Bank's Approach to Power Tariffs    *24*
Utility Rates and Economic Efficiency    *30*
Other Financial Covenants    *32*
The Application of Financial Policies    *33*
Some Major Borrowing Countries    *49*
Perspective on Financial Results    *64*
Progress with Efficiency Pricing    *65*
The Effects of Financial Stringency    *66*


3. Institutional Development in the Power Industry                          *68*

The Power Agency    *70*
The Organization of the Power Industry    *79*


4. Investment Planning and Project Implementation                          *98*

The Evolution of Project Appraisal in Electric Power    *98*
Extensions of the System: Rural Electrification    *102*
Forecasting Demand    *104*
The Execution of Projects    *107*
Effects of Cost and Time Overruns    *113*

5. The Bank's Role in Power Development: Past and Future          *121*

   Changing Approaches to Development     *121*
   Electric Power and the Energy Sector     *126*
   Investment Requirements for Electric Power     *129*
   The Role of the Bank     *131*


Appendix. Country Summaries                                        *145*

   Asia     *145*
   Africa     *149*
   Middle East and North Africa     *155*
   Latin America     *158*


Appendix Tables                                                    *161*

Index                                                              *183*

# *Preface*

The World Bank has long been conscious of the desirability of giving a public account of its operations—an explanation of its policies and objectives as they are reflected in the projects it assists and their results. I first became interested in the possibility of writing about the Bank's experience during the late 1970s when I was assigned to the Bank's Operations Evaluation Department, which is responsible, among other things, for auditing Bank-assisted projects. With encouragement from some colleagues but also with some trepidation, I set about collecting the material which eventually resulted in this book.

The book is likely to be of interest principally to those concerned with foreign aid and the operations of aid agencies. Since it deals with electric power I hope it will also be of some value to those concerned with electric power development in Third World countries. It is not, however, a technical book and does not assume any familiarity with the electric power industry on the reader's part.

One problem with a study of this kind is how much ground to cover. On the one hand, the Bank's lending operations involve so many projects and countries that it is impossible to be comprehensive. On the other hand, in too much of the discussion of the effectiveness of foreign aid, and of the Bank in particular, critics cite a project which they claim has failed and defenders respond with one or a few which they argue have succeeded. To avoid this inconclusiveness some attempt at a wider perspective is essential. I have therefore tried to cover most of the major borrowing countries, at least to some extent, and enough of the others to avoid any suspicion of using a biased selection. This concern is also the reason for including in the appendixes brief descriptions of operations in selected countries.

The character of the book as an objective account of policies and events has meant that some aspects of the Bank's relations with its borrowers are perhaps underemphasized. Some projects proceed along the pipeline from conception to construction and operation meeting few problems and marked by easy cooperation on both sides. Others sometimes become embroiled in disputes of one kind or another, with both sides taking apparently irreconcilable positions. This can lead to tension, anxious and difficult decisions, and sometimes even high drama before a compromise can be hammered out. I have not attempted to describe such encounters in any detail—even assuming I could—although it should be clear to the reader where they must have occurred.

The author of a book such as this is peculiarly dependent on assistance from others. It deals with many projects and countries and with various subjects including financial analysis, utility economics, investment planning, and occasionally with the technology of electric power supply. There are specialists in the Bank who are more familiar with each of these subjects and countries than I am myself. The Bank's Energy Department under its director, Yves Rovani, provided me with the necessary support and information; I received much assistance from the department's power staff, particularly Richard Sheehan, James Fish, Edward Moore, Jeremy Warford, Mohan Munasinghe, and John Davis. Many others commented on the book or on specific points, including Warren Baum, Jack Beach, Ralph Bloor, Roger Carmignani, Ricardo Halperin, Arturo Israel, James Jennings, Salvatore Liberatore, Ipe Mathai, Bernard Montfort, Rafael Moscote, Robert Reekie, Arturo Roa, Robert Sadove, Ralph Turvey, Mervyn Weiner, Everardo Wessels, and Hans Wyss. All these did their best to help me get the facts straight and the perspectives clear. The burden of typing was cheerfully done by Sibophay Kong, Novikio Clark, and Rita Capon, and special thanks are due to Kamlesh Gillespie, who spent many hours searching for and assembling information and data.

For most of the time I worked on this book I was a staff member of the Bank and hence had complete access to all its reports and files. No one in the Bank ever attempted to influence or censor what I wrote. Nevertheless, as a staff member of the Bank for many years, I might possibly be regarded by some as less than completely objective. For this reason I have tried to let the facts and analyses speak for themselves. If the reader does come across an opinion in these pages, however, it is of course mine, not that of the Bank.

*Hugh Collier*

October 1983

# Developing Electric Power

Thirty Years
of World Bank Experience

# Introduction

THE PURPOSE OF THIS BOOK is to describe and extract some lessons from the World Bank's lending for electric power development, to review not only the objectives the Bank has deemed important for the success of its operations in this field, but also the policies and methods it has followed to reach those objectives, and to provide some assessment of the results. The Bank is the world's largest development agency and can reasonably claim to be the most influential. It is known to have high standards of project appraisal. It also has policies and requirements that it tries to ensure are followed in the execution and operation of the projects it finances. It has gathered experience over more than thirty years with lending operations in every part of the Third World. It claims that its contribution to developing countries is not confined to the funds it makes available but that it also strengthens its borrowers' ability to carry out projects; that is, "institution building" is an important aspect of its work. What, then, is the result of all this activity? What are the Bank's appraisal methods and what results have they achieved? What policies has it followed? How well have they achieved their objectives, and what does this indicate about the best methods to develop electric power? This book tries to answer, or to provide the material for an answer, to this kind of question.

The extensive literature on foreign aid contains remarkably little in the way of "postevaluation" material. The process of growth in developing countries has been intensively studied both in theory and in practice, as well as in general and as applied to specific countries. The World Bank has contributed not a little to this literature. It has issued numerous books, pamphlets, and working papers intended for the general reader and the professional economist on all kinds of development-related topics. Its Country Economic Reports describe and analyze the situation in specific countries. In 1978 it began a series of annual *World Development Reports* that comment on the problems and progress of the various parts of the Third World. In common with other international and national aid agencies, it issues annual reports that contain all the easily ascertainable facts on matters such as how much money has been committed to which countries and for what projects, and that often describe in general terms the broad objectives and policies of the Bank. But there is little available on how projects and policies actually work out. *The World Bank since Bretton Woods*, by Edward S. Mason and Robert E. Asher, appeared in 1973.[1] It contains two chapters entitled "Beginnings of a Balance Sheet"; the first consists of five country vignettes, and the second is a brief account of the sectoral impact of operations. At the beginning of the first of these chapters the authors remark, "Our objective has been to analyze the Bank's policies and their evolution rather than to make a systematic appraisal of its lending operations. Had we attempted the latter, we would have found ourselves on more treacherous terrain, both because of the scarcity of 'hard' data and the difficulty of interpreting such data as can be addressed." This book can thus be regarded as an initial foray into this more treacherous terrain.

The scarcity of hard data has been somewhat relieved since 1973. Over the past decade there has been a growing emphasis on monitoring and evaluation of all kinds of governmental economic and social programs to assess their effectiveness. These methods are also being introduced by foreign aid agencies to assess their own operations and are beginning to be used by some developing countries. The Bank established an Operations Evaluation Unit in its Programming and Budgeting Department in 1970, and this was later expanded into a separate department.[2] A major part of this department's work is to issue Project Performance Audit Reports (PPARS) on every project after it is completed. Since 1974 the Operations Evaluation Department (OED) has prepared an annual review of the PPARS for the previous calendar year, and those for 1977 and subsequent years have been published. They contain a considerable amount of information on the projects covered, but they reflect the project-by-project approach which underlies the evaluation system and which is designed to compare the results of each project with the estimates and intentions at the time of appraisal.

Although comparisons of this nature are valuable, they examine the immediate output of the project, not the effect of this output on the rest of the economy via forward and backward linkages and so on. In this study also, it is simply assumed that an adequate and reliable supply of electric power at a reasonable cost is a necessary condition for economic growth— no matter what kind of growth or which strategy was used to achieve it. This seems a reasonably safe assumption. The effect of linkages arises in a meaningful sense only in connection with rural electrification. Then the

1. (Washington, D.C.: Brookings Institution.)
2. An account of its objectives and methods may be found in the pamphlet "Operations Evaluation—Standards and Procedures" (Washington, D.C.: World Bank, 1979).

question is whether the additional benefits (that is, the benefits in addition to the value of the electricity delivered) exceed or fall short of the subsidies required to keep the cost to consumers low enough to ensure that the electricity will indeed be used. These additional benefits may be either social, such as raising the quality of life in the countryside, or economic, such as having a catalytic effect on local agriculture or small industry. This study does deal with the rural electrification loans the Bank has made and with some of the problems encountered. But its chief concern is the process by which capital, technology, organization, and economic analysis are combined to provide power for the various classes of consumers. It is not concerned with the purposes to which the consumers may put it.

The concepts essential to any evaluation of the Bank's operations[3] — such concepts as the efficient use of the Bank's funds, the financial soundness of the borrower, and the economic justification of projects — can be fully understood only as they apply to specific cases. For this reason it is necessary to concentrate on a specific type of operation. The Bank's lending for electric power has some advantages for a case study of this kind. Its problems are reasonably typical of most infrastructure investment, which has claimed a large proportion of Bank lending, particularly in the early years. Because electric power was one of the most important areas of lending from the start of World Bank operations, many of the Bank's basic policies arose out of its experience in this field. Finally, the importance of electric power has recently been reemphasized because of the world energy situation.

Since the purpose of the book is to set out and analyze the Bank's response to major problems in the expansion of electric power systems, the approach is a functional one. Each issue is presented separately, together with illustrative case material, and the evolution of relevant Bank policies is discussed. The issues themselves are divided into three broad categories. First are the financial issues. Electric power is a very capital-intensive economic activity and financial problems are of paramount importance; they arose immediately the Bank began to lend for electric power and have continued at the center of its concern ever since. The second group of problems revolves around the organization of the power

---

3. Throughout this book references to the Bank and Bank loans include the International Development Association (IDA) and IDA credits. IDA is the Bank's soft-loan affiliate and makes credits, repayable over fifty years, without interest but with a service charge of 0.75 percent a year. The difference between Bank loans, which are made on conventional terms, and IDA credits is significant for the debt service of the borrowing country, but it does not affect the project, the agency carrying it out, the Bank's project appraisal methods, or its project policies, which are the main subject of this book.

industry, whether an individual utility or a country-wide system of many utilities. This subject is often referred to as "institution building," although in the case of electric power the financial situation so influences the efficiency of an agency that it could be regarded as an aspect of institution building. The third set of problems concerns investment planning, project appraisal, and the execution of investment projects. The successful solution of these problems—that is, the execution of an economically justified investment program—is the ultimate objective to which all the other factors, financial and institutional, contribute. The last chapter summarizes the Bank's policies and experience in power lending and sets them in the context of the evolution of general ideas on economic development and the Bank's response to them.

To grapple with the issues in investing for electric power, it is necessary to set out the main features of the electricity supply industry. In so doing, the emphasis has been placed on the financial, institutional, and economic problems with relatively little space devoted to technical and engineering matters. This is not because the technology of electric power is not important or because the Bank is not concerned with it. But the technology is not altered when transferred to developing countries, and the process of acquiring the necessary expertise is not essentially different from the process in developed countries. The transfer of technology is carried out partly by engineering consultants working with power agencies and partly by manufacturers of equipment. In addition, the agencies usually have their own training programs and send personnel to developed countries when necessary to familiarize them with new technologies. This transfer is an essential part of the investment process and takes place whatever the source of finance. The role of the engineers on the Bank staff is primarily to ensure that the project is technically sound. They also participate in many discussions of technical issues during the preparation and supervision of projects, but they are not the primary channel for the transfer of technical assistance. The role of the Bank in pressing for financial and organizational improvement might not be played at all, however, if finance were provided by commercial sources.

As mentioned already, many of the Bank's major lending policies were either devised in connection with its power lending or are reflected in this experience. This study is not, however, intended to cover all the Bank's lending policies or to assess how they have been applied in other sectors. Some background information has been provided on general policy matters only when it was necessary to understand their significance for lending for power.[4]

4. For further information and discussion of the Bank's lending policies, see Mason and Asher, *The World Bank since Bretton Woods,* particularly chaps. 6, 8, 9, 10, 11, 13, and 14.

# 1. A General Perspective

THE WORLD BANK was conceived by its founders as primarily a financing institution whose major purpose was to bring stability to international capital markets. Its Articles of Agreement stated, however, that its loans should normally be for specific projects. This provision reflected the widespread conviction that international capital markets had collapsed during the depression of the 1930s largely because the proceeds of loans had been used for unsound purposes. An essential and novel element of Bank lending was therefore that the Bank should know what its loans were used for and should ensure that they were for productive purposes.

## The World Bank as a Project Lender

It soon became apparent that it was not enough simply to make an economic appraisal of the proposed project and then, if the appraisal were favorable, make a loan. To carry out an investment project—and to use the Bank's money "with due attention to considerations of economy and efficiency," as required by its Articles—the borrower had to have the necessary organization, management, and experienced manpower. The Bank soon realized that not every borrower could be assumed to possess these essentials, and its appraisal reports began to assess not only the soundness of the project but also the capacity of the borrower to carry it out. Similarly, loan agreements began to contain covenants stipulating how the borrower should carry out the project (for example, with the assistance of consultants) or that certain measures should be taken to improve the efficiency of the borrowing agency. In this way the notion of project appraisal was extended. In 1960 the Bank's first systematic statement of its appraisal methods stated that as many as six different aspects of projects had to be investigated.[1] Only two criteria had to do

---

1. "Some Techniques of Development Lending" (September 1960). The substance of what was said on project appraisal in this pamphlet was later incorporated into "The Project Cycle" by Warren C. Baum, *Finance & Development* (June 1970 and December 1978). Baum's article has since been revised and issued as a booklet, "The Project Cycle" (Washington, D.C.: World Bank, 1983).

7

with the merits of the project itself, while the remaining four concerned the capability of the borrower and the way the project would be carried out.

The first concern was the calculation of the economic return on the project. The second was the technical aspect which included the cost estimate, possible need for engineering consultants, and so on. The third and fourth were the managerial and organizational aspects which later tended to be treated together as institutional issues. The fifth was called "commercial aspects," but this really referred to the proposed procurement procedures; in later expositions this was treated as a matter of implementation rather than appraisal. Sixth was the financial aspects, which included whether the investment cost of the project was adequately covered and whether the prospective operations of the borrower would generate an adequate margin to meet fixed financial obligations.

Although this general description of the objectives and methods of project appraisal was formulated in 1960, it is still a good account of the Bank's approach. Within this approach, however, significant changes of emphasis have occurred as a result of the Bank's experience, changes in developing countries, and changing attitudes about the appropriate objectives of foreign assistance. One such change has been the gradual broadening of the concept of what was relevant for project appraisal. The notion that a project should be considered in a wider sectoral context is derived from economic analysis, which may have more or less validity in specific cases. But in the case of electric power, as systems expanded, a wider approach became necessary and individual projects had to be appraised as part of an overall investment program. More recently, the context has been further expanded to present investment in electric power as part of the whole energy picture.

Another change reflects the newer emphasis of development policy on alleviating poverty rather than on promoting economic growth as such. Attention is now paid to increasing the proportion of the population served by electric power, both by physically extending the system to rural areas and by making some power available to the poor in urban areas. Another development stems from the application of economic principles to utility operations: "cost-related" or "marginal-cost-based" electric power tariffs direct attention not just to the level of tariffs but to their structure as well. More attention to the environmental effects of projects is an indication of the growing concern of both developed and developing countries. The specific ways in which all these changes have been reflected in the Bank's lending operation will be taken up in subsequent chapters.

## The Project Cycle

The nature of the Bank as a project lender has determined its operational procedures. These have been described in general terms in some of its publications (see, for example, "The World Bank and International Finance Corporation," Washington, D.C., 1983), but the most systematic account of the way the Bank goes about its work is contained in "The Project Cycle" by Warren C. Baum (see note 1 above).

The cycle refers to the various stages through which an investment project passes from the time it is first identified as a need or an opportunity; these stages are usually listed as identification, preparation, appraisal, negotiation, implementation, and evaluation. After the initial identification there follows a period of preparation during which the project is investigated, the costs and benefits are estimated and compared with possible alternative projects, and any specific technical or institutional problems are studied and solutions proposed. This process culminates in the appraisal stage, in which the Bank prepares an appraisal report that analyzes the technical, institutional, economic, and financial characteristics of the project. The report deals with all the problems investigated during the preparation of the project and sets out the measures agreed on to deal with them. The appraisal report forms the basis for the final negotiations, sessions at which the Bank and the borrower agree on the legal documents.

By the time of negotiations it has almost always been established that the project is economically worthwhile and is, or can be made, acceptable to the Bank for financing. If for any reason a project is not satisfactory this generally becomes clear at an earlier stage, and either something is done to rectify the matter or the project is dropped. Thus in practice the negotiations between the Bank and its borrowers are normally not about whether a loan is to be made but about the steps which are necessary or desirable to ensure that the project can be carried out and operated satisfactorily. In the case of electric power projects, for example, a frequent subject of negotiation is the level of power tariffs and hence the revenues of the power agency. This is a crucial issue because it directly affects the financial soundness of the agency and the amount of money it can generate internally to help finance its investment program. In addition, any major problems concerning organization, the financial position of the borrower, official policy toward the power sector as a whole, or the planning of future investment may come up during negotiations. Normally agreement is reached on what is to be done to deal with them.

The negotiations result in a loan agreement, in which the Bank agrees to lend the borrower a given sum of money and the borrower undertakes to carry out the project described in some detail in a schedule to the loan agreement. The provisions of the loan agreements can generally be divided into three broad groups. First, standard provisions lay down the terms of the loan such as repayment period, payment dates, interest rate, disbursement procedures, and the right of the Bank to receive information about the project, to send its staff to visit it, and so on. Second, wherever relevant—and in all power loans—there are protective financial covenants designed to ensure that the borrower retains a sound financial position. Third, there are provisions concerned with procurement, the use of consulting engineers, or other aspects of how the project is to be carried out. The formal description of the project often covers not merely the investment project in the strict sense but also the technical assistance which the loan funds can be used to purchase. Technical assistance is usually provided by consultants and may cover a broad range of services such as engineering, management and organization, financial or account- ing procedures, the preparation and operation of training programs for the borrower's staff, or the study of future investment needs or of the structure of tariffs. The Bank's evolving policies are often revealed in the purposes to which its technical assistance funds are devoted and in the type of covenants appearing in its loan agreements.

After negotiations are completed the loan is normally approved by the Bank's Executive Directors, and the loan documents are signed by the Bank and the borrower without delay. After an interval, which may be as short as six to eight weeks, the loan is declared effective by the Bank and the borrower is entitled to draw upon it. In many cases the only condition the Bank requires before making a loan effective is the receipt of a legal opinion from the government of the borrowing country confirming that the loan documents are legally valid and binding. However, the Bank and the borrower may, and frequently do, agree on additional steps as a condition for the loan to become effective. For example, other loans necessary for the financing of the project may need to be concluded, legislation affecting the borrower may need amendment or enactment, or a specific increase in power tariffs may be necessary. Where conditions of this kind are laid down it takes longer, sometimes many months, before the loan becomes effective.

Once the loan has been declared effective the borrower can draw on the proceeds for the implementation of the project. While the project is being constructed, Bank staff visit the borrower periodically on so-called supervision missions.[2] These missions normally visit the borrowing country every six months. Their main purpose is "to help ensure that projects achieve their development objectives and, in particular, to work with the borrower to identify and deal with problems that arise during implementation. Thus supervision is primarily an exercise in collective problem solving, and as such is one of the most effective ways in which the Bank provides technical assistance to its member countries."[3] After the project is completed and the loan has been fully disbursed a project completion report is prepared by the Bank staff, and the Bank now requires its borrowers to prepare such reports as well. They are intended to compare the actual results of the project, particularly its costs and benefits, with those expected at the time of appraisal, and they form the basis of the Bank's postevaluation system. In this way, it is hoped that lessons can be learned from experience and incorporated into future projects.

The evaluation process is the final stage of the project cycle as it is normally described; the cycle then begins again with a new project. In the electric power sector this cyclical or continuous nature of the process is particularly marked. The demand for power grows continuously, and even though investment in power may be uneven or "lumpy," the process of investment planning and implementation tends to be continuous. Although investment planning studies undertaken by power agencies frequently cover a period of several years, the resulting plans have to be adjusted with the passage of time to account for changing costs or demands. Through the periodic supervision missions, Bank staff keep in touch with and to some extent participate in this investment and implementation process. Individual missions do not confine themselves to reviewing the progress of a specific project. They also become concerned with the steps necessary to plan and investigate the next project. In this way, particularly in large countries, the Bank is in continuous contact with its power borrowers, and there may be a number of projects in different stages of the project cycle. For this reason any evaluation of progress and results cannot be based on a single project. Only when the process of investment planning and

---

2. This is something of a misnomer; it derives from the idea of supervising the expenditure of funds in the sense of checking that they are not diverted to unauthorized uses. The implication is not that the Bank staff supervises the actions of the borrower. An attempt has been made to replace this term—at least for use outside the Bank—with the term "project review missions," which is a more accurate description.

3. Baum, "The Project Cycle," *Finance & Development.*

implementation is studied over a period that encompasses several projects can the patterns of change be seen.

## The Evolution of Electric Power Systems

The practical application of the Bank's project approach and the substantive problems with which it deals obviously vary according to the type of project. Some knowledge of the distinctive features of the electric power sector is therefore essential to an understanding of the Bank's objectives and policies in this field.

That electric power is a capital-intensive form of investment is well known. It has been regarded as particularly suitable to receive foreign aid since it involves a substantial transfer of resources. For this reason financial problems and policies have been the subject of considerable thought and discussion within the Bank and have occupied a prominent place in the Bank's relations with its borrowers.

The way in which electric power systems grow has peculiar characteristics that form the background to and are the subject of many of the policies and objectives of the Bank in this field. Since the Bank made its first power loan in 1948, the electric power systems of most developing countries have undergone a vast transformation. This change has naturally gone furthest in the more advanced, so-called middle-income countries, but in almost all developing countries the same kind of change is under way. The technology of electric power generation, transmission, and distribution imposes a typical pattern or process of development that can be seen, with individual variations, in all countries.

Thirty years ago in most developing countries the supply of electric power was confined to one or a few large towns. It was produced by small thermal or diesel plants or a small hydroelectric plant often developed to supply a single enterprise such as a cement mill or a mining operation. Since then the power sector in developing countries has become, or is on the way to becoming, an integrated network of various kinds of power plants operated and developed as a system.

Electric power was usually provided first to the capital city, sometimes by a government department or special agency established for the purpose, sometimes under a concession granted to a private company, often a subsidiary of some large utility company in North America or Europe. Industries and local authorities also generated power to meet their own needs since it often turned out to be more convenient to do so and no more expensive. But as the major consuming sectors expanded and as local industrial and commercial demands increased, it became worthwhile to take advantage of one of the most important economic features of electric power generation, namely, the great economies of scale. Consequently, new generating capacity might take the form of a hydropower plant on the most economic site or a large thermal plant whose location would be determined by the kind of fuel used. This requires the construction of high voltage transmission lines which then provide the opportunity to supply power to other consuming centers within economic distance of the main power line. In most countries this sort of development begins in several different areas. As the load increases, it becomes advantageous to link up areas, and eventually a nationwide integrated grid is constructed.

There are numerous benefits from a large integrated system. It becomes economic to construct very large plants. The proportion of reserve capacity required decreases since capacity in any part of the system can be used to make up for shortages, breakdowns, or maintenance in any other part. And the maximum advantage can be obtained by using different kinds of generating plant to supply base or peak loads. For all these reasons the economic pressure to construct an integrated system becomes very great. Physical construction, however, has to be accompanied by substantial institutional changes in the organization of the sector, the handling of its financial problems, and the planning and implementation of investment. These changes are generally more difficult to carry out than the physical construction, and the efficiency with which they are made may well determine the success of the whole system.

There is no generally agreed best method of organizing a country's power sector. In some countries there is only one agency, in which case the problem of coordination is minimal. In others there may be two or three agencies, each with different responsibilities; one may be responsible for operating the major power plants and the associated transmission network, while another or others may be responsible for the supply and distribution to the largest cities or industrial areas. In recent years some countries have established new agencies to promote rural electrification. In large countries several large utilities may supply different parts of the country, with numerous small public, and sometimes private, suppliers and distributors in small towns. Since the small companies have to purchase power from the large generating utilities, they are normally easily controlled, but coordinating the activities of a number of large utilities can be difficult. Some regulatory agency is needed with enough authority to ensure that the sector is operated and its expansion planned and implemented as a system. Such an agency may be part of a government ministry or established separately for the purpose. Utilities, even public ones, which are accustomed to running their affairs independently, may well resist the establishment of such authority. Consequently, the organizational changes necessary for the formation of an integrated network can be slow and painful to some of the participants.

These organizational changes must usually be matched by some financial changes. It becomes desirable to prepare the accounts of the various utilities in the system on a uniform basis. The terms on which power is to be purchased by one utility from another have to be agreed. Questions arise as to whether rates should be uniform and whether and how surplus earnings in some utilities should be used to meet the investment needs of others.

Finally and perhaps most important, the investment planning for an integrated network has to be system-wide. For a large network the questions of what types of plant to add next, where they should be, and when they will be needed become very complex. There may be hundreds of different options to be analyzed or at least explored. This is in sharp contrast to the situation in a small system where the next investment may be so obvious as hardly to require analysis.

In general terms, the final objective of all these changes is to provide sufficient coordination to ensure that activities which have to be carried out system-wide are implemented efficiently. Different countries, however, show considerable variation in how they approach this objective. Nevertheless, in the power sector, much of what is called institution building can fairly be regarded as the adaptation of existing institutions or the formation of new ones to bring about this process of integration and coordination. The Bank's role is frequently to encourage or prod its borrowers to move faster along these lines.

## The Choice of Projects for Lending

In its early years the Bank took a somewhat passive attitude toward the question of which projects to finance; it acted more or less like a commercial lender in that it was content to consider the projects proposed by borrowers. Later the Bank became more active in seeking out projects and making suggestions to borrowers about suitable projects. Since the Bank finances quite a large variety of projects, it is necessary to understand the significance of its choice of one project over another within the power sector.

In a fairly small power system the investment required to meet demand may well consist of only one new generation project together with the associated transmission lines and substations. In this simplest of situations the Bank would normally determine the size of its loan by estimating the foreign exchange expenditure required for such a project; the borrower would be expected to find the balance of the capital either from its own cash generation or from local borrowing. The practice of determining the size of a specific loan by estimating the probable foreign exchange cost derives from certain provisions in the Bank's Articles of Agreement. This policy has been the subject of considerable discussion from time to time,[4] but in the case of power projects it usually results in an acceptable answer—some proportion between, say, 40 and 75 percent of the total cost of the project. If the foreign exchange cost of a project is unusually low—so low that the borrowing country would be unable to finance the balance itself—the Bank loan is generally larger than the foreign exchange cost. In such cases, which are much more common in other sectors, the determination is normally made as part of the analysis of the funds required for the project and the possible sources available.

As power systems grew, the investment requirements (or, strictly speaking, the foreign exchange requirements) often exceeded the amount the Bank could make available. The larger power agencies began to develop programs to carry out a number of generation and transmission projects more or less concurrently. This provided the Bank with the opportunity, indeed the necessity, to select which project it would finance. In these circumstances the Bank began to select projects on the basis of where its influence could have the greatest impact. Projects financed by the Bank do tend to be given some priority over other projects in the allocation of both funds and attention. If, for example, the Bank believed that the distribution system in a country was particularly in need of expansion and improvement, it would concentrate its lending in distribution. Altogether, between 1967 and 1982 the Bank made more than twenty loans solely for distribution. In other countries the Bank has concentrated on investments to promote or strengthen the establishment of a country-wide integrated network. The financing of the central interconnection in Colombia is one such case, and in India the Bank made a series of transmission loans between 1965 and 1976 which helped link up the major systems in different parts of the country. This has been followed by the financing of a number of very large thermal projects, to be owned and operated by the central government of India, which will be crucial in integrating the different state and regional systems.

The Bank's emphasis on overcoming rural poverty is reflected in the growing number of rural electrification projects. Although loans explicitly categorized as being for rural electrification are a recent innovation, many

---

4. Since the practice is inscribed in the Bank's Articles, it is sometimes wrongly deduced that it must therefore have some logical justification.

power agencies have had programs of rural or village electrification for some time. In fact, some village or small-town electrification usually occurs as a matter of course as transmission lines are constructed to link generating plants to industrial centers or to connect such centers together. It then becomes economically worthwhile to provide power to areas close to the transmission network. The policy issue is to determine how far it is economically or socially desirable to extend lines into rural areas when the expected demand is too small to recover the necessary capital expenditure in a reasonable time.[5]

The rise in the price of petroleum since 1974 has had important consequences for the electric power industry, among which is a greater emphasis on developing hydropower and other non-oil-using forms of generation. Several countries with favorable geological conditions are investigating the possibility of using geothermal energy. The Bank's first loan specifically for a geothermal project was made to El Salvador in 1973. More recently it made an engineering loan to investigate geothermal resources in Kenya in 1978 and a subsequent loan for the project in 1979.

As an international institution the Bank could be expected to take a particular interest in projects which have an international aspect. Power projects may affect more than one country (1) when power is produced in one country and exported to a neighboring one, (2) when a hydroelectric project is constructed on a river that forms the boundary between two countries, and (3) when a hydro project is located on a river that flows through more than one country, in which case the Bank's only international interest is to be satisfied that the riparian rights of the other countries are not infringed. Early in the Bank's history two projects of the first kind were financed in Austria. One loan in 1954 was to a company which exported part of its output to Italy, while the other in 1955 was to a company whose principal function was to provide power to southern Germany. Another project in Norway, financed in 1959, provided about half its output to Sweden. However, there have not been many such projects because of political difficulties, particularly the reluctance of countries to become dependent on a source of power beyond their control. The Bank made a loan for the Owens Falls project on the Nile in Uganda, an important part of the justification being the sale of power to Kenya. It also contributed to the Kariba dam on the Zambezi between Zambia and Zimbabwe. At the time these loans were made, however, the countries concerned were under the control of the United Kingdom. Had this not been so, the conclusion of the necessary agreements would have been much more difficult, if not impossible.

5. For an exposition of these issues, see chapter 4 below and *Rural Electrification*, A World Bank Paper (Washington, D.C., October 1975).

International connections have been the subject of much investigation in Central America. The Economic Commission for Latin America has completed a general study of the potential benefits of connecting the power systems of the Central American countries. The analysis of this question has been going on for many years, and some progress has been made. In 1972 the Bank made simultaneous loans to Honduras and Nicaragua which included funds for each country to construct transmission lines to the border. At that time one of the major objectives was to enable Nicaragua to purchase power from the proposed El Cajon hydro project in Honduras. Because the necessary arrangements took a long time, the El Cajon project was considerably delayed, and in fact work on it did not begin until 1980.

The economic, financial, and technical issues underlying international electric power connections are not, in principle, different from those involved in connecting different regions within the same country. This subject is analyzed further in chapter 3, and the examples just mentioned can be seen against that background.

As these examples illustrate, the Bank can choose to finance projects which enable it to concentrate on areas where its contribution can be greatest. Sometimes, however, the choice of a specific project may be based only on pragmatic considerations of simplicity or convenience. As has already been mentioned, when a power agency has a large investment program, the entire program is the subject of the Bank's appraisal since any specific project can be appraised only within the context of the program as a whole. There may then be no strong reason for choosing one project rather than another, and the choice may depend, for example, on which project has a convenient foreign exchange content. Quite commonly the Bank is one of several lenders who are each providing part of the foreign exchange cost. In these circumstances the lenders often have different rules for the use of their funds—that is, some funds are tied to purchases in specific countries while others may be untied—and consequently the program or project is divided among the lenders to satisfy these conditions. Another possibility is that, rather than finance a project in the normal sense, the Bank may provide funds to meet a proportion of the borrower's foreign exchange requirements over a given period, usually two or three years.

## Bank Activities Other than Lending

The policies and practices just described have all been directly concerned with the Bank's lending operations. However, some Bank activities, although intended to influence lending operations in the long run, are carried on with varying degrees of independence from them.

One such activity is the preparation of sector studies or reviews. This kind of work is carried out for all sectors, and its principal purpose is to provide the Bank with the necessary background information to support its project appraisals. These studies can vary from quite elaborate in-depth investigations by a mission in the field to much shorter desk studies which sometimes do little more than summarize the major facts about the sector. There have been numerous studies of the electric power sector in different countries, but with the increased emphasis on energy problems the Bank has recently embarked on a program of sector studies of energy problems as a whole, with electric power as only a part, or subsector, of the area studied. In countries with an integrated power network operated by a single agency that borrows from the Bank, an appraisal of this agency automatically covers the whole sector, and there may be no need for a separate sector study. The sector studies dealing with electric power tend to concentrate on the economic issues. There is usually an analysis of trends in demand and the probable financial implications of meeting it and some analysis of the tariff structure, its relation to costs, and its consequences for the supply of power to various consumers including the rural and urban poor. Any problems concerning the organization of the sector are also discussed.

In addition to sector studies of the power industry in particular countries, the Bank's Central Projects staff has produced a series of studies varying from major research projects to short notes on current issues in the electric power field.[6] The two most important areas of interest have been the appraisal of electric power projects and the theoretical and practical problems of public utility pricing. As in the case of the country sector studies, interest in recent years has focused on providing power to the rural and urban poor and on the problems of the energy sector as a whole.

## Volume and Distribution of Lending for Power

From the start of its operations until June 1982, the Bank and the International Development Association (IDA) committed a total of $17.8

---

6. For two that have been published, see Ralph Turvey and Dennis Anderson, *Electricity Economics: Essays and Case Studies* (Baltimore, Md.: Johns Hopkins University Press, 1977), and Mohan Munasinghe and Jeremy J. Warford, *Electricity Pricing: Theory and Case Studies* (Baltimore, Md.: Johns Hopkins University Press, 1982).

billion for electric power projects. This represents about 17.0 percent of total commitments and is exceeded only by agriculture ($26.5 billion) and transportation ($18.7 billion).[7] However, the category "agriculture" includes many different kinds of projects such as agricultural development banks, irrigation projects, crop development projects, rural development projects, and extension projects, while "transportation" includes highways, railways, and ports, so that electric power represents the largest single purpose for which Bank funds have been used.

Bank lending for electric power has covered 86 countries, in which some 413 projects have been financed. The largest share—some $6.6 billion or 37 percent—has been lent to Latin American countries, followed by countries in South Asia (20 percent), East Asia (19 percent), Europe, the Middle East, and North Africa (15 percent), and Africa south of the Sahara (9 percent). These totals include loans to 13 countries in which the Bank no longer lends, namely, the industrialized countries in Europe, Japan, Australia, New Zealand, and South Africa. The remaining 73 countries include about all the Bank's current active borrowers.

Since electric power is a universal requirement for economic development, no special explanation is needed for the wide spread of the Bank's power lending. The number of countries receiving loans for power is, in fact, still growing. Among the countries which have borrowed for power for the first time in the recent past are Burma, the Dominican Republic, Guinea, the Ivory Coast, the Republic of Korea, Mali, Senegal, and Zaire. The four French-speaking countries in Africa had been able for many years to obtain adequate capital and technical assistance from France, and Korea had received substantial sums from the United States and the Asian Development Bank. That these countries are now supplementing their other sources by borrowing from the Bank illustrates the growing demand for power investment and the present constraints on the supply of capital for developing countries. Most of the countries to which the Bank has made no loans for power are small; many have joined the Bank fairly recently and Bank lending to them is inevitably small. In these countries the government or the Bank may prefer to use the limited Bank resources in some other sector. In addition, there are oil-rich countries that either have never borrowed or no longer borrow.

A detailed statement of the amounts lent for electric power and the number of projects financed in all the countries for which loans have been made is given in appendix table 1 at the back of the book. Six countries—India, Brazil, Colombia, Indonesia, Mexico, and Thailand—account for

---

7. "Billion" is used throughout in the sense of thousand million. Dollars are all U.S. dollars.

half the total commitments of $17.8 billion and about 30 percent of all the projects. Furthermore, the thirty most important borrowing countries account for 83 percent of all the commitments and 63 percent of all the projects. This degree of concentration may appear remarkable at first sight, but it is not, in fact, significantly different from the pattern found in Bank operations as a whole. The analysis in this study is based primarily on the experience of these thirty countries, although examples from others have been used to illustrate specific points.

## The Trend of Power Lending

In the early years of the Bank's existence, lending for power increased rapidly, in line with the growth of its total lending. Annual average commitments and disbursements for the first twenty years of its lending operations for power are shown in table 1. This represented approximately 30 percent of total lending. The figures are in current dollars, but since the rate of inflation at that time was fairly modest, the trend they reveal is not seriously misleading.

Commitments for any year are the total value of all loans approved by the Bank during that fiscal year. Since Bank loans are disbursed gradually over the period of construction of the project, however, disbursements lag behind commitments. Normally, only a small part of any loan is disbursed in the same year in which it is approved; most of a year's disbursements come from loans made in previous years. When lending is increasing rapidly, the gap between commitments and disbursements can be sizable.

For the period since 1968, the effect of inflation is much more pronounced so that in order to analyze the trend in Bank lending it is necessary to express the nominal amounts in constant dollars. Table 2 shows Bank and IDA commitments and disbursements for power loans in constant dollars for fiscal year (FY) 1981. This table clearly shows the combined influence of inflation and of the Bank's decision to emphasize

Table 1. *Annual Average Lending for Power Projects*
(millions of current U.S. dollars)

| Period | Commitments | Disbursements |
|---------|-------------|---------------|
| 1948–53 | 65 | 41 |
| 1954–58 | 134 | 85 |
| 1959–63 | 262 | 205 |
| 1964–68 | 323 | 271 |

Table 2. *Annual Average Lending for Electric Power*
(millions of FY1981 U.S. dollars)

| Period | Commitments | Percentage of total commitments | Disbursements | Percentage of total disbursements |
|---|---|---|---|---|
| 1964–68 | 1,633 | 28.6 | 1,531 | 31.3 |
| 1969–73 | 1,397 | 18.3 | 1,115 | 25.5 |
| 1974–78 | 1,369 | 13.4 | 924 | 15.0 |
| 1979–82 | 1,800 | 15.3 | 903 | 13.2 |

*Note:* To obtain commitments and disbursements in constant dollars the Bank's commitment and disbursement deflators have been used. For an explanation of these indices see the note to appendix table 3.

lending for other sectors, particularly agriculture. Bank lending for electric power in real terms during 1974–78 was actually about 17 percent less than it was ten years earlier. During 1964–68, however, the Bank was still lending to a number of developed countries to which it no longer lends (Denmark, Japan, New Zealand, Norway, Singapore, and Venezuela). If the loans to these countries are subtracted, the average annual lending rate for 1964–68 would be (FY1980) $1,335 million. Thus, power lending to developing countries did, in fact, remain much the same in real terms from 1964–68 to 1974–78. The average for the four years FY1979 to FY1981 is unusually high as a result of a sudden random increase in power commitments in FY1980. It must be remembered, however, that the installed capacity in developing countries has increased approximately sixfold since 1960. Moreover, the real cost per installed kilowatt is higher now than it was in 1960 because greater emphasis has been placed on hydro power and the most economic sites have already been used. Therefore, as a proportion of its borrowers' investment needs, the Bank's power lending has decreased significantly.

Table 2 also shows the behavior of disbursements on power projects. Disbursements are a more realistic measure of the Bank's contribution to power financing in any period. They tend to run significantly below commitments because commitments have generally increased every year and disbursements follow commitments with a lag spread over several years. The table shows that whereas commitments in 1974–78 were about the same as in 1969–73, disbursements continued to decline. Some part of this is explained by the normal lag between commitments and disbursements, but the effect of the lag was accentuated by the behavior of prices. The increasing inflation of the 1970s affected the real value of commitments made in 1969–73 (which were disbursed after prices had risen) more than that of disbursements.[8]

## Bank Disbursements and Investment in Developing Countries

To assess the capital contribution by the Bank to investment in power in developing countries the data on disbursements should be compared with estimates of power investment in the borrowing countries. Unfortunately, data on power investment are not easily available. Investment is estimated in different ways in different countries, and often no separate estimate of power investment is available at all. In theory it is possible to make a very rough estimate by taking the growth in installed capacity and making some assumption about the cost per megawatt and adding an allowance for transmission and distribution. But the large margins of error in this procedure mean that the result is little more than an educated guess.

Appendix table 4 presents estimates covering fifteen of the Bank's borrowers and accounting for 55 percent of all the power lending. The data give Bank disbursements and investments for those years for which investment estimates are available. Since these years differ from country to country, it is not possible to make a global comparison of Bank disbursements with total power investment in developing countries. Such a comparison would not in any event be very significant in view of the great variety among the Bank's borrowers. What can be gathered from the data, however, is an indication of the relative significance of Bank lending in different countries. The table shows how very greatly this varies, particularly between large and small countries. At one extreme are large countries such as Brazil, India, and Yugoslavia which, despite the large amounts that have been lent, represent only 2 to 4 percent of total power investment. At the other extreme are the small countries where the whole investment program may consist of only one project and associated transmission and distribution. If the Bank finances such a project, it would normally make a loan equal to the foreign exchange cost of the project, which might be as much as 60 or 70 percent of its total cost. Indeed, the table does show a wide range of proportions, with five countries receiving from the Bank around 20 percent or more of their total power investment.

For all the countries in the sample the Bank financed 4.7 percent of their total investment. However, this average is heavily influenced by the

8. For 1969–73, the average commitment deflator was 68 percent higher than it was for 1964–68, but the disbursement deflator was only 25 percent higher.

large countries (Brazil, India, and Yugoslavia), and if they are excluded the proportion becomes 10 percent. But any judgment of the extent to which the Bank is contributing to the power development of its borrowers, or of the extent to which its lending yields it some influence over the total investment program, must take into account the large variation among countries and between different times within a country. Furthermore, many, if not most, Bank loans are associated with specific projects which may play a key role in the development of the sector.

# 2. *Financial Policies and Results*

In its earliest appraisals of the prospects for repayment of loans made either to private borrowers or to any agency organized along commercial lines, the Bank made a distinction between the ability of such a borrower to generate funds in local currency and the ability of the government of the country to convert these funds into foreign exchange. The first question required an analysis of the financial strength and prospects of the borrowing company or agency, and the second required an analysis of the economic situation and balance of payments of the country. The former analysis might be regarded as unnecessary, since the Bank is required to obtain a government guarantee for all its loans and a government can always provide its own currency. The Bank, however, has never used a government guarantee as a justification for lending to any borrower whom it regarded as not financially acceptable. This was particularly important during the Bank's early years when it needed to establish its reputation as an institution with high standards so as to further its ability to sell its own bonds.

## Evolution of the Bank's Approach to Power Tariffs

Since the financial strength of electric power utilities depends heavily on the regime which governs the tariff rates they can charge, it was not long before the Bank had to face the tariff issue. It arose for the first time in connection with two loans for the Mexican Light and Power Company (Mexlight) made in 1949 and 1950. The first loan, for $10 million, was an interim loan intended to be refunded by a larger loan after a financial reorganization of Mexlight to put it into a sound condition. In connection with this reorganization the Mexican government agreed, and a letter from the secretary of the Ministry of Economy confirmed, that Mexlight would be allowed to charge higher rates, which would permit it to earn a "reasonable return." The new rates were introduced and the second loan for $26 million was made in April 1950. Shortly thereafter, however, increases in wages reduced the effect of the higher rates, and the Bank made representations to the government for a further increase, which was eventually agreed to in 1953. At that time, the Bank regarded the problem as primarily involving the application and interpretation of the law regulating utilities. In another loan made to the Comisión Federal de Electricidad (CFE) in Mexico in 1952, the Mexican government promised to take all steps within its power to ensure that power rates were adjusted "diligently and promptly" in accordance with procedures provided for in the relevant laws, decrees, and regulations.

In early loans to Brazil for power projects, the issue was somewhat different. Although the legislation itself was satisfactory, its application had left most companies in a weak financial situation because they had not been allowed to calculate depreciation on the basis of assets revalued to allow for inflation. The Bank considered asking for an assurance that the law's provisions would be strictly adhered to, but it did not do so because the Brazilian authorities claimed it would be politically embarrassing.[1]

The Bank's first loans to Japan were made in October 1953 for three power companies. Because of inflation coupled with government control of power rates, the prices charged for power had risen much less than other prices. As a result, some rate increases were inevitable if the companies' revenues were to cover the costs of operation and bring an appropriate return on invested capital. To take care of the problem the guarantee agreement specified that the government was to permit the borrowers to charge rates which would allow them "to finance, by means of retained earnings, issuance of share capital or borrowings, the provision of facilities adequate to meet present and future power requirements" in their areas of supply. This was the first rate covenant to appear explicitly in a loan or guarantee agreement. It was supplemented by a side letter which added little of substance except for a government promise to review the position of power companies regularly to ensure that rate adjustments were made expeditiously in accordance with the guarantee agreement.

1. In the fall of 1953, because of its concern in this area, the Bank requested the Harvard Law School to sponsor a study of the regulation of power utilities in Latin America. For a variety of largely accidental reasons, this study (David F. Cavers and James R. Nelson, *Electric Power Regulation in Latin America* [Baltimore, Md.: Johns Hopkins University Press, 1959]) was not completed until 1959, by which time the Bank's own approach to the whole problem of adequate rates had advanced substantially. Although the book did deal with many of the problems that occupied the Bank, such as the appropriate rate base and how to determine the rate of return, it appeared too late to have much influence on the Bank's policies.

Between October 1953 and the middle of 1957 the Bank made some twenty loans for power projects, but during this period no major issues of principle arose. In several cases the loan documents included a provision or a supplementary leter from the government to the Bank stating that power rates would be such as to provide "a reasonable surplus for new investment" or to provide for "necessary improvements and extensions in accordance with sound public utility practices." The president's report on a loan to Colombia in March 1955 referred to the rate covenant and stated: "This covenant has been included because the Bank believes that future expansions should normally be borne at least in part by electric power consumers." This was the first reference to any objective or principle other than that the power agency should be financially sound. But neither in this case nor in any of the others was there any indication of what the Bank might regard as a "reasonable" surplus for new investment. In all cases the Bank had examined the regimes covering the determination of rates and the financial prospects of the borrower and had regarded them as acceptable.

A significant advance occurred in 1957 when the Koyna hydroelectric project in Indian was proposed to provide power largely for the area around Bombay. At the same time, the Bank had received a "Review of Power Tariffs" by the Damodar Valley Corporation (DVC) to which it had made two loans, in part for power generation. After considering this review and the preliminary report on the Koyna project, the Bank concluded that in both cases the proposed power rates were too low. It therefore sent a memorandum with a covering letter to the Ministry of Finance. These documents were the first to set out the Bank's views on this subject.

In the letter to the Ministry of Finance, the vice president of the Bank wrote:

> I should like to describe briefly the background to the Bank's thinking in the matter of rate policies for public utilities of this kind. We have always impressed on our borrowers the advisability of setting rates at "economic" levels, that is, rates which will permit the undertaking to cover its costs, repay its obligations and set aside funds to contribute towards the cost of normal expansion. We regard this as desirable in any circumstances, but especially so in developing countries where capital is short.

The memorandum on the "Review of Power Tariffs" stated:

> The Bank's main concern is with the overall financial results to be realized by the DVC's electricity operations rather than with the fixing of individual tariffs, which is essentially a matter for the Corporation itself

to decide. The Bank does not therefore wish to comment on the sections of the Review which are devoted to the composition of the various tariffs, with particular reference to the proportions represented by demand and energy charges respectively. On the other hand, the Bank would like to offer certain observations on the broad issues of rate policy involved, and these are set out in the following paragraphs.

In its appraisal of public power undertakings in developing countries, the Bank considers that an appropriate test of the adequacy of the power rates is whether the projected earnings are sufficient:

(a) to meet all operating, maintenance and administrative expenses, including taxes, interest charges and depreciation calculated on a realistic basis;

(b) to create a surplus out of which

    (i) to make suitable provision for the repayment of all loans and advances, in so far as this is not covered by depreciation, and in addition,

    (ii) to set aside a reasonable sum for investment in the expansion of the enterprise.

The vice president's letter also included the following:

The main question is therefore what contribution the authority should make, over and above the service of its loan capital, to the cost of future expansion. The Bank would not wish to suggest any particular proportion; however, the preliminary report indicates, by way of illustration, that as much as 46% of the estimated costs of Stage II construction could be met from earnings without the rates charged to the ultimate consumers in the Bombay-Poona system being raised by more than 5–7% above the maximum that would be consistent with the application to Koyna of the Sixth Schedule to the Electricity (Supply) Act.

By first stating that the Bank did not wish to suggest any particular proportion and then proceeding immediately, in effect, to suggest one, the Bank obviously wished to have it understood that at least some proportions, for example, 2 or 3 percent, would not, in its view, be regarded as reasonable.

The question of how to distinguish between a reasonable proportion and an unreasonable one was still not answered, however, and this unanswered question gave rise to considerable thought and discussion within the Bank over the next few years. The attempt to formulate some position regarding power tariffs involved a number of key questions. Was it appropriate to concentrate attention on the notion of a contribution to further expansion, or would it be better to follow the traditional method

used in the United States and many other countries and fix an overall rate
of return which a utility should earn on its "rate base"? If so, how should
the rate base be defined and how should the rate of return be determined?
Was there any difference in principle between the rate of return approach
and one based on cash generation or contribution to future expansion? If
not, what were the pragmatic advantages and disadvantages of the two
approaches?

The outcome of these discussions was an implicit recognition that in
judging the financial prospects of a utility, and hence the level of its rates,
no hard and fast rules could be used. The contributions utilities could
make to the cost of their own expansion varied widely because of
differences in their capital structure and in the size of their expansion
programs. Equally, there was no way an appropriate rate of return could
be precisely determined. Some of those involved in the discussion felt that
the rate of return ought logically to be related to the opportunity cost of
capital in the economy, but the margins of error in estimating such an
opportunity cost were so large that the principle, even if correct, was of
little use.

An internal Working Party was established early in 1961 to consider
the whole question of power rate covenants. In its report it assumed that
when the Bank made a loan it had thoroughly appraised the financial
prospects of the utility concerned and had "negotiated any measures
which may be necessary to ensure that it is or will be in a sound financial
position, with adequate earnings." The purpose of a rate covenant should
then be "to ensure that the Borrower will maintain this satisfactory
condition over the life of the loan." The report further assumed that "in
the appraisal of the financial condition of the utility, the rate of return on
investment and the need for expansion funds will have been taken into
account." By assuming that all the difficult questions of financial
soundness, funds for expansion, and the rate of return had already been
solved, the Working Party was then able to consider the form of the rate
covenant on purely pragmatic grounds. Even though a rate of return
covenant seemed an attractive concept, the report noted some practical
difficulties such as the definition of the rate base when, for example, the
book value of assets needed to be adjusted, and the determination of an
appropriate rate of return. Mainly for these reasons, the Working Party
concluded that a covenant providing for a contribution to investment
would often be more suitable.

In practice, the rate of return approach has tended to be used more often
than the contribution to investment or cash generation approach. The cash
generation approach does have the advantage of addressing the central
practical problem of raising capital, whereas the rate of return method can

appear more abstract, and some governments object that it makes the power agency look as if it were making a profit at the expense of consumers. The cash generation method runs into practical complications, however: because of variations in capital expenditure from year to year it is necessary to formulate the covenant in terms of multi-year averages, which makes it difficult to test.

The rate of return approach has the advantage of being familiar to many borrowers as a widely accepted method of regulating utilities. The definition of the rate base did not prove a major difficulty, although with the accelerating inflation of the 1970s the problem of revaluing the assets making up the rate base became increasingly important. Furthermore, fixing a rate of return turned out to be less difficult in practice than it had seemed to be in theory. Some countries already had rate regulation systems incorporating rates of return, and some companies already had concessions which authorized them to earn a specified return. Where these rates yielded an acceptable level of earnings the Bank could request an assurance that the rate concerned would be continued and adhered to. This occurred for the first time in Mexico, in May 1958, in connection with a loan to the Comisión Federal de Electricidad (CFE). The Mexican Tariff Commission had approved a rate of return of 9 percent on the rate base for certain of the larger systems then operated by CFE, and the Bank was assured that the government regarded this rate as reasonable and that CFE would be permitted to earn a reasonable return. Another case was the first power loan to Argentina in early 1962 where the borrower's concession authorized a return of 8 percent.

From these and other cases there developed a tradition that a rate of return of 8 or 9 percent or more was generally regarded as acceptable. It was true that the Bank could not provide a logically convincing explanation of why it wanted an 8 percent return, instead of 7 percent. On the other hand, borrowers faced a similar difficulty since they could not support an opinion that 7 percent was preferable to 8 percent. Actually, almost all borrowers themselves had the same objectives as the Bank. They recognized the advantages of a financially strong power agency and the desirability of reducing the burden of power investment by means of power revenues. Consequently, negotiations over power rates, though often difficult, were about matters of degree rather than matters of principle, and it was almost always possible to reach an eventual agreement. In this context, the absence of cut and dried theories was probably an advantage.

Throughout the 1960s and 1970s it was standard practice to include some form of rate covenant in Bank loan agreements. Similar covenants were also used in lending for telecommunications, railways, ports, urban water supply, and, with considerable modification, irrigation water. In fields other than telecommunications and ports, however, this type of covenant was subject to many limitations. Railways, for example, face competition from road transport and are often unable to increase revenue by raising rates. In water supply and particularly irrigation projects, social considerations tend to be more important than financial ones, and the issue tends to be regarded more as one of tax policy.

For electric power projects, however, and on the basis of strictly financial considerations, an adequate rate of return remains the central concern. An internal memorandum in the late 1950s described the objectives of the Bank's financial covenants, of which the rate of return covenant was the most important: "Basically the primary purpose of all financial covenants is to assure the lender that the enterprise will be able to meet its debts as they come due. This is what is implied by the term 'protective' as applied to them. In the Bank's case, however, there is a secondary objective arising out of the aims and purposes of the Bank itself. That is to assure that the enterprise will flourish and fulfill the service to the country for which it was designed." The secondary objective—that the enterprise should flourish—lies behind the notion that revenues should be sufficient to make a reasonable contribution to investment. Although an enterprise that earns an adequate return would normally meet both objectives, the two are nevertheless conceptually distinct, not just two ways of saying the same thing. As will emerge in the discussion of specific cases, the question of which should receive the primary emphasis may become significant.

## Utility Rates and Economic Efficiency

The Bank's evolving attitude toward power tariffs, described in the preceding section, was based on the assumption that tariffs should be determined by reference to financial criteria. This corresponded with the approach to rate regulation traditional at that time, namely, that utilities should earn an adequate return on their invested capital. A utility which did so would be able to pay the current interest rate for new capital and so expand to meet increased demand. It was also believed that consumers should pay the full costs incurred by producers in providing the service, a principle regarded as being not only equitable but also in accord with the demands of economic theory. However, the apparently simple notion of earning a return on invested capital had always been subject to serious ambiguities. There was, for example, the question of whether invested capital should be valued at historic or replacement cost. This issue might at first sight appear to be a matter of accounting, but it led to other questions revolving around the meaning of "cost." If power tariffs were to reflect costs in an economic sense, it was not enough to base them on financial expenditures or accounting costs because there could be important differences between accounting costs and the real economic cost of producing power. For example, the real cost of power at periods of peak demand is much greater than that of off-peak power. Consideration of this and similar problems led to an increasing application of economic ideas in the setting of utility rates.

The modern debate over these issues began in the late 1930s when economists began to apply principles derived from welfare economics to problems of utility pricing. The starting point was that prices should be equal to marginal cost, since only in this case would consumers be charged an amount which correctly measured the value of the resources they were using. Utility rates would then perform in the same way as prices determined by competition in an open market. There was much discussion of the appropriate definition of "marginal cost" and of ways of determining it in practice. In the lengthy controversy over these issues, those who followed the traditional approach tended to regard the economists' ideas as academic and impractical, while the economists tended to regard the traditionalists as sadly in need of enlightenment. Although not all the issues have been settled, the idea of marginal cost pricing has become much more influential over the past two decades, particularly in electricity pricing.

Setting power rates on the basis of marginal costs—or efficiency pricing, as it is often called—can have significant effects on a utility's financial position. If rates are set on the basis of economic considerations a utility's financial position becomes an effect, or by-product, of the rates. This is the reverse of what happens under the traditional approach, whereby the financial position of the utility is the cause and the rates the result. Thus, under efficiency pricing, a utility's financial return depends on the relationship between expected long-run marginal costs and the valuation of its existing assets. In practice, if a power system is experiencing economies of scale so that expected marginal costs are declining, rates based on them could produce a low return or even a deficit. This was often the case during the 1960s, and the possibly adverse financial effects of efficiency pricing became a serious objection to it. During the 1970s, however, there was a very significant change as many countries passed the point of major economies of scale and began to face rising real costs in the expansion of their systems—for example, because the remaining hydro sites were less favorable and equipment and fuel were more expensive. Most recent studies in both developing and industrial countries show that rates based on marginal costs would be substantially higher than prevailing rates. Efficiency pricing has thus become an important argument for higher rates, one consequence of which is that those who operate power utilities are now more receptive to the ideas of economists than they used to be. However, efficiency pricing is often resisted on the grounds that electric power is a public service and should therefore be sold at a price sufficient only to recover the historical investment.

The discussion of the financial implications of efficiency pricing pointed up the fact that power rates serve more than one function. From an economic point of view they act as a signal for the allocation of resources. From a financial point of view they protect a utility's credit and hence its ability to borrow, and they can increase public savings by contributing to power investment. But they can also have other social and economic effects. Keeping rates low can facilitate rural electrification and encourage the development of rural areas. So-called lifeline rates—especially low rates for a limited amount of power—can bring electric power to the urban poor. Some countries adopt nationwide uniform tariffs partly to encourage development outside major urban centers and partly to avoid feelings of discrimination. Thus financial, social, and general economic considerations may justify departures from strict marginal cost criteria; but even where such departures are made, a knowledge of marginal cost will provide a measure of the cost they impose on the rest of the economy.

Bank economists working on power problems have contributed to the development of the theory and applications of efficiency pricing. During the 1970s much progress was made in transforming the rather abstract theory of marginal cost pricing into a set of practical procedures for preparing a tariff structure, and the Bank began to encourage its borrowers to adopt tariffs based on a calculation of efficiency prices.

Despite its encouragement of efficiency pricing, the Bank still retains a rate covenant expressed in financial terms in its loan agreements. Since efficiency pricing generally requires rates higher than those of traditional financial criteria and since actual rates in most countries are now below what is needed for either purpose, this does not create any inconsistency and seems unlikely to do so in the foreseeable future. A financial rate covenant does, of course, reflect the Bank's interest as a lender of money, and it is therefore likely to be maintained however widespread efficiency pricing may become.

## Other Financial Covenants

The rate of return or, more generally, the level of earnings of its borrowers has always been at the center of the Bank's financial concern in its power lending. It has generated by far the most discussion within the Bank and between the Bank and its borrowers. But the Bank has other financial concerns reflected in covenants in its loan documents. These covenants are used, of course, for loans not only to power agencies but also to any borrower who operates on commercial lines and for whom they would be appropriate.

Some form of debt limitation has become a standard covenant. It is intended to prevent the borrower from incurring debt which might cause future debt service to be excessive and endanger the borrower's financial viability. A debt limitation covenant might specify a debt-equity ratio or a debt-assets ratio or require that interest or debt service be covered by earnings with a specific margin. If a proposed borrowing operation would reduce this margin beyond the agreed amount the Bank's consent has to be obtained.

Another standard covenant obligates the borrower to have its accounts audited by an auditor satisfactory to the Bank and to forward the audited accounts to the Bank within some stated period, normally four or six months.

A covenant sometimes employed in power loans places a limit on investment by the borrower. The justification is that, if the project being financed by the Bank is part of a larger program, the effectiveness of the project may well depend on the larger program being carried out as planned. The analysis of the financial position of the borrower, in particular the sources and applications of funds, will have been based on an analysis of the investment program as a whole. The Bank can therefore claim that the basis on which its loan has been made should not be changed without its agreement. In some formulations this covenant is essentially a financial test of whether the proposed addition to the investment program can be appropriately financed without interfering with the implementation of the program already agreed. In other versions there is also a reference to the economic merits of the proposed new investment so that, irrespective of the method of financing, the Bank could withhold its agreement if it believed the investment was economically unjustified. This type of provision is not practical in some large countries where the Bank's lending is only a small part of the total program.

## The Application of Financial Policies

In all countries electric power tariffs are controlled—generally by legislation, by a concession agreement, or simply by government practice—because power agencies normally possess some degree of monopoly. Governments are often under strong pressure to keep tariffs down in the interests of consumers. It would be wrong to say that the interest of power agencies is simply to keep rates up; those who run these agencies do endeavor to keep costs as low as they can. When faced with rising costs, however, they have to apply for increased rates to protect their finances and their operations. In this situation the interest of the agencies' creditors, including the Bank, is the same as that of the agencies themselves. In a period of substantial inflation and rising energy costs such as that of the past ten years, the Bank therefore tends to appear as a persistent advocate of higher rates.

When a power agency, supported by the Bank, tries to obtain rate increases to match its rising costs, its efforts are very visible, and much of the following account is concerned with them. But there is another side which must not be overlooked. In the 1950s and 1960s several expanding power agencies found that the lower operating costs of their newer and larger projects more than offset the effect of the relatively slow inflation in those years. Because the pressure to lower rates when costs fall is far less than the pressure to increase them when costs rise, these power agencies were often able to maintain their rates roughly constant for many years, or even reduce them, while at the same time increasing their financial strength.

Several examples of this process can be given. When the Bank began to lend for power in Honduras in 1959, rates had been set high enough to discourage the unnecessary use of energy in view of the shortage of capacity at the time, but it was expected that the rates would be reduced as capacity expanded. The financial rate of return at that time was about 20 percent. In 1964, after the Canaveral hydropower project had been completed, there was a 30 percent reduction in rates. Despite this, the agency's financial rate of return averaged 11.8 percent between 1965 and 1975 without any rate increases.

In Nicaragua, upon completion of the first major project financed by the Bank, a 30 megawatt steam plant, the government introduced a 40 percent rate reduction. Since this was much more than was justified, the power agency operated at a deficit during the following year, 1959. During negotiations for another Bank loan for a hydro project it was agreed that much, but not all, of the reduction would be rescinded, and the new rates were eventually set at about 16 percent below the original ones. There were then further reductions in rates charged for different types of consumers between 1965 and 1968, and the agency did not have to increase its rates until after the energy price rise in 1975.

The Bank's first loan to Malaysia was made in 1958 for the Cameron Highlands hydroelectric project. At that time rates were set to cover the cost of the small thermal plants already operated by the power agency.

When the new hydro project was completed in 1964 the cost of power declined, but there was only a small reduction in power rates. This project was followed by large thermal plants at Port Dickson and Prai. As a result, the power agency was able to maintain a financial rate of return exceeding the agreed figure of 8 percent and to make substantial contributions to its investment program, sometimes exceeding 70 percent, despite the fact that there was no rate increase between 1958 and 1977.

In Thailand the Bank's first power operations were four successive loans, made between 1957 and 1967, for the Yanhee project, a multipurpose power and irrigation project. This was a large, capital-intensive investment, and rates were initially set fairly high with the expectation that they would be reduced as the load expanded. There were, in fact, periodic rate reductions between 1961 when the Yanhee Authority began operations and 1974 when rates were increased to meet the rise in fuel costs. Nevertheless, the power agency was able to make a satisfactory contribution to investment over this period, generally averaging about 30 percent.

The same pattern occurred in other developing countries, and some of the most efficient power utilities among the Bank's borrowers are those which were able to build themselves up in this way. The agencies in Malaysia, Thailand, and Honduras are examples of this; the agency in Nicaragua has had other difficulties, but for many years at least they were not complicated by financial problems. In many countries the reductions in the nominal prices for power during the 1960s involved even greater reductions in real prices, with the result that despite the nominal increases that occurred during the inflation of the 1970s, the real price of power in 1980 was still less than in 1960.

## Inflation and Regulatory Lag

As the rate of inflation has increased in recent years, it has created problems for utilities throughout the developing world that have to sell their output at controlled prices. But countries with a longer history of fairly rapid inflation had to face these problems earlier. One of the more instructive of these cases is the Bank's largest borrower for electric power, namely, Brazil.

Bank lending for power in Brazil began in 1949 with a loan to the Brazilian Light and Power Company. By June 1959 it had made nine loans to various power agencies in Brazil for a total of $240 million. In all of these, the Bank had relied explicitly on Brazil's legislation and regulatory regime; the rate covenant simply obligated the borrowers to take such steps as were necessary to ensure that they earned the maximum revenues permissible under the law. By 1959, however, the Bank was becoming concerned because, with the cruzeiro depreciating by 20 percent a year, the rate base of the utilities was being eroded and they were unable to attract either private or domestic capital. Because of Brazil's economic difficulties all Bank lending to the country ceased between June 1959 and February 1965. During this period there was serious inflation, and Brazil accumulated external debt that was substantial—at least by the standards then prevailing. In April 1964 there was a change of government. The new government negotiated a debt rescheduling agreement and took steps to stabilize the economy and improve the position of the public corporations. By the early 1960s the low revenues of most power companies had made them unable to generate any cash or to attract outside capital. Maintenance was being neglected and the expansion of the distribution systems had virtually ceased. To remedy this situation the new government permitted power companies to revalue their assets with the use of official annual correction factors based on cost of living indices. As a result, when the Bank decided to resume lending to Brazil in early 1965, it was able to finance two power projects on the basis of substantial rate increases.

Immediately after the new revaluation provisions were introduced, however, they encountered a number of problems. The most serious, at least in the Bank's eyes, was that revaluation was not compulsory, merely permitted, and the corresponding tariff adjustments were obtained only after some delay. Other problems concerned, for example, the procedures for depreciation and amortization and those for comparing at year end the actual and permitted returns on investment. The result was that in 1965 many different tariff policies were being pursued by different utilities. Furnas and USELPA, two agencies that borrowed from the Bank early in 1965, had, in accordance with their agreements with the Bank, increased their tariffs on the basis of assets revalued through 1964; other agencies, including CEMIG, to which the Bank made a loan in March 1966, had revalued their assets only to 1963.[2] Since inflation in 1964 was 74 percent, CEMIG's assets were valued at only about half their true value and its rates were substantially lower than those of Furnas, from whom it was intending to purchase power.

All these matters were discussed at length between the Bank and the Brazilian authorities, particularly in connection with four proposed loans for distribution to be made to utilities in different areas of Brazil. In the

---

2. The agencies referred to are Central Elétrica de Furnas, Usinas Elétricas do Paranapanema (USELPA), and Centrais Elétricas de Minas Gerais (CEMIG).

negotiations for these loans the Bank proposed a rate covenant which provided for compulsory revaluation of the borrowers' assets at least once a year on the basis of the latest official cost indices. It also provided for a reduction in the amounts allowed for depreciation and amortization and a change in the treatment of certain surcharges on customers' electricity bills. (The two main surcharges, the "sole tax" and the "compulsory loan," together added about 45 percent to the average tariff; the proceeds of these surcharges were used for financing power expansion programs.) The Brazilian authorities did not disagree in principle with the Bank's basic approach, but they were concerned that the covenant might conflict with Brazilian law and that it might be unduly rigid. The negotiations were complicated and difficult, and at one point they were suspended pending clarification and consideration on both sides. But in 1966 the Brazilian tariff law was modified to provide for compulsory annual revaluation of assets and to reduce the electricity surcharges. This opened the way to an eventual agreement described in the appraisal report as follows:

(1) The Government . . . and the . . . Distributions Companies agreed to a covenant under which (a) as provided by Brazilian legislation, tariffs will be set so as to produce revenues at a level consistent with sound financial and public utility practices, using straight-line depreciation which shall not be less than that based on the useful lives of depreciable assets in operation, and (b) as permitted by Brazilian legislation, assets will be revalued and tariffs will be correspondingly adjusted at least once every calendar year.

(2) A change in legislation which shall adversely affect the setting of tariffs at the level stated above, shall be an event of default.

(3) In a letter to . . . the . . . Distribution Companies the Bank will define the standard which it would use to analyze a change in the legislation for the purpose of (2) above. This standard shall be whether revenues from the sale of electricity are sufficient to: (a) cover all of the Borrower's operating expenses, including straight-line depreciation of gross revalued fixed assets in operation, at rates based on useful lives of assets and (b) produce a reasonable annual rate of return on the revalued averge net fixed assets in operation (which under presently foreseeable conditions would be of the order of 10%).

The four distribution loans were eventually approved in December 1966, and the agreement described above has formed the basis for the rate covenant in all subsequent Bank lending for power in Brazil. The basic policy, as reflected in Brazil's legislation, has been implemented by the agency in charge, DNAEE.[3] It has improved and modified its methods of implementation, but the financial position of all the major utilities has been generally well maintained for many years, despite continued inflation and the rise in oil prices. The main modifications since 1966 are a law adopted in 1971 that stipulates all utilities must earn a return of 10 to 12 percent on their investment, and a policy introduced in 1974 to equalize tariffs throughout the country. With this objective, a Global Guarantee Fund was established so that surpluses generated by utilities with lower costs could be transferred to those whose costs were higher.

The operation of this system for setting tariffs has worked remarkably well. For many years it enabled the power sector to make a substantial contribution to its investment needs—more than 50 percent, for example, in 1971–75. In the past few years, however, the increasing rate of inflation has meant that the government of Brazil, like many other governments, has delayed approving rate increases. Consequently, the volume of internally generated funds in the sector has declined, and the financing of future power needs may become a difficult problem.

A somewhat similiar situation arose in Chile after the change of government in September 1973. The Bank had made five loans to Empresa Nacional de Electricidad (ENDESA), the principal power utility in Chile, the last of which was in December 1966. After this loan was made the Bank and the Chilean government were in frequent contact because ENDESA was not meeting the agreed rate covenant. The tariff problem became significantly worse after the Allende government came into office in November 1970. From then until September 1973, ENDESA received only one rate increase of 26 percent despite a rapid increase in inflation. In 1973, ENDESA was unable to cover its operating costs, but in October 1973 a 500 percent rate increase was permitted and further increases, amounting altogether to more than 5,000 percent, were permitted during 1974. Even with these increases, however, ENDESA was only barely able to meet its operating costs.

In connection with the next loan, made in December 1976, extensive discussions took place concerning Chile's power legislation and its application. It was agreed that a number of changes in the law should be made. The more important provisions were for improved procedural rules for the Tariff Commission, for more frequent revaluations of the rate base and applications for tariff increases, for more rapid review of those applications, and for abolishing discounts for governmental purchasers of power. These and other changes were made a condition of effectiveness of

3. The National Department of Water and Electric Energy, which is a part of the Ministry of Mines and Energy.

the loan. In addition, the loan agreement provided for a 9 percent rate of return to be earned in 1979 and for intermediate rates in the intervening years, 1977 and 1978.

A major part, but not all, of the agreed changes were, in fact, put into effect in 1977. The Bank accepted an assurance by the government that the items left out would be observed in practice as a matter of policy. In the meantime, however, ENDESA had not received the full increase in rates that had been expected, and there was a long delay before the loan was made effective. Eventually the intermediate values for the rate of return were put back by two years, and the loan was made effective in December 1978, some two years after it was approved. In 1979 ENDESA's rate of return was about 4.1 percent as against a target in the loan agreement of 4.7 percent.

Since 1977 the central point of the discussion on ENDESA's rates has shifted away from the question of legislation. The government has expressed reservations about the desirability of a 9 percent return—or, indeed, of any fixed and guaranteed return—on the grounds that a guaranteed income militates against efficiency. Ensuring that public monopolies operate efficiently, in the managerial and technical sense, is a perennial challenge which has played its part for years in discussions of utility regulation. It is, of course, understandable that governments do not want to reward with rate increases an agency they may regard as inefficient. Nor do they wish to recognize rate bases which, as in the Chilean case, may be inflated because of inefficient investment in the past. A particular difficulty with power utilities is that the preponderance of fixed charges in the cost of production often makes it virtually impossible to put pressure on the controllable costs by holding down prices. Many cases illustrate the point that governments do not like to raise rates for power agencies when the supply of power is unreliable. But there is no evidence that agencies which earn high rates of return are less efficient than those which earn low rates. There is an important role here for a good regulatory authority which can maintain some surveillance over a power agency's controllable costs, in which case necessary tariff increases might be more easily accepted.

Although proper regulatory legislation is important as a basis for the operation of power utilities, there is always some scope for changes in the interpretation of legislation to reflect official policy. In Chile a policy matter is now a more fundamental issue than the form of Chile's legislation. In Brazil the increasing pressures arising from inflation have caused the authorities to lean on the regulatory agencies in their interpretation of the law—a good example of the conflict, now growing more acute in most developing countries, between the desire to control inflation and the need to raise funds to meet the demand for investment in power.

One result of this conflict is a tendency for the lag between cost increases and rate increases to lengthen. Moreover, if a power agency's rate base is calculated on historic asset values, a fixed rate of return will mean that power tariffs rise less than the general inflation rate. For this reason the Bank has urged all its borrowers to revalue their assets regularly and to introduce provisions into their tariff whereby increases in operating costs can be quickly reflected in the rates charged. This has been particularly important with regard to fuel costs. Many Bank loan agreements include provisions by which the borrower agrees to introduce these changes into the determination of power tariffs.

## Financial Implications of the Organization of the Industry

Most countries have more than one major power utility. Separate distribution agencies, often operated by municipal authorities, are common, and in larger towns and particularly in many capital cities the local power agency generates power as well. In large countries, as numerous sizable utilities become linked into a system, the coordination of their financial problems is an important part of a financial and tariff policy for the system as a whole. But in any country with more than one agency generating power, the relationship between agencies can have important financial consequences.

In many countries, including most Latin American countries, power for the capital city was first supplied by a foreign company operating under a concession. Most of these companies were subsidiaries of the American and Foreign Power Company or of some other large American, Canadian, or European utility. The establishment of a government-owned agency, often more or less intended as a "chosen instrument" for the national development of electric power, came later. Thus the operations of the national agency had to be coordinated with those of the concessionaire, and one of the most important subjects at issue was the price at which the national agency would sell its power to the concessionaire, whose concession frequently included the most profitable market. This situation frequently had a major impact on the financial position of the government agency, and the eventual solutions differed widely according to local circumstances. The organization of the power sector is dealt with in the next chapter, but its financial implications are sufficiently important to deal with separately here.

A situation of this kind was a predominant influence on the financial position of the Bank's borrower in the Philippines for many years. The

Bank made its first loan to the National Power Corporation (NPC) in 1957 and has since made seven more loans, the most recent in 1978. NPC was formed in 1937 as a government agency primarily to develop hydro power. Power was provided to the Manila area, much the largest market, by the Manila Electric Company (MERALCO), a subsidiary of the General Public Utilities Corporation of New York. When, during the 1950s, NPC began to expand its construction program, MERALCO apparently regarded this as a threat to its own position, a view which eventually turned out to be justified. Relations between the two organizations were marked more by competition and conflict than by cooperation. In 1961 MERALCO was purchased by a local Philippine group, but this in no way diminished its influence and the competitive relationship continued. This situation affected not merely NPC's financial situation but all the problems of planning and operating the system. Moreover, in this relationship, NPC tended always to be in the weaker bargaining position. It was a newer and smaller institution, and in its early years priority was given to construction activities more than to utility operations. It sold over 80 percent of its generation on Luzon island to MERALCO. MERALCO was a well-organized, well-staffed, and efficient utility, and its owners had political influence.

The Bank's first loan, for the Binga project, was made in November 1957 on the understanding that NPC would seek a rate increase sufficient to increase revenues by 25 percent. Getting this increase approved and implemented took about two years. A major problem was that NPC's contract for the sale of power to MERALCO contained no provision for an adjustment in the price. Moreover, it was subject to cancellation only after three years' notice. A few years later, in 1962, NPC was authorized to increase its tariff by 17.5 percent, an increase which MERALCO refused to accept. NPC thereupon gave notice of cancellation of its contract, which took effect in 1965. A new contract was signed in 1966 which provided for a 19.6 percent increase in the average price of energy. In addition to this major problem with MERALCO, the legality of NPC's rate increase was contested in the courts by other purchasers represented in the Philippine Electric Plant Owners Association. The result of these delays was that NPC could not meet the agreed target for contribution of 25 percent of investment expenditure; it provided only 17 percent of an investment program considerably smaller than expected. One result was that in the Bank's fourth loan, made in April 1967, the rate covenant with NPC was changed from a cash generation basis to an 8 percent rate of return.

The first significant steps to solve these problems were the establishment of the Power Development Council in 1970 and the revision of the charter for NPC in 1971. To avoid rate increases by NPC from being contested in the courts, the new charter provided that sole jurisdiction over appeals against NPC's tariffs was to rest with the Public Service Commission and the Supreme Court. Nevertheless, delays in rate increases between 1967 and 1971 made it impossible for NPC to meet the stipulated 8 percent rate of return; in 1970 it was only 3 percent and in 1971 it was 2.6 percent.

The establishment of the Power Development Council reflected the need for a coordinated and systematic development of the power sector. This was not just a question of the relationship between NPC and MERALCO. It also involved all the problems of organizing and developing power in a country consisting of many islands and with numerous small public and private power agencies. Although the Power Development Council was only advisory, all these subjects were discussed with the Bank, and in a loan agreement made in March 1972 the government undertook to prepare specific proposals for the coordination of the planning and implementation of power development.

Later in 1972 the government issued "Presidential Decree No. 40 Establishing Basic Policies for the Electric Power Industry." This decree set out the objective of total electrification of the country. It also recognized NPC as the "authorized implementing agency" of the state with responsibility for setting up transmission systems and constructing associated generation facilities in Luzon, Mindanao, and major islands. This was a major change in policy. The generating plant of MERALCO, which amounted to 60 percent of the total for the country, was to be transferred to NPC, and MERALCO would then operate only as a distribution agency. MERALCO had encountered quite serious financial difficulties after 1970. Until then it had been able to finance its investment by the sale of bonds abroad, but the devaluation of the peso in 1970 and MERALCO's inability to secure approval of tariff increases created a severe liquidity crisis. MERALCO's problems in effect provided an opportunity for the government to make major changes to solve the organizational problems of the sector.

All these changes implied substantial new responsibilities for NPC, and the Bank's loan for the seventh power project in June 1977 included funds for consultants to provide management advisory services in organization, planning, and day-to-day operations.[4] In addition, after 1972 NPC's financial position began to improve. There were tariff increases in 1972, 1973, and 1974 and the rate of return improved over this period from 4.5 to 6.4 percent, which, since it coincided with the first rise in fuel prices, was noteworthy. After a decline in 1976 the rate of return reached 7.6

---

4. This was not the first time the Bank had provided funds for NPC for management consultants; the 1967 loan had done the same.

percent in 1978—still below, although not much below, the figure of 8 percent included in Bank loan agreements since 1967.

Since Bank lending to NPC began in 1957 it might seem that much time passed and many loans were made—seven for a total of $220 million— before NPC began to approach what the Bank regarded as a satisfactory financial condition. And, indeed, the appraisal report for the 1967 loan, after noting NPC's various problems, remarked: "The question of whether the proposed loan should be considered despite these shortcomings of administration has been the subject of considerable discussion within the Bank. This discussion led to the conclusion that on balance a loan was justified." The other loans were also supported by the need to encourage the implementation of some price increase or some measure to improve NPC or the organization of the sector.

Moreover, the problems facing NPC were unusually difficult and mostly not of its own making. Although at times progress seemed slow, the underlying situation was changing. During the 1970s NPC's position began to improve, and since 1977 the change has been substantial. A new financial director was appointed, largely at the insistence of the Bank, and his appointment was followed by others, including a new president. There have also been a number of organizational changes and considerable emphasis on a training program. These changes prepared NPC for the job of taking over MERALCO's generating properties and implementing a much larger investment program. Thus the recent improvement in NPC's financial position, as well as the earlier experience when improvement was hardly detectable, are really part of a total process both within NPC itself and as regards its role in the power sector. It is often said that institution building takes time. This experience illustrates the point.

The situation in the Philippines was particularly difficult, but similar situations are not uncommon. The financial relations between government agencies and private concessionaires have also been an issue in Central American countries. In El Salvador the Bank's first loan was made to the Comisión Ejecutiva Hidroeléctrica del Rio Lempa (CEL), a government agency established in 1945 to develop the hydro resources of the Lempa river. The loan was made in 1949 for the Guayabo project, and it was recognized at the time that, owing to the size of the project in relation to the market, CEL would need subsidies from the government until the load on the system had had time to increase, a period originally estimated at four years. About 80 percent of CEL's output at that time was sold to CAESS,[5] a company generating and distributing power in San Salvador, the

5. Compañia de Alumbrado Eléctrico de San Salvador, a subsidiary of International Power Company of Montreal.

capital city. But when the Guayabo project was completed in 1954, the rates set for sales to CAESS represented a 20 percent reduction. Consequently, it was necessary for the government subsidy to be continued. The rates charged to CAESS were increased in 1959 and again in 1963. CEL covered its operating costs plus interest for the first time in 1958, and the government subsidies were finally terminated only in 1963. Once it had reached this point, CEL was able, on the basis of its low-cost hydro power, to build up its financial position without raising rates. By 1974 there had been no significant rise in rates charged to final consumers for about twenty years, and CEL was one of the Bank's financially strongest borrowers.

In Guatemala the government agency responsible for developing the country's power resources is the Instituto Nacional de Electrificación (INDE), which was established in 1959. It was responsible for the supply of power in all areas except Guatemala City where a concession was held by the Empresa Eléctrica de Guatemala S.A. (EEG), a subsidiary of American and Foreign Power. EEG was established in 1922 and had been a well-organized company for many years before INDE was set up. Cooperation between the two agencies proved difficult, and INDE's financial position remained weak largely because it could not charge adequate rates to EEG. The government acquired 93 percent of the shares of EEG in 1972, but this alone did not solve the general problems of sector organization. However, since the low earnings of INDE were offset by correspondingly higher earnings of EEG, when both organizations were government owned it was possible to transfer any surplus earnings of EEG to INDE to meet its needs for investment.

The foregoing examples illustrate the problems that can arise when one agency must sell a large part of its output to another strong power agency. But a similar situation arises whenever a purchaser of power is able to exercise bargaining power through either economic or political influence. Many power agencies sell power under long-term contracts to industrial or mining concerns; for example, in Ghana the Volta River Authority sells a large proportion of its power to the Volta Aluminum Company. These contracts often involve lengthy negotiations to revise.

A problem closely related to that of raising the prices charged to influential consumers is that of obtaining payment on time. The standard method of dealing with nonpayment is to cut off the supply, but this may be politically impossible if the purchaser is an important government department or a large municipality—or even, in some countries, an influential person. In situations such as this the Bank often endeavors to include in its loan agreements a provision that overdues shall be brought down to some agreed target figure. But the problem is difficult because the solution is often not within the power agency's control. If it cannot cut off the power supply to an important consumer it may have no other weapon. Hence pressure on the consumer has to come in some other way. In Brazil, for example, the DNAEE, the government's central regulatory agency, uses its control of the Global Guarantee Fund for this purpose. To ensure access to the Global Guarantee Fund (which is used to supplement the earnings of the less profitable utilities), a utility has to have a valid agreement with the state in which it operates for the payment of all bills in arrears by state government agencies. Thus, unless a state ensures that its agencies pay their bills, it will lose access to some central government funds.

## Sectoral Organization and the Financial Rate of Return

As the organization of a power sector evolves with the separate agencies being either consolidated or linked together under some supervisory body, the significance of the finances of each separate agency diminishes and that of the system as a whole increases. This shift is reflected in the way the Bank has applied its rate covenants. Should each separate agency earn a stipulated return or is it sufficient if the system as a whole does so?

Some of the cases described in the preceding section illustrate this problem. In Guatemala INDE could not earn the agreed 9 percent return largely because of the low rates charged to EEG, the generating and distributing agency for Guatemala City. But it was obvious, particularly after the government acquired ownership of EEG in 1972, that the two agencies should be regarded together, and that the precise nature of the financial transactions between them was not a matter of direct concern to the Bank. Consequently, for the last two loans the rate covenant has taken the form of government assurance that the "Power Sector," defined as INDE and EEG together, should earn the stipulated rate of return, and that the rates set for power sales from INDE to EEG should be such as to transfer to INDE all funds in excess of EEG's requirements for its operations, debt service, and capital expenditures.

Both Costa Rica and El Salvador had a similar organizational arrangement, with the principal government agency (ICE in Costa Rica and CEL in El Salvador) selling power to companies distributing power under a concession in the capital city (CNFL in Costa Rica and CAESS in El Salvador). Although in the early period of the Bank's lending operations, both ICE and CEL had difficulty charging an adequate price for power sold to CNFL and CAESS, this problem was eventually overcome in both countries. There was therefore no need for an explicit recourse to a sector-based rate covenant. The loan agreements with ICE in Costa Rica do contain a provision whereby ICE—which owns 92 percent of CNFL—is obligated to ensure that CNFL's earnings are sufficient to comply with its concession. This provision was not included in the first instance, however, because the Bank wanted the whole sector to meet some minimum earnings test; it was included in a loan made in 1969 after ICE purchased CNFL under an arrangement which involved issuing $9.5 million of negotiable notes maturing over seventeen and a half years. CNFL's concession was revised to provide that it be granted tariffs sufficient to enable it, among other things, to provide ICE with the funds necessary to service these notes. The Bank's main concern was that CNFL's rates were in fact sufficient to do this.

In El Salvador, once the problem of the low rates charged by CEL to CAESS was overcome in 1959, the existence of the two agencies did not produce any financial complications. CAESS operates under a concession which permits it to earn an 8 percent return; it usually has done so and the Bank has not required any specific undertaking for the sector as a whole.

Although the organization of the power sector was very similar in these three countries, the Bank's technical application of its rate of return policy differed somewhat from country to country. In Guatemala one explicit rate covenant applied to the entire sector, and in line with this approach the appraisal report contained consolidated balance sheets and income statements of the two agencies. In Costa Rica there were two separate rate covenants, one for each agency, and the accounts of both agencies were given in the appraisal report but were not consolidated. In El Salvador no rate covenant was applied to CAESS, although its financial position was described and the appraisal report noted that "the Bank would continue to monitor CAESS's earnings levels during project execution."

In the Philippines, despite the fact that two main agencies, NPC and MERALCO, were supplying power for the Luzon grid, the appraisal reports did not adopt any kind of sector approach to financial matters. In view of MERALCO's position as a private company and its competitive relation with NPC, the Bank could not have obtained any assurances about rates from MERALCO. Nevertheless, it might well have been pointed out that, if the Bank's rate policy is based on the view that consumers of power should make a reasonable contribution to the cost of expansion, then consumers in MERALCO's concession area were presumably doing so. One appraisal report, referring to NPC's financial problems, particularly before 1972, said, "The problems were not as serious as they would have been had NPC been responsible for meeting projected load growth rather than financing selected hydropower projects." In other words, the financial position of the "Luzon sector" was not as unsatisfactory as that of NPC, and the Bank could have claimed that this constituted some justification for persevering with NPC despite its persistent problems.

The way the power sector is organized has often affected the way the Bank has tried to achieve its financial objectives. Three further examples illustrate this situation. In Thailand, by 1977, the Bank had made eight loans to the Electricity Generating Authority of Thailand (EGAT), formerly the Yanhee Electricity Authority. EGAT is the principal agency responsible for generation and transmission. There are two other important agencies, the Metropolitan Electricity Authority (MEA), which distributes electricity to the Bangkok area, and the Provincial Electricity Authority (PEA), which supplies electricity to the rest of the country. EGAT accounts for 94 percent of all electricity generated, the balance being produced by PEA in areas not connected to the grid and by several industries that generate their own supplies.

Until 1977 the rate covenant with EGAT was based on a contribution to investment criterion, principally because the Thai authorities feared a rate of return covenant might imply that EGAT was making a high profit, which would draw political criticism. In 1977 the Bank negotiated its first loan to PEA for rural electrification. It became clear PEA could not generate a contribution to investment as did EGAT, because PEA operated in the provinces and its operating costs were higher than those of the other agencies. Nor could PEA charge higher prices because the government had adopted a policy of uniform prices throughout the country. This created a problem because the three agencies are administratively of equal status, and PEA did not wish to have a different rate covenant from that of EGAT. The solution was to include a rate covenant in the guarantee agreement by which the government ensured that the three agencies together earned a specified return on their consolidated assets. PEA's obligation was simply that its earnings should be consistent with the specified sector return.

In Brazil the government also adopted a policy of unified rates throughout the country, and it established the Global Guarantee Fund to facilitate this policy by transferring funds from utilities with lower costs to those whose costs were higher. To fit in with this approach the Bank modified the wording of its rate covenant to include in the definition of "revenues" any sums obtained from the Global Guarantee Fund. This meant that the rate of return achieved by any borrower need not be derived from its own operations but could be supplemented by earnings derived from other parts of the sector. There was no need for any general undertaking by the government for the sector as a whole since this was, in effect, laid down by Brazil's legislation.

The organization of the electric power in Yugoslavia is exceptional, but it illustrates this same kind of problem. In 1972 the Bank made a loan to expand the transmission network. At that time the organization of the whole electric power industry was extremely decentralized, and the loan was made to eleven transmission enterprises in six of the Yugoslav republics. Each enterprise undertook to maintain its rates at a level sufficient to finance 35 percent of its investment in power facilities. In 1977 when a second loan for the expansion of transmission facilities was made, the appraisal report contained the results for the eleven enterprises for the 1971–75 period. All except four had reached the 35 percent target. Two of these four were in Croatia, and the appraisal report commented, "In the case of Croatia, the borrowers have argued that the covenant would be fulfilled if all the four borrowers in Croatia . . . were considered together. There is force in this argument since the additional measures [that is, to increase revenue] were determined by the Republic on the basis of their impact on the entire sector in Croatia and not on one particular enterprise; therefore it may be considered that the intent of the covenant has been fulfilled." By the time the second transmission loan was made, the separate power enterprises in each republic had been formed, or were at the time being formed, into "composite organizations." One of the institutional objectives of this loan was to strengthen these composite organizations, and one element of this effort was to consolidate the financial statements of their constituent enterprises. Accordingly, the rate covenant tests were applied only to the composite organizations and not to the separate enterprises which formed them.

Although all these examples differ in detail, the process underlying them is the same: the growing importance of the financial position of the whole sector. As was pointed out earlier, the Bank's financial covenants have a dual purpose of ensuring that the enterprise meet its debts when due and that it fulfill the service for which it was designed. The move toward sector-wide rate covenants reflects the importance of the second of these purposes and recognizes that the financial position of a single agency often cannot realistically be regarded in isolation. The way the Bank approaches the financial problems of its borrowers depends on the details of the power sector concerned. Does it make sense to regard a particular borrower as necessarily solely responsible for its own debts, or is it such an integral part of a larger system that this attitude is unrealistic? Can the Bank reasonably use a sector approach when its lending may be confined only to one agency among many? Not only do the answers to such questions involve an element of judgment, but in any one country the answers may change with the growth and integration of the power system, and the Bank has to adapt its financial approach to these changes.

## Some Major Borrowing Countries

Some of the power agencies just described—for example, those in Brazil, Malaysia, and Thailand—are borrowers who have coped with their financial problems with a considerable degree of success. This could also be said of many others. But before a more general discussion of the financial experience of the Bank's borrowers, it is necessary to consider some cases in which financial difficulties have played a much larger role. In the six countries selected—India, Mexico, Indonesia, Turkey, Argentina, and Uruguay—financial issues have been only one of the concerns of the Bank, and, particularly in the latter three countries, they were just one aspect of more general problems facing the borrowing agencies.

### India

India is the largest single borrower of Bank and IDA funds and also the largest borrower for electric power. By June 1982 the Bank and IDA had lent $3,059 million to India for electric power development. This represented 20.5 percent of all Bank and IDA lending to India, a figure which is somewhat higher than the average for all borrowers (16.7 percent) and which reflects the substantial power lending for India's large thermal projects in recent years.

Lending for power in India falls into three fairly clearly defined periods. The first period began in April 1950, when the Bank made its first loan, and lasted until June 1965 when a loan for the first of four transmission projects was made. Loans for these four projects were made between June 1965 and January 1976. Since 1976, in the third and current lending period, the Bank has concentrated on financing several very large thermal plants being constructed by the government of India.

During the early period of power lending in India the Bank made four loans for the Damodar Valley Corporation (DVC), a government agency patterned somewhat after the Tennessee Valley Authority in the United States. It also made two loans for the Trombay project which served the area around Bombay and was owned and operated by the Tata Power Company, a private group. In 1959 the Bank's first loan for the Koyna project was made after considerable discussion with the Indian authorities. The appraisal report for this loan stated, "The Government of India and the Bombay State Government have agreed with the Bank's views on rates, namely, that they should be set at a level to ensure that the earnings derived from the operation of the project, after provision for all operating expenses including taxes, adequate depreciation and interest and repayment of all loans and advances available to the project in so far as it is not covered by depreciation, are sufficient to make a reasonable contribution towards the cost of future expansion in the State." A covenant containing approximately this language was included in the loan documents without a specific definition of a reasonable contribution. But in loans (for the fourth DVC project and the second loan for the Koyna project) made in 1962, the documents included side letters which stated that the agencies concerned intended to charge rates sufficient to earn a 7 percent return on net fixed assets in operation. In 1963 a loan was made for the Kothagudem project to be constructed by the Andhra Pradesh State Electricity Board, which undertook to earn an 8 percent return.

In 1965 a major development in the Bank's assistance for power in India was the first loan for a transmission project. This loan was for $70 million, an amount substantially larger than all previous power loans (the largest of which had been for $25 million) and was for the benefit of virtually all the State Electricity Boards (SEBS) in India, as well as for a few other agencies such as the Delhi Electricity Supply Undertaking. Some account of the organization of the electric power sector in India at that time is necessary for an understanding of the significance of this project.

The Constitution of India provides that both the central government and state governments may legislate on the subject of electricity—it is a "concurrent subject." The Electricity (Supply) Act of 1948 determined the structure of the industry and made the SEBS responsible for the generation, transmission, and distribution of electricity. It also laid down certain rules for the financial operation of the SEBS. It required that they should not be run at a loss, but this requirement was interpreted strictly in a cash sense. Depreciation was regarded not as an annual expense which had to be provided for in the tariffs but as a contribution to a reserve for replacement or renewal of plant or for repayment of certain loans, subject to a revenue surplus being available. The 1948 act authorized the SEBS to borrow but placed no obligation on state governments to allow rates sufficient to service their borrowings. Instead it laid down an order of priority for the distribution of revenues, "as far as they are available," after payment of operating and maintenance costs and taxes. This order of priority began with the payment of interest on certain bonds and concluded with appropriations to a development fund to be used for electrical development in the state or the repayment of advances from the state government.

Between 1950 and 1961 SEBS were established in all the Indian states and took over the power installations from the older state electricity departments. In 1964 at a meeting of state ministers of irrigation and power, it was agreed that the financial position of most SEBS was unsatisfactory. A committee was then convened by the government of India to suggest means of improving the finances of the SEBS. The recommendations made by this committee were the basis on which the Bank agreed to make its first transmission project loan.

The most important of the committee's recommendations was that the SEBS should aim at a return of 11 percent, a figure which included an allowance of 1.5 percent for electricity tax and left 9.5 percent for the SEB's own earnings. The Indian government informed the states that the 11 percent should be regarded as a minimum, and in connection with negotiations for the Bank loan a series of target dates was set for the various SEBS. It was also agreed that the Indian government would obtain assurances from state governments that SEBS would adopt commercial systems of accounts as the national auditor-general had recommended.

This loan was followed by three credits for transmission projects in 1971, 1973, and 1976 and one for rural electrification in 1975. These loans were the occasion for a more or less continuous dialogue between the Bank and India concerning the rates of return earned by the SEBS and their financial practices. The initial targets, which provided that all SEBS would earn 9.5 percent, excluding duties, by 1970–71, were soon perceived to be unrealistic and new target dates, often allowing another three years, were adopted. Even so, many SEBS still did not reach them. The situation up to 1977–78 is shown in appendix table 7. Altogether, nine of the fifteen agencies earned 9 percent or more either in that year or the previous one, which was a considerable advance over the initial position even though it had taken much more time than expected. However, the figures overstate the real return since they are based on historic costs. Two factors militated against the financial position of the SEBS: the rural electrification program and the financial implications of the 1948 Electricity (Supply) Act.

After 1964 the Indian government's program of rural electrification was greatly expanded. This program was carried out by SEBS, and state governments made large loans to them for it. The SEBS had to bear the costs of operation and maintenance of the program and were also expected to pay interest on the loans. But because of the concessional tariffs and the low demand on the rural systems, financial losses were inevitable. The

Bank did not object to the rural electrification program itself and, indeed, in 1975 and again in 1979 made credits to assist it. It urged, however, that the state governments subsidize the losses. To do this, financial records had to be kept in a way that would enable the SEBS to calculate the effects of the rural electrification program. The Indian government concurred, and when the Bank made its credit for rural electrification it was agreed that, to qualify for financing, state governments would have to subsidize the SEBS to make up for the losses they incurred on the program. The effect of the rural electrification program on the financial return of the SEBS is also shown in appendix table 7.

The Bank had expressed the view, right from the first transmission project in 1965, that the Electricity Act of 1948 should be revised. In practice it meant that SEBS had little incentive to repay debt to state governments or even to pay interest. Consequently many SEBS accumulated substantial arrears of interest and developed very unfavorable debt-equity ratios, all of which occurred in accordance with the provisions of the act. Although the state and national governments had adopted the 9.5 percent rate of return, the financial system did not put any pressure on the SEBS to achieve this target. Consequently, the volume of internal cash generation was low. (The 1964 Energy Survey Committee of the Indian government had recommended that the SEBS aim at generating 35 percent of their capital requirements, but this recommendation was not accepted.)

At first the Indian government was not prepared to revise the 1948 act—it believed difficulties would arise with state governments since electricity was a "concurrent subject" under the Constitution—but eventually it accepted the idea. The revision was concerned not only with financial problems but also with problems of organization and planning. The revised financial provisions, which were passed in 1978, put the operation of the SEBS on a more commercial basis. The state governments had to specify the annual surplus which should be earned if the SEBS were to comply with the amended legislation. An important step toward overcoming the problems of India's power sector was the appearance in 1980 of the report of the Committee on Power, a high-level committee established in 1978 to study and make recommendations on all major aspects of the power sector. It recommended that the SEBS earn a return of 15 percent on their average capital base and that the sector as a whole aim to generate 50 percent of its expected capital expenditure from internal funds. This would represent a substantial increase over the average of 17 percent actually generated from 1974–75 to 1978–79.

## Mexico

Mexico is the fifth largest borrower from the Bank for electric power. It was also one of the earliest countries to borrow for electric power, and mention has already been made of the early loans to the Mexican Light and Power Company and the Comisión Federal de Electricidad (CFE).

In 1958 the Bank made a loan to CFE for $34 million to assist in financing four high-priority power projects. The Mexican Tariff Commission had allowed CFE to earn a return of 8 percent. For a number of reasons, including delays by the commission in approving increases in rates to offset increases in the cost of fuel and labor, CFE had not, however, been able to earn the 8 percent return. The significance of these delays had been brought home to the Bank in the previous few years in connection with the two loans to Mexlight. This company had requested a loan in June 1955, and the Bank had said that it could not approve any loan until an increase in Mexlight's tariffs had been approved by the government. The necessary increase was not approved until December 1956.

For the 1958 loan to CFE, which followed shortly after the Mexlight loan, the government and CFE agreed that CFE should earn a more adequate return. Therefore a return of 9 percent was to be allowed on the "larger systems" and adjustments of tariffs were to be accelerated. This was the first time the Bank had obtained, from any of its borrowers, an assurance about power revenues expressed as a specific number.

This loan was followed by five loans to CFE between 1962 and 1972. All were disbursed against total investment by CFE over a period of two or three years so that they came to be regarded as sector loans, as distinct from loans for a single project. The last four were explicitly called "Power Sector Loans," but the first one was essentially of the same kind. Another distinctive feature of these loans was that the Bank made explicit arrangements with a number of countries for joint financing of part of CFE's investment program. Contracts were awarded after international competitive bidding, and, for orders placed in a country participating in the joint financing, payment was made partly by the Bank and partly by the lending institution in the supplying country. The objective of these arrangements was to encourage the flow of financial assistance to Mexico and at the same time to ensure that it was provided on reasonable terms and was, in effect, untied. For example, these arrangements raised $31 million in connection with the second sector loan in 1968 and $70 million in connection with the third sector loan in 1970.

For the first of these five sector loans, there was considerable discussion between the Bank and the Mexican authorities about the financial situation of CFE. In 1959 the Bank had been approached by CFE about further lending but had taken the position that CFE's financial situation was not sufficiently strong to support the large investment program on which it was embarking. Moreover, the return on net fixed assets was well below the figure of 9 percent which had been agreed as reasonable in connection with the Bank's previous loan. As a result of the Bank's refusal to lend, CFE obtained a number of large suppliers' credits. These credits were raised by the Nacional Financiera (NAFINSA), a government agency established as a channel for official borrowing, and passed on to CFE. The service of these credits substantially reduced CFE's ability to contribute funds to its expansion program.

Eventually, in January 1962, new tariffs for the entire sector were introduced, and these provided the basis for the Bank's first sector loan. The debt limitation covenant was modified to cover debt borrowed not only by CFE but also by government agencies on behalf of CFE, and the rate covenant was changed to stipulate that CFE would generate one-third of its investment expenditure. By changing to a cash generation covenant the Bank hoped to focus attention on the need to raise capital. But the test incorporated in the covenant depended on future and hence uncertain estimates of investment and earnings, and in practice it proved difficult to determine whether it was being observed. Consequently, the rate covenant in the subsequent loan was changed back to a rate of return on assets. (In later cash generation covenants with other countries the test was defined more precisely and made less dependent on future estimates.) In any event, actual cash generation by CFE fell well below the target. Because of higher labor costs and lower sales than expected, cash generation for the four years 1961–64 was only 13 percent of investment expenditure. Moreover, this 13 percent was possible only because NAFINSA itself serviced the debt it had incurred on behalf of CFE. Had it not done so, the sector's cash contribution to investment would have been only 0.9 percent.

In response to this situation, the financial plans agreed on for the 1965 loan included measures to refinance the power sector's debt and an increase in the power consumption tax. The rate covenant was made to apply to the whole power sector. In addition, it was agreed to review the power sector's financial position annually to determine whether any rate adjustments were necessary. The idea of an annual review of the financial situation was also a significant precedent. Later, as inflation gathered speed in many developing countries, the Bank came to make increasing use of such annual reviews in its efforts to mitigate the effects of regulatory lag on power agencies' finances.

After this loan was made there was a substantial financial improvement, and by the time of the 1970 loan the power sector's capital structure and financial position were generally sound. This was partly the result of the increased power consumption tax, the proceeds of which were turned over to CFE, but owed more to the measures to moderate CFE's heavy burden of debt. In 1969, for example, a large refinancing operation was carried out with the government covering $89 million of debt maturing within five years.

After 1970, however, the power sector again encountered financial problems. Because investment expenditure on the sector program exceeded the estimates by 29 percent in 1970 and 41 percent in 1971, there was additional borrowing of some $228 million in those years. Since CFE was not able to meet the interest coverage test, it had to obtain the Bank's agreement to this additional borrowing. The Bank could not, in the circumstances, realistically attempt to prevent CFE from borrowing, but it did persuade it not to borrow for less than a five-year term. It also urged the Mexican authorities to raise the power tariff, and this became one of the important matters discussed at the negotiations for the fourth (and last) power sector loan in 1972.

In November 1971 a Mexican study group on energy policy recommended a 17.5 percent increase in electricity rates, and the effectiveness of the Bank's fourth sector loan was made dependent on this increase, which was expected before the end of 1972. Despite this prospective increase, the financing plan provided that investment would be covered by borrowing to the extent of 87 percent in 1970–71 and 70 percent in 1972–74. The Bank included in its loan agreement a cash generation covenant requiring that the power sector's net internal resources should contribute 18 percent to investment in 1973 and 25 percent thereafter. The covenant in the previous loan requiring an 8 percent return was to remain in force so that there would, in effect, be two rate covenants in operation.

As events turned out, neither of these financial targets was met and the position of the sector deteriorated further. Part of the explanation was the delay, from December 1972 to October 1973, in introducing the 17.5 percent tariff increase, but the major reason was the increasing rate of inflation in Mexico and the government's policy of price control of key commodities, including electric power. The combination of lower net income and the higher costs of investment, also resulting from inflation, meant that for 1972–75 the sector's contribution to investment, instead of being 18 percent as originally expected, was actually negative. Low earnings and low or negative cash generation have been characteristic of the power sector ever since. Consequently, the Bank has made no loans to Mexico for electric power since 1972. Mexico is the only country in which there has been no lending for power for such an extended period because of differences over financial policies. In many other countries specific loans have been delayed because of negotiations over rates, but in all other countries some agreement has eventually proved possible.

The continuation of this situation throughout the 1970s should be seen in conjunction with Mexico's rapidly growing earnings from its oil production. One of the Bank's major arguments in favor of power agencies making a substantial contribution to the cost of their investment programs was the high capital needs of power development and the shortage of capital in developing countries. When a country finds its available resources greatly increased by external price changes, as did Mexico, this argument loses much of its force—if not in theory, at least in practice as the budgetary problem of providing resources to the power sector is eased.

Even though no power loans were made to Mexico after 1972, the possibility of a resumption of lending has been discussed on more than one occasion. The Mexican authorities have never regarded their differences with the Bank as a matter of principle. Indeed, the original target of a 9 percent return on assets was adopted by the Mexican government itself and accepted by the Bank as reasonable. Recently an interministerial group was set up to study and make recommendations to improve the financial situation of the power sector. It recommended that investment in power should be financed to the extent of 25 percent by internal cash generation. However, this would have required an immediate increase in rates of more than 40 percent, and the government was not prepared to go so far.

Neither in this case nor in those of other oil-producing developing countries has the Bank been prepared to modify its heavy emphasis on the importance of public saving, even though public savings were already high. For one thing, to do so would have made it much more difficult to pursue a consistent policy in other cases. Another reason is the undesirability of lending to an agency that is dependent on some form of government subvention to maintain its financial position. Economic considerations of efficiency pricing add a further argument. In Mexico, for example, for most of the 1970s, not merely electric power but most other energy prices were well below international levels. With energy problems playing such a large role in world economic development, it would have been difficult for the Bank to resume power lending in Mexico unless some action was being taken to remedy the financial situation of the sector.

## Indonesia

Bank and IDA lending to Indonesia began only in September 1968, about two years after the Suharto government replaced the previous regime. The Bank established a resident staff in Indonesia in mid-1968 to assist the new government in a number of ways, including the preparation of sector programs and projects. Thereafter Bank and IDA lending to Indonesia increased rapidly. The first power credit was made in October 1969 to improve the distribution system in Jakarta, and a second credit for a similar purpose was made in 1972. From then on a substantial loan or credit for electric power has been made every year except 1974.

All the earlier loans and credits were made in the context of a major program of technical assistance for the Indonesian government's power agency, the Perusahaan Listrik Negara (PLN). Because of the disorganized state of the sector and of PLN itself, it was not possible to appraise the project along customary lines. In particular, PLN's financial records were described as "essentially meaningless," and therefore the appraisal report was not able to provide the usual financial analysis. These financial problems, together with other problems of organization, management, operational efficiency, and planning, were to be tackled with the assistance of management consultants, financed from the credit. The terms of reference for the consultants covered a wide range of subjects, including the establishment of a modern system of uniform accounts, training in financial management and financial planning techniques, a review of the level and structure of tariffs, and assistance with the evaluation of PLN's assets. The credit agreement also included a rate covenant that tariffs would be set, within thirty-two months of the effective date of the credit, so as to enable PLN to finance a reasonable proportion of its capital expenditures. It was expected that the thirty-two months would give PLN a full year after the evaluation of its assets to introduce its new tariffs.

By the time of the third credit to PLN in 1973, the consultants had completed an evaluation of its assets and had prepared accounts for 1971 and preliminary budget figures for 1972. These revealed that PLN's financial situation was even weaker than the Bank had previously thought; it could not meet its expenses even before depreciation. The Bank, the government, and PLN then worked out a financial recovery program which PLN was to carry out with the assistance of its management consultants. This plan was to reduce PLN's operating costs by improvements in management, including operation and maintenance of the system, planning, finance, construction, and personnel. A comprehensive training program was to be introduced. The government also agreed that, as long as PLN continued to operate at a deficit, it would provide the necessary covering funds. The objective of the financial recovery program was that, by means of cost-reducing improvements in efficiency and tariff increases, revenues would cover 80 percent of operating costs by 1974–75, 90 percent in 1976–77, and 100 percent by 1978–79. The operation of the covenant in the previous loan requiring PLN to make a reasonable contribution to its investment was postponed until 1979.

This program was followed by a substantial improvement in PLN's financial situation. By late 1976 much progress had been made with regard to finance, accounting, and operations; less in improving construction and planning. PLN's capabilities in accounting and fund management were deemed comparable to those of other utilities in the area. Improvement in operations was reflected in increases in installed capacity per employee of over 60 percent and in customers per employees of about 20 percent between 1972 and 1976. Fuel efficiency had also increased and the training program had made a good start.

The financial targets which had been agreed on in connection with the 1973 credit were actually overfulfilled. Whereas it had been hoped that PLN would cover its operating costs by 1976, they were 97 percent covered three years earlier. This result owed a great deal to increases in electricity tariffs of 145 percent between 1973 and 1976. This extremely rapid increase seems to be virtually unique in the Bank's experience. The individual increases were often larger than those the Bank had suggested as appropriate. It was obviously to PLN's interest to free itself from financial dependency on the government, and it made a series of proposals for rate increases. But there is no obvious explanation of why these increases were accepted so readily by the government except that it was not under the usual pressures to keep rates low. There was no noticeable public protest when the rate increases were introduced; possibly they were regarded as part of the price of repairing the economic distortions left by the previous regime. Whatever the explanation, by 1979–80 it ceased to operate, and the Indonesian government became as sensitive as most others to the problems of rising electricity rates.

After the targets of the financial recovery program had been achieved, it was agreed that a cash generation covenant should be adopted. It provided that by 1984–86 PLN should charge rates sufficient to generate 30 percent of its investment during that period with interim targets of 12 percent (FY1980 and FY1981) and 18 percent (FY1982–83). To meet these interim targets a 38 percent increase was approved, after some delay, in June 1980, and a similar increase occurred in January 1983.

During the mid-1970s when power rates were increasing rapidly, the government of Indonesia was receiving a substantially increased flow of revenues from its oil production. But since the government felt under no pressure to keep power rates down, the earnings from oil did not have to be used to provide resources for the power sector. What will happen in the 1980s, when the government is much concerned about inflation, remains to be seen. But in retrospect the financial recovery of PLN from its disorganized situation in 1969 to a position of considerable financial strength by 1976 represents one of the most rapid institutional improvements in the Bank's experience of power lending.

## Argentina

The Bank's first power loan to Argentina was made in January 1962 to the Servicios Eléctricos del Gran Buenos Aires (SEGBA), the principal agency providing power to Buenos Aires. Since then the bank has made three further loans to SEGBA, in 1968, 1969, and 1976. In addition, two loans have been made to other agencies, one to HIDRONOR (Hidroeléctrica Norpatagonia) in 1968 for the El Chocon project and one in 1979 to EBY (Entidad Binacional Yacyreta-Apipe) for the large Yacyreta project on the Paraná river, which forms the border between Argentina and Paraguay.

The first loan was made after a large amount of preparatory work on the organization of the power supply for Buenos Aires and the role of the newly reorganized SEGBA (see chapter 3). A new concession to SEGBA permitted it to earn a return of 8 percent on its net fixed assets. For a time SEGBA's earnings were reasonable, but toward the end of 1963 there was a change of government in Argentina. The new government was not committed to all the reforms and policies that had formed the basis of the first SEGBA loan, and it did not accord SEGBA the rate increases necessary to meet the terms of the concession. Consequently, SEGBA's financial return fell to 2.1 percent in 1964. In 1965 and 1966 (when there was another change of government) rates were increased, however, and SEGBA's situation improved. The rate increases had to be substantial because of the rapid depreciation of the peso and the consequent devaluations during the 1962–67 period. By 1968, power rates were 4.7 times their level at the end of 1961. As a result, SEGBA's earnings in 1968 and 1969 exceeded the requirements of the concession. It was against this improving financial background that the second and third SEGBA loans were made.

As it turned out, 1969 was the last year SEGBA earned a return exceeding 8 percent. In an effort to fight increasing inflation in Argentina, the government once again did not permit SEGBA to charge rates in accordance with its concession. In 1972–73 rates in real terms were 40 percent lower than in 1967–68, whereas SEGBA's costs were only 20 percent lower. SEGBA's return declined to less than 1 percent in 1973, and in 1974 and 1975 its earnings were negative.

In March 1976 there was yet another new government, which took steps to deal with the financial problems of all the public enterprises.

SEGBA was authorized to increase its rates by 10 percent a month. At the time the fourth SEGBA loan was made, in September 1976, the monthly increases were expected to continue until December 1978, after which SEGBA would be able to earn the 8 percent on net revalued assets as stipulated in its concession. During 1977 and 1978, despite a clear improvement in SEGBA's situation, its return reached only about 5 percent instead of 8 percent.

In 1979 the situation deteriorated again, and there were renewed discussions about rates between the Bank and the government. Although the government had adopted an explicit policy of increasing rates each month by an amount estimated to exceed the rate of inflation, power rates in real terms had in fact declined because inflation proceeded faster than had been expected. But the financial problems of Argentina's power sector, as they appeared in 1980, were not confined to obtaining adequate rates. SEGBA had been compelled to borrow substantial amounts of short-term debt, the service on which reduced its cash generation; in 1979 SEGBA's cash generation was negative. In the discussions with the Bank, the Argentine authorities argued that if one of the financial tests was to be the proportion of cash generation to investment, the analysis should be done on the basis of the power sector as a whole. Their analysis consolidated the accounts of the major Argentine power agencies and made corresponding adjustments for the taxes paid by the agencies, the government's equity contributions to them, and the operation of the so-called electrical funds. These funds are derived from surcharges on sales of electricity and hydrocarbons and were used to finance investment in electric power. The government's analysis also included only *net* borrowings by the whole sector. Since debt service by the sector agencies was very high, this naturally improved the cash generation considerably. By thus netting out the serious problem of high debt service, this consolidated sector analysis avoided the problem of the financial viability of the separate agencies. The Bank, however, was not prepared to accept an approach which implied that the financial soundness of major agencies, such as SEGBA, was a matter of little consequence. In other cases, the Bank might agree that a particular agency could, for a valid reason, earn a low return if it was part of a larger system that was financially sound overall. But in Argentina, so many of the important agencies have difficult debt service problems that the sector as a whole cannot solve its problems without government action on rates and debt.

The financial problems of the Argentine power sector illustrate the point made earlier in this chapter that it is not possible to derive precise conclusions about the desirable level of power rates from financial analysis alone. Financial analysis always needs a judgment as to what rate of return or contribution to investment, however defined, is or is not "reasonable." Three separate but related issues are involved in any power sector analysis, all of which arose in the case of Argentina. The first is the question of rates. In Argentina a recent study of the structure of rates, based on marginal cost principles, shows that the present rates are significantly below long-run marginal costs. If it were agreed that rates should be at least equal to marginal costs, then two other problems would remain. There is the question of the financial viability of the separate agencies. This is largely a matter of dealing with the burden of accumulated debt by, for example, converting it to a longer term or providing some form of refinancing guarantee. Then there is the question of financing the investment on the major hydroelectric projects that are necessary to meet the economy's energy requirements. This is a question of public finance and borrowing policy, and for this purpose an analysis of the consolidated financial situation and hence the savings and investment position of the sector as a whole is a relevant approach.

## Uruguay

The power agency in Uruguay, the Administración Nacional de Usinas y Transmisiónes Eléctricas (UTE), has faced financial problems somewhat similar to those found in Argentina and to some extent for similar reasons. Since the late 1950s Uruguay has encountered serious economic and social problems as governments attempted to meet the demands of its predominantly urban and educated population by transferring income from a resource-rich agriculture to the urban areas. These policies led to slow growth and often rapid inflation, culminating in acute social conflict in the early 1970s. These events naturally affected UTE, not only its finances but also its management and operational efficiency.

The Bank has made five loans to UTE, the first three between 1951 and 1957 when UTE was a relatively well-managed and efficient utility. The fourth loan, in 1971, and the fifth, in 1980, both followed agreements between the Bank and Uruguay on measures to improve the financial position and efficiency of UTE. The 1971 loan was not followed by any improvement because of the serious inflation and social problems of the early 1970s. Then in 1974 it became clear that the country's economic problems, which had been exacerbated by the rise in the price of oil, required a fundamental change in policy. The government moved to improve resource allocation and productive efficiency through greater reliance on the price mechanism. There was a considerable liberalization of domestic price controls and of the trade and payments system, and these and other policies brought about a reversal of the economic decline.

In a mid-1976 review of the power sector the Bank outlined a plan to regulate the sector and improve UTE's operations. The government accepted the recommendations, and this eventually formed the basis for the fifth loan in early 1980.

After the new economic policies were adopted UTE's financial situation significantly improved. The rate of return reached nearly 7 percent in 1976 and was estimated to be over 10 percent in 1977 and 1978. The oil price increase of 1979 has made further rate increases necessary, however, if improvement is to be maintained. The improvement of the 1970s followed a long period of problems. Since the late 1950s UTE had not only financial difficulties but also management problems and a serious shortage of experienced staff owing to the limits placed on the salaries it was authorized to pay. Although the attempt to stem inflation by controlling prices, including power rates, was the major cause of its financial problems, UTE's other problems reinforced the government's reluctance to grant rate increases because of a belief that UTE could not use increased earnings efficiently. Reversing this vicious circle, whereby low earnings contribute to inefficiency which in turn makes it difficult to raise rates, is likely to be a major task after such a long period.

## Turkey

Economic conditions in Turkey, as in Uruguay, have been usually difficult since the first rise in oil prices in 1973. Turkey is so heavily dependent on imported oil that, after the 1979 increases, its oil import bill was about equal to its earnings from all merchandise exports. The Turkish Electricity Authority (TEK) was established in 1970 after a study financed by the Bank, and the basic law governing its structure and operations was also discussed with the Bank. This law provides that TEK should earn an 8 percent return, but in practice it has never done so except in 1972. The main reasons have been the familiar lag of rate increases behind inflation and the decline in the foreign exchange rate. In addition, TEK's operating costs were increased because it frequently had to make use of old plant owing to delays in the construction of projects, delays to which its financial difficulties contributed.

TEK has also had continual difficulties in collecting the amounts due from municipalities. The municipalities tend to divert their revenues from the distribution of electric power to meet the deficits incurred on other municipal services, particularly urban transport. The result has been that, periodically, the government has to consolidate the intra–public sector debts. In 1977 and 1978 the government took over all the municipal overdues to TEK more than three months old and reimbursed TEK from taxes collected from municipalities. This alleviated the symptom but did nothing to deal with the underlying problem, namely, the inadequacy of municipal revenues.

These serious problems were the subject of continuous discussion and negotiation between Turkey and the Bank, and for one loan there was a gap of two years between the date of signing and the date it was made effective while the Bank waited for some action on tariffs. After the rise in oil prices in 1979 the economic situation in Turkey became so critical that the government announced a series of far-reaching economic reforms and policy changes in the context of negotiations for assistance from the International Monetary Fund and other official and private creditors. These reforms and policy changes formed the basis for a structural adjustment loan from the Bank in March 1980. The government also proposed a radical reform of the finances of Turkey's state economic enterprises, of which TEK was one. After agreement on targets for cash generation by TEK and terms of reference for a review of the financial situation of the power sector, a further loan for TEK was signed in May 1980.

Bank lending for electric power in Turkey has not been confined to TEK. One loan was made for the distribution system in Istanbul and four loans have been made for the Cukurova Electric Company (CEAS), which supplies power to the three provinces of Adana, Icel, and Hatay on the Mediterranean coast. This company arose out of a loan made in 1952 for a multipurpose irrigation and power project involving a dam on the Seyhan river which flows through the Adana plain on Turkey's southern coast. Largely at the urging of the Bank, the government agreed that the power installations should be taken over and operated by a new private company. The company, CEAS, was established in 1953 and subsequently received four loans from the Bank between 1963 and 1971. By 1974 it had an installed capacity of 192 megawatts and provided 7 percent of the total power generated in Turkey. Although CEAS was established as an entirely private company, the government, through TEK, now owns 25.5 percent of its shares.

This small company has not had to face any of the difficulties which TEK has encountered. Being small, its rate increases could not be regarded as seriously interfering with the government's efforts to counter inflation. Not being a state economic enterprise, it could pay adequate salaries and thus avoid the serious shortage of experienced manpower which has plagued TEK throughout its history. It did not suffer unduly from large unpaid bills because those who purchased power knew that it could not fall back on the central government budget and would therefore be forced to cut off supply to any purchaser who became seriously delinquent. CEAS had other advantages. Since 1971 more than half its capacity was hydro, which lessened the effect of the rise in oil prices. And it could count on the strong support of both the Bank and the local businessmen, one of whom has been its chairman since it was first set up. With all these factors in its favor, CEAS succeeded in obtaining the rate increases necessary to maintain a strong financial position and managed to provide a reliable supply of power to the economically important areas it served. In 1978, after CEAS was linked to the central network, the government decided that all future expansion should be the responsibility of TEK.

## Perspective on Financial Results

To give a broader perspective on the financial performance of the Bank's power borrowers, appendix table 6 sets out the rate of return on net assets for power borrowers in thirty-three countries accounting for 68 percent of power lending. This indicator is given because it generally appears in the relevant covenant in the Bank's loan agreements and therefore becomes the most important single test of financial soundness. However, the limitations of the data and of the indicator itself must not be overlooked. Although the Bank has tried to follow a consistent method for calculating the rate of return, there are limits to what can be achieved when dealing with the accounts of so many different agencies. More important, the indicator does not reflect the debt service coverage of an agency. An agency may have an adequate return and yet be burdened by heavy debt payments and therefore unable to make a significant contribution to investment. Finally, the rate of return is affected by external factors such as the price of fuel, the level of wages, and, for a hydro system, the availability of water. It cannot, therefore, be taken by itself as the sole measure of efficiency.

The high and often steady return of many borrowers with strong financial situations emerges clearly. There are several instances in East Asia, such as Malaysia, Thailand, Taiwan, Singapore, and, more recently, Indonesia. In Latin America and Africa the picture is mixed. Brazil, Peru, Bolivia, and some countries in Central America, particularly Costa Rica, El Salvador, Nicaragua, and Honduras, generally maintained adequate earnings for many years. In Africa, Kenya, Tanzania (until recently), and Malawi have escaped serious financial problems but Nigeria, Ghana, and Sierra Leone have not. Finally, there are the countries whose serious financial problems have been described in the preceding section.

A few patterns can be discovered in this varied picture. Not surprisingly, many of the strong borrowers were set up in the early postwar period, or even before, and have enjoyed strong and stable governments. This is true of Malaysia, Thailand, Singapore, Taiwan, and, since the Bank began lending to it, Indonesia. In Africa, the governments in Kenya, Tanzania, and Malawi have all been strong and stable since their independence, while those in Nigeria, Ghana, and Sierra Leone have been much less so. In Argentina, Uruguay, and Turkey serious social and economic conflicts have sometimes been aggravated by rapid inflation. In Argentina the organization of the power sector was fragmented and without a strong central body to represent its interests. In Mexico and Nigeria the situation was different because public revenues from oil enabled the governments to meet any deficit arising from low power rates. In other countries, of which the Philippines is perhaps the clearest example, relations between the power agencies may generate conflicts that have adverse financial consequences on the sector or on some part of it.

Another pattern to emerge from appendix table 6 is the evolution of financial experience over time, particularly since the energy crisis. For example, some thirty of the thirty-three countries had agencies which, in either 1972 or 1973, were earning a return of 8 percent or more. After 1973 many borrowers showed a decline in their rates of return, which reflected both the direct effects of rising fuel costs and a more pronounced lag of power rates behind increasingly rapid inflation. In some countries the effect was temporary, but even financially strong borrowers are being affected. In Brazil, for example, the DNAEE has tried to limit rate increases by disallowing the inclusion of certain expenditures in the rate base, with the result that the rate of return may not reflect a decline in the agency's financial position. In Malaysia the National Electricity Board (NEB) was traditionally treated, for tax purposes, exactly as a commercial company. Recently the government has departed from this policy, however, and reduced NEB's tax payments in an attempt to mitigate increases in power rates.

## Progress with Efficiency Pricing

In recent years the Bank's efforts to protect and improve the financial position of its borrowers has been supplemented by what has become a major effort to encourage the use of efficiency pricing. The first significant step in this direction occurred in 1972 when the Bank initiated a research project on electricity pricing in developing countries. Some theoretical studies and pilot case studies were carried out. Later a practical methodology for determining marginal costs and preparing tariffs was developed, which took into account other constraints and policy goals, including financial viability, subsidies for poor consumers, problems of metering and billing, second-best considerations, and other objectives such as providing incentives for rural or regional development.

The results of this work were disseminated by publications and by seminars for senior managers and staff of utilities and government officials. Between 1978 and 1980 five one-week seminars were held, two in Asia, two in Latin America, and one in Africa.[6] The Bank has also urged its borrowers to undertake efficiency pricing studies, and by early 1982 forty-four studies had been completed and twenty-five more were under way. Some twenty countries had incorporated efficiency pricing principles, either fully or partially, into their tariff structures. All appraisal reports for power projects now comment on power tariffs in relation to marginal costs and discuss the implications for resource allocation. In a report on its research program the Bank recently wrote: "Over the past five years the principles of marginal cost pricing have been incorporated in a series of policy guidelines to Bank project staff. What in the late 1960s was considered to be 'academic' and 'impractical' is now little short of routine practice." This represents a major change since the Bank informed the Damodar Valley Corporation in 1957 that it had no wish to comment on the structure of its tariff.

## The Effects of Financial Stringency

The immediate effect of low earnings on a power agency is to present it with a problem of finding additional funds to carry out its investment program. One possibility is that the government may provide it with the necessary funds, perhaps in the form of additional equity, particularly if the government has funds available from oil revenues or some other source. In this case, as in Mexico and Nigeria, there may be very little

6. Some of the early results appeared in Ralph Turvey and Dennis Anderson, *Electricity Economics: Essays and Case Studies* (Baltimore, Md.: Johns Hopkins University Press, 1977). This contains chapters on the basic theory of marginal cost pricing and the first case studies on Thailand, Tunisia, and Sudan. Mohan Munasinghe and Jeremy Warford, *Electricity Pricing: Theory and Case Studies* (Baltimore, Md.: Johns Hopkins University Press, 1982) contains a systematic account of the methodology for preparing a marginal cost–based tariff and case studies on Indonesia, Pakistan, Philippines, Sri Lanka, and Thailand, all of which grew out of the two seminars held in Asia in 1978 and 1979.

effect on the power sector, but a reduction in resources available for investment elsewhere. A much more likely consequence is that the power agency is forced into additional borrowing, generally on fairly short terms. This solves the immediate problem but at the cost of reducing net cash available for investment in the longer run, so that the financing problem is only postponed. An agency that is constructing a major project, however, may be able to restore its financial position after the project is completed, if given enough time.

If the financial problems persist, they will probably affect the investment program and, eventually, the supply of power. Since electric power is generally recognized as a high-priority investment, most countries will try to allocate enough funds to it to avoid a serious interruption to the projects under construction. Nevertheless, low cash generation can contribute to a shortage of capital and affect the investment program. In principle, it could force power agencies to postpone capital-intensive hydro projects and build thermal plants instead. In practice, hydro projects are often constructed later than they should be, but lack of advance planning and delays in construction are usually to blame. A shortage of capital, however, can contribute to these problems and appears to have done so on occasion, for example in Yugoslavia and Chile.

The adverse consequences of financial stringency increase substantially if it is at all prolonged. The most serious effect is that high-priority expenditure or distribution and maintenance is neglected with the inevitable result that losses mount, the quality of service declines, and customers refuse to pay higher prices for poor service. This process is at the root of most of the power supply problems in many countries, large and small, and it can become so serious that investment in additional maintenance and more efficient distribution can have a much greater effect on output than the addition of generating capacity.

# 3. *Institutional Development in the Power Industry*

INSTITUTIONAL DEVELOPMENT or institution building can embrace a wide spectrum of topics having to do with the implementation of projects and the operation of many kinds of economic units. Certainly, in the power sector, the financial situation of a power agency is an essential element in its ability to operate efficiently. But this chapter is concerned with institution building in a narrower sense as it refers to the more strictly organizational problems that affect project execution.

The importance of ensuring that the executing agency has the capacity to carry out the project was brought home to the Bank soon after its early loans were made. One clear example occurred in connection with an early power loan to Brazil. The state of Rio Grande do Sul requested assistance in financing a program of electrification. The Bank agreed provided, first, that the agency responsible for it, the Companhia Estadual de Energie Elétrica (CEEE), an office in the state Secretariat of Public Works, was established as an entity independent of the state administration, and, second, that the state government should itself make a substantial financial contribution to the program. The first condition was met early in 1952 when the state legislature passed an act constituting CEEE as an autonomous state agency, and the second was met by a decision that the proceeds of the state electrification tax for 1952–60 should be paid to CEEE. The Bank's loan was made in June 1952 for $25 million.

Toward the end of 1953 and throughout 1954 it became clear that the project was encountering serious delays. After a number of visits by Bank staff, a special mission was sent to reappraise the project in early 1955, and its report was circulated to the Bank's Executive Directors, the Brazilian state and federal authorities, and CEEE. At that time, although the loan had been made three years earlier, the borrower had not made any drawings on the loan. The Bank then suspended the borrower's right to draw.

The root cause of the problem was that CEEE was attempting to carry out a much larger investment program than it ever had before, and it was using the same methods as in the past. Neither CEEE nor the Bank had foreseen the nature of the problems that would arise. The Bank's appraisal report had concentrated on an analysis of the investment program; it had only one paragraph on management, which said that CEEE had carried out earlier projects successfully and should have little difficulty in recruiting additional personnel if necessary.

The report of the 1955 mission emphasized a considerable number of matters, which later became incorporated into the Bank's normal appraisal and lending approach. For example, the report pointed out that CEEE had attempted to do virtually all the engineering work on the program, a task which proved beyond the capacity of its staff. Similarly, CEEE had tried to undertake construction jobs exceeding the capacity of its personnel and had used outside contractors only for limited purposes; moreover, some of the contractors were not sufficiently experienced for the job. The report was also critical of the absence of any long-term investment and financial planning based on estimates of future market demand.

At that time, CEEE prepared only annual budgets, which were necessary to comply with state law. The report therefore included a tentative estimate, prepared by the mission, of CEEE's probable capital needs and sources of funds for the following five years. This emphasis on the importance of forward planning also became a familiar subject in the Bank's relations with its power borrowers.

Another problem the report considered was the accounting procedures of the agency, which made no clear distinction between operating expenses and capital expenditure. It was thus impossible to ascertain the real cost of power production or to establish a proper rate policy. It was also impossible to know whether the proceeds of the electricity tax which had been turned over to CEEE had been used for investment or to subsidize consumption.

Two other significant factors contributed to CEEE's difficulties. One was that the federal government, through one of its agencies, was responsible for the construction of the civil works in the program although they had been designed and would be operated by CEEE. Since there was no clear distinction between the responsibilities of the federal agency and CEEE, each tended to hold the other responsible for any delays or mistakes. The second factor was that the organizational structure of CEEE concentrated too much responsibility at the center of the organization, particularly on the general manager. Part of the organization was thus "disastrously overworked," which caused much delay and inefficiency.

The problems the CEEE project encountered were not unique, but they are rather clear and well documented. Similar problems of execution that arose in a few Bank-financed projects during its early years of lending led to the extension of its ideas of project appraisal. From being concerned only with an economic and technical evaluation, appraisals began to investigate the method of execution and the ability of the borrower to execute efficiently and subsequently to operate the project. In turn this naturally led to a concern for strengthening the borrower's organization and procedures if it was thought necessary—in other words, to a concern for institution building.

With this extension of its concern the Bank's task became both more difficult and more apt to arouse controversy. The economic and engineering costs and benefits of a specific investment present a technical problem about which the appropriate experts should be able to reach agreement relatively easily. But the capacity of an agency to carry out a project calls for a much more qualitative judgment, impinging on matters into which some agencies might feel the Bank should not intrude. Hence these issues of institution building have come to occupy an important place in Bank-borrower relations. The final negotiations between the Bank and its borrowers, which take place just before loan proposals are presented to the Bank's Executive Directors for approval, are generally much more occupied with how the project is to be carried out than with what to do or whether or not to do it.

In the electric power sector two important aspects of institution building are, first, the organization and efficiency of the agency or agencies responsible for the provision of power and, second, the organization of the sector as a whole. In countries with only one or two agencies the second question may not be important, but in large countries with many agencies it can become a crucial matter. These two problems form the subject of the remainder of this chapter.

## The Power Agency

### Organization and Authority

The question of what kind of entity should be responsible for the provision of electric power has given rise to much debate. Since electric power is produced for sale, any electric power supplier has a strong commercial orientation. At the same time, since electricity is a necessity for virtually any economic development beyond the most elementary, governments anxious to foster development must ensure that sufficient power is available. An electric power system is also a natural monopoly, which constitutes another basis for government concern. To deal with all these elements governments have traditionally followed one of two possible approaches. The first is to establish the utility as a company, either wholly or partly private, with a concession defining its responsibilities and generally laying down the financial principles under which it will operate. The second is for the government to provide the power itself by giving some agency specific authority and objectives. In practice, the difference between these approaches has tended to diminish as the private companies have been nationalized or at least partly taken over, while the government agencies have often acquired considerable independence in their operations.

Of more significance than the legal form of any power agency is the way in which it can operate in practice. The Bank has directed its attention to this issue whether it has been concerned with private or semi-private companies operating under concessions or with government agencies operating in accordance with some general legislation. In numerous instances the Bank has participated with governments in discussions preparatory to the establishment of a new power agency.

In the early 1950s, in connection with its first power loan to Nicaragua, the Bank urged the government to set up a separate agency to supply power. The government moved the existing agency from the State Railways to the Department of Public Works and agreed to engage consultants to recommend measures to improve its organization and administration. The consultants investigated all aspects of the agency's organization, management, administrative procedures, rates, financial status, and accounting practices, and their recommendations were generally adopted. Accordingly, the Empresa Nacional de Luz y Fuerza became an autonomous public corporation. To strengthen the staff, the consultants helped recruit additional engineers, a chief accountant, a personnel officer, and others; they also supervised the initial operation of the project—a steam plant—and trained local operating staff.

The part played by the Bank in establishing TEK and CEAS in Turkey has already been mentioned. CEAS, however, was a unique case; it was the only time the Bank used its influence to establish a private electric power company.

The Bank was also directly involved in establishing the Swaziland Electricity Board and the Electricity Authority of Malta. In both these small countries, a new agency was set up when it became necessary to embark on a major power project. The legislation establishing both these agencies was worked out in close consultation with the Bank.

Reference has also been made to the Bank's role in the rehabilitation of PLN in Indonesia, a major instance of the use of consultants to assist the borrower with all aspects of management and administration. The contract for management services was signed in June 1970, extended in 1973, and completed in 1976. During this period, with the assistance of the consultants, new legislation was enacted to increase autonomy for PLN and make it responsible for project construction and some procurement of goods and services. A new accounting system was introduced and physical assets were classified and revalued. The consultants made recommendations on a new tariff structure and on personnel administration and the design of a training program.

Although there were, not unnaturally, some problems in the course of all this work—for example, the main consultants were French, which sometimes lead to language difficulties—the efficiency of PLN greatly improved. In 1969 PLN's situation had been so confused that it was impossible for the Bank to apply its normal appraisal methods to its first project. But by the mid-1970s, with the assistance of the consultants and as a result of the Financial Recovery Program (see chapter 2) PLN was financially viable and, although it still had numerous problems, was regarded as the best of the Indonesian government agencies.

In Sri Lanka the Bank also played a significant role in the establishment of the present Ceylon Electricity Board (CEB). Although the Bank's first power loan was made in 1954, there have been only six loans in the twenty-six years since then. The long gaps in lending reflect the quite difficult economic conditions which from time to time made the Bank reluctant to lend to Sri Lanka at all. Since about 1974, however, this situation has improved and Bank lending has been more regular.

As early as 1951, the Bank made a major economic survey of Sri Lanka. At that time, electric power was provided by the Department of Government Electrical Undertakings, and the Bank urged that the government set up an independent unit instead. The government said that such a unit was not feasible when the first loan was made, although it did agree to have an expert look into the problem. The expert concluded that an independent board should be set up, and by the time of the second loan in 1958 the government had the matter under study. In 1961 when the third loan was made, the government did agree to establish an independent board. The proposed legislation ran into political opposition, however, and was not passed until 1969, some fifteen years after the first loan. The fourth loan, made in 1969, provided for consultants' services to help establish the new board, reorganize the accounting system, and revalue the assets.

Many other examples could be given of the Bank's role in encouraging and assisting in the establishment of autonomous power agencies. As a result of these experiences, the Bank came to attach importance to certain attributes it believed were essential if a utility was to have sufficient authority to carry out projects and operate efficiently. First, the agency should have a competent management and preferably a separation between a board of directors responsible for policy and a management charged with its execution. Moreover, the management should have a high degree of continuity. If senior managers are subject to change with political changes in government, the consequences can be serious— particularly if long-term construction projects are under way, as is often the case. Second, the agency should have the authority to set wages and salaries so as to attract and retain staff and the authority to engage and dismiss staff. Third, the agency should be financially independent and viable. Fourth, it should have the primary responsibility for the procurement of goods and services. Of these, the financial issues have been discussed in chapter 2. To complete the picture, the following sections deal with the questions of management and staff, and of procurement.

## Management, Manpower, and Training

An experienced and capable staff is a prerequisite for any efficient institution. Of particular importance are the experience and ability of senior staff and the person who has final executive responsibility, whether as chairman, president, or general manager. One problem the Bank has had to face, particularly when a potential borrower was to be newly established or reorganized, was that the success or failure of its project was likely to be heavily or even decisively influenced by one person. If, as sometimes happened, a loan was signed before the new agency head was appointed, it did not seem unreasonable to ask that the person eventually selected be acceptable to the Bank, or at least that the Bank be consulted about the appointment. This led to a great deal of discussion both between the Bank and its borrowers and within the Bank itself. Many governments felt that requests of this kind infringed on their sovereignty. Hence the Bank tried to soften the wording of its proposed covenants; instead of requiring that an agency head be "acceptable," the Bank asked only to be consulted or even merely informed of the proposed appointment in sufficient time to comment.

In addition to the sensitive questions of principle, there were purely practical questions—for example, could the Bank be sure that a certain person would or would not be a successful agency head? The Bank was wary of political appointments—which are not uncommon, and not only in developing countries—but it was far from clear that it should object or that its objections would be considered. There were, of course, occasions when some people in the borrowing country welcomed the possibility of the Bank's taking a position on a proposed appointment because they believed it would be a beneficial influence. But in other cases such as Argentina this issue became a serious irritant. As experience accumulated, the Bank came to believe that the costs usually exceeded the benefits, and provisions of this kind are now infrequent.

Salaries are another major issue. Power utilities need trained engineers, accountants, and other personnel, and they often have to compete with the private sector for their services. If governments do not permit power agencies to pay adequate salaries, it is difficult to attract and hold a capable staff. Hence the Bank has often urged governments to allow higher salaries and, if possible, to grant an agency the necessary authority to determine its own salary policy. This matter can be both important and difficult.

In discussions which led to the establishment of TEK, the main government agency for the supply of power in Turkey, the Bank tried hard to persuade the government to permit TEK to determine its own salaries. As a State Economic Enterprise (SEE), however, TEK was subject to the same policies and regulations applying to SEEs generally. As a result, it has had considerable difficulty in building an adequate staff. From time to time the government has tried to ease the situation, but TEK's salary difficulties are part of the larger problem of the general efficiency of Turkey's SEEs. In cases like this, issues concerning institution building extend beyond the Bank's borrower itself to include not only the industry or sector but even the whole economy. It is hardly possible to tackle these problems within the context of a loan for a single project; they have to be dealt with on a wider basis, such as in the economic dialogue which is a part of the Bank's general relationship with its member countries.

The last main element in the Bank's efforts to assist borrower's with manpower problems is staff training. The technical requirements of operating a power system mean that some form of training is essential. Traditionally, suppliers of equipment to developing countries have trained local people to operate it. Some utilities established their own formal training programs or arranged for their personnel to be trained with utilities in Europe or North America. In its early years the Bank apparently found these arrangements adequate; moreover, the Bank did not then regard itself as an appropriate agency to organize or finance training. After the establishment of its affiliate, the International Development Association, in 1961, however, the Bank and IDA began to finance education projects and built up experience and a qualified staff in the field of education. Thus more attention was paid to the arrangements for staff training in borrowing agencies, while at the same time the need for such training grew as systems became more complex and projects became larger.

The project performance audits, which started around 1973, also emphasized that many projects were hampered by a shortage of well-trained personnel. Not only the power sector, but all sectors were affected. For example, transport systems suffered because of the time needed to make repairs, and farmers were unable to obtain the full benefit of irrigation when the system's management and maintenance suffered from inadequately trained staff.

These experiences, which were shared by other agencies working with education, indicated that responsibility for training should be divided between government and the various agencies in industry, agriculture, and the public services and that training should be both formal and nonformal. Formal training would be provided by the educational systems, but it should be supplemented by nonformal training by entities directly concerned with the construction or operation of projects.

The Bank began to supplement its direct lending for education by providing funds to finance specific training needs—such as for power station technicians, water and sewerage plant operators, locomotive drivers and maintenance staff, and lighting maintenance staff—in projects other than education projects. Project-related training expanded rapidly during the decade of the 1970s. In FY1972, out of 140 projects financed by the Bank and IDA, 52 included training components which together were allocated $6.58 million, or 0.25 percent of total financing. By FY1979 the number of projects with training components had risen to 152 (out of 247), but the amount of money provided had increased to $139.7 million, or 1.5 percent of total financing. This represents an almost ninefold increase in constant dollars. Since FY1975 about 10 percent of all the funds allocated to project-related training has been for power projects; power therefore ranks third after agriculture, which took 47 percent, and transport, which accounted for 21 percent.

What kinds of project-related training were most effective, how best to organize it, and the main factors determining success or failure also received much attention during the 1970s. Normally regarded as constituting project-related training are, first, study tours and fellowships that enable personnel to train abroad or simply to visit similar projects in other countries. Second is "off-the-job" training in technical schools or colleges or specially established training institutions. This is useful when there is a substantial number of trainees as, for example, in distribution system maintenance. Third and most useful is on-the-job training, if the right people can be found to do the training. Project managers and other senior staff can do some on-the-job training as part of their normal duties, but the quality of such training tends to be uneven because it is given lower priority than constructing or operating the project. Consultants are often used and some now specialize in training. Consultants can be very successful if they have the necessary experience and are able to work effectively in the country concerned. The best method is to build up a permanent professional training staff with full-time responsibility for training. To do this, however, obviously takes time.

Since a great deal of the Bank's lending for project-related training is fairly recent, little information is available about the results. Some factors, however, clearly influence the degree of success. A frequent problem is to ensure that training is given a high enough priority. Project managers are not always sufficiently convinced of the benefits of training to devote the necessary time and money to it. Training inevitably tends to interfere with day-to-day operations; supervisors must devote time to it and staff have to attend courses.

When consultants are employed to prepare and carry out training programs, it is essential that they have a clear understanding with the agency about not merely the objectives of the program but also how it is to be carried out. In practice, the agency must be organized to make proper use of the expertise being provided—that is, it must have the necessary "absorptive capacity." This point is well illustrated by one loan operation that clearly failed to accomplish its objective.

In 1975 the Bank made its third loan to the Liberian Electric Company (LEC), solely for technical assistance to improve management, particularly financial management and long-term planning, and to facilitate the process of Liberianization by training qualified nationals. The progress achieved under this loan was negligible. The experts were recruited individually and, not unnaturally, could not operate as a team. Moreover, personnel changes in LEC and in the government hampered the government's support for the scheme. The result was that the efforts of the expatriate experts were almost wholly absorbed by operational work. Although the consultants may well have provided useful services while they were working in LEC, they left behind little by way of additional trained personnel. Hence the fourth loan, in 1978, provided for a different approach, with technical assistance provided by a team from Tata Consulting Engineers, a division of Tata Sons Ltd., of India. The Tata group operates a large power system in the Bombay area, and the use of experts from such a source has several advantages. The team would have the backing of an experienced utility with large resources. Individual experts would have job security, and anyone who did not work out could be easily replaced. If necessary, specialized personnel could be sent from headquarters for specific tasks. These advantages are considerable, although technical assistance furnished by this method does tend to be more expensive. In this particular case, the management team was expected to draw up a comprehensive program and to devote about half its time to staff training. Funds were provided to establish a training school for technical, accounting, and administrative staff. The program was also to use the services of the Monrovia Vocational Training Center, which had been financed under a separate education loan from the Bank, and some training was to be provided by one of the local iron mining companies. Altogether considerable preparatory work was done for this component of the fourth project, and the experience of the third project was taken into account.

The shortage of skilled and experienced personnel tends to be greater in low-income countries, but there are opportunities for the Bank to assist with training problems even in higher-income countries. In 1976, for example, a power loan to Brazil, probably the most sophisticated of the Bank's power borrowers, included a substantial training component. Although a comprehensive training system for the power sector in Brazil already included numerous programs in universities and special training centers, the growth of the interconnected system and the emergence of new technologies associated with extra-high-voltage transmission made it necessary to organize another training program in this specialized field. The Brazilian authorities asked the Bank to include funds in the loan to meet the foreign exchange costs of sending some 1,800 staff from various power companies to seminars, short courses, and periods of attachment to power companies at a similar stage of development in the United States and Europe. Thirty-six professors from engineering schools in Brazil would be included so that they could establish the necessary courses in their own faculties on their return. The total cost of this program was estimated at $15.4 million, of which the Bank would provide the necessary foreign exchange, $4.3 million. This is, of course, a relatively small proportion of the total loan of $82 million, and it was very small indeed by comparison with the total volume of investment in power in Brazil. The power agencies found it useful to have the Bank's approval of the program, however, to help justify it to other parties in Brazil and, since the Bank was providing the foreign exchange, to avert any possible criticism of staff traveling abroad.

## Procurement

That the Bank has a legitimate interest in the consultants and contractors employed on projects it finances is now generally accepted by the Bank's borrowers. Covenants stipulating that consultants and contractors used for the project should be acceptable to the Bank are now a standard feature of loan and credit agreements. The borrower has the final decision on which consultant or contractor is awarded a contract, but the Bank has the right to withhold use of the loan if it finds the contract for some reason unacceptable. The Bank's normal practice is to review the list of prequalified bidders, the bid documents, evaluation of bids, and the proposed award. In this way, the Bank is kept informed about the progress of procurement and has an opportunity to comment at any stage. In almost all cases any differences of view can be agreed or compromised before the final award is made. Although these issues often provoke considerable discussion, only rarely do disagreements persist so far that the Bank declines to proceed.[1]

The Bank's concern with procurement arises not only because experienced consultants and contractors are essential for the efficient construction of a project but also because procurement by international competitive bidding can mean substantial economies for the Bank's borrowers.[2] Although there are very few data on precisely how large these economies are, the indications are that they can be substantial. For example, in 1969 the Bank was asked to finance a power project in Ethiopia for which bids had already been received. Because the financing was tied, these bids had been confined to suppliers in a single country and were much higher than the engineer's estimates. After the Bank agreed to finance the project new bids were requested under international competitive bidding, and those received were substantially less than the original bids—some little more than half the first prices quoted.

International competitive bidding for Bank-financed projects ensures that potential suppliers in all member countries have a fair opportunity to secure orders placed by the Bank's borrowers. Since orders for Bank projects—not only for electric power but for other sectors as well—are eagerly sought by suppliers, the Bank has to make sure that the procedures followed by its borrowers are as fair and equitable as possible. It has gradually evolved a set of guidelines for procurement which are now, in effect, incorporated into its loan agreements and which borrowers are required to follow unless there is good reason not to. A substantial part of

---

1. For example, in early 1981, the government of India had decided to award a contract to a certain firm for engineering services on the construction of a fertilizer plant, and the Bank had accepted this decision. When the government later awarded the contract to a different firm, the Bank regarded the change as unjustified and withdrew from the project. This incident was sufficiently unusual that it received a great deal of publicity.

2. International bidding is possible because the Bank's funds can be used for purchases in any of its member countries and in Switzerland. When the practice of restricting the use of Bank funds to member countries was introduced in 1956 it was thought appropriate to make an exception for Switzerland because it was an important purchaser of Bank bonds.

the time of the Bank's technical staff is devoted to following procurement problems, and the Bank conducts regular courses on procurement both in Washington and in member countries. Since its early operations, when the Bank simply requested its borrowers to use international competitive bidding and assumed that the meaning of this term was more or less self-evident, the Bank has moved toward setting standards for international bidding. By following procurement procedures closely and attempting to improve the procurement skills of its borrowers, it helps ensure that its loans are used "with due attention to considerations of economy and efficiency."

## The Organization of the Power Industry

The structure of the electric power industry in developing countries—as in developed countries—varies considerably depending on the size of country, the nature of its power resources, and historical accident. In many developing countries that were formerly dependent territories, the organization followed that of the mother country. Commonly, the first power was supplied by a government department, often the Public Works Department. As the system developed, responsibility was often transferred to some autonomous public agency, which was the government's "chosen instrument" and often given a monopoly position. This sequence, familiar in many small and medium-size countries in Africa and Asia, is one of the simplest examples of structural evolution. In Latin America it was usual to arrange for a private utility to provide power in accordance with a concession agreement.

Considerably more complicated is the situation in many larger countries in which power development was initiated by private companies or municipalities in a number of centers. When it becomes economic to link the centers together and build larger plants, some form of cooperation becomes essential for the efficient operation and development of the system as a whole. A network consisting of a number of agencies requires a centralized load-dispatching system to ensure that power is generated and transmitted to where it is needed in the most economical way.

The proper development of an integrated network has to be centrally planned. If there are separate agencies the planning has to be done cooperatively or some central agency needs to have enough authority to ensure that its plans are carried out. Adequate institutional arrangements for this purpose are difficult to make, since individual agencies may need to come under greater central control or be merged, both of which they often resist.

## The Growth of Integrated Networks in Large Countries

In a few large countries, such as France and Indonesia, one organization is responsible for electric power supply for the whole country. But in most large countries, networks in different parts of the country have expanded and been linked up in a gradual process of organizational change and consolidation. In some countries, particularly in Latin America, the process of organizing the growing power sector has been closely linked to the nationalization of the numerous private power companies, usually foreign-owned, that provided most of the power at the end of World War II. The way this process occurs can be seen in the following examples of the development of integrated networks in Mexico, Brazil, and India.

MEXICO. The main government-owned power utility in Mexico, Comisión Federal de Electricidad (CFE), was first established in 1937. After the war its installed capacity began to expand rapidly, and it also purchased a large number of small power companies. In 1960 the Mexican government purchased the assets of the American and Foreign Power Company's subsidiary in Mexico and acquired the shares of the Mexican Light and Power Company. In the years following, CFE purchased more than fifty operating companies, and by 1965 the government controlled all but 2 percent of the public power supply. Only two major entities other than CFE remained in the power field. One was Industria Eléctrica Mexicana, S.A. de C.V. (IEMSA), to which had been transferred the assets of the American and Foreign Power Company, and the other was Compania de Luz y Fuerza del Centro (Centro), formerly Mexlight, now government-owned, which provided electric power to Mexico City.

Although the private companies had been taken over and the industry was all government-owned, it was not a unified organizational system. In most cases the original organizations still continued to operate, even though they might have a new name and a new owner. Originally the government had intended to consolidate all its power holdings into one integrated national organization. In 1962 a report by Electricité de France and the French consultants, SOFRELEC, recommended that a single autonomous agency be set up. Two years later a committee appointed by the government prepared a comprehensive report on the power sector and came to much the same general conclusions: there should be a new organization with complete responsibility for the planning, organization, development, and coordination of the public power sector.

The consolidation of the sector proved to be slow and difficult. A major obstacle was that the various power agencies and companies had different labor unions, and an agreement had to be reached between them before any full mergers could take place. In 1966 an agreement between two labor unions enabled IEMSA, together with eighteen of its subsidiaries, to merge with CFE. This left two major agencies in the power sector: CFE and Centro. In 1969, under the pressure of financial problems, CFE became responsible for debt and fund management for the sector. Three members of CFE's board were also put on the board of Centro, and in 1970 the director general of CFE became president of Centro as well. However, Centro still preserves its separate identity.

Throughout this process, Bank appraisal reports and loan documents reflected its continual concern with the sectoral organization and its constant endeavors to persuade the Mexican authorities to push ahead with consolidation of and long-term investment planning for the entire sector. The appraisal report for its 1958 loan pointed out the areas in which the Bank believed investment planning needed to be improved. It stated that the various investment projects had not been coordinated with those of other companies in the interconnected system. Consequently, there had been some duplication of investment, and some plants had been constructed which were much smaller than would have been justified if the interconnected system had been considered as a whole. CFE agreed with the Bank that "substantial economies could be made in the future cost of generation in the interconnected systems by strengthening the facilities for exchanging power between the Commission [CFE] and the interconnected companies, and by coordinating the future plant investments of the parties to these systems." The Bank informed CFE that it considered this coordination to be of such importance that it would like to see substantial progress made before pursuing the possibility of further financing.

The following loan, made in 1962, included a covenant that CFE would conclude agreements with Mexlight and IEMSA to coordinate the operation of their systems and the planning of their investments over a five-year period. A side letter set out details of how this coordination should be carried out: the investment plan should be revised annually, and there should be studies on the advisability of interconnecting the major systems and standardizing the country's frequencies.[3]

3. In Mexico at that time, the generation facilities of CFE operated at 60 cycles per second (Hz) but those of Centro were 50 Hz. A study done in 1963 confirmed the economic advantages of converting Centro's system to 60 Hz to obtain an integrated operation. The documents for Bank loans made in 1965 and 1968 provided for completion of the first stage of a frequency unification program, but nothing was accomplished. A new master plan was prepared, and the documents for the 1970 loan provided that the first phase of a frequency

*(continued on next page)*

By December 1965 when the Bank made the first of its four sector loans, some further progress on coordination had been made. The government had agreed that CFE would review the budgets of all entities within the power sector and would have full budgetary control over the operations and expansion of such entities. The investment program of Centro would be limited to the expansion of transmission and distribution facilities and to maintenance and improvement of its generating facilities. The appraisal report for this loan contained a lengthy discussion of the history and problems of the power sector, with particular emphasis on organizational and financial matters. It summarized the Bank's views of the situation at the time:

> In order for the proposed loan to have the maximum of coordination in the sector, the ideal arrangement would be to have a single organization be the borrower, responsible for the planning, operation and financing, and subject to the Bank's loan covenants and requirements. Such an entity does not yet exist; and since its formation at this time would require the prior solution of such serious problems as different wage scales of the three labor unions and the dissolution of Mexlight, it is proposed: (a) to accept as a transitory measure CFE as the borrower, (b) to have CFE make available part of the loan funds to CLFC [Centro] and IEMSA on terms and conditions satisfactory to the Bank, and (c) to base the rate and debt limitation covenants on the consolidated figures of the three entities.

After 1965 consolidation of the sector gradually moved ahead. By 1972 when the Bank made its last power loan to Mexico, it was concerned not with sectoral coordination but with the internal efficiency of CFE in the face of its rapidly expanding responsibilities. Emphasis was on the implementation of CFE's new computerized system for budget control and for control of the construction program. The Bank was also urging CFE to prepare an investment program for generation and transmission based on a

---

unification program should be completed by September 1972. Again, although new equipment was purchased, no conversion was actually carried out. The frequency unification program was apparently delayed because the Mexican authorities feared widespread protests by the consumers affected by it.

   In May 1972, two weeks before the negotiations for the next loan, a Frequency Unification Committee was established and proposed yet another schedule. This time the program was accomplished. In fact the entire conversion was completed by November 1976, one year ahead of schedule and at a cost, in real terms, 18 percent below the forecast. The rate of return on the conversion was estimated at 12 percent at appraisal, but because of the lower costs and speedier execution the ex post rate of return must have exceeded this. In the event, there were no protests by consumers.

twenty-year time horizon, and the loan included funds for consultants to prepare such a program.

BRAZIL. Before World War II, private companies on the coast provided most of the power in Brazil. After the war the federal government entered the power industry by establishing the Companhia Hidro-Elétrica do São Francisco (CHESF) to provide power for the development of the Northeast. During the 1950s both the federal and the state governments established additional companies in the different regions of the country.

In 1961 the Brazilian government created the Centrais Elétricas Brasileiras S.A. (ELETROBRAS), primarily to act as a holding company for the utilities owned by the government. It has since become one of the key organizations in the whole sector. In 1964 it took over the Brazilian assets of American and Foreign Power and was later made responsible for administering public funds allocated to the power sector. It has also become responsible for investment planning and for coordinating the operation of generation and transmission facilities throughout the country.

The influence of ELETROBRAS arises from its control over the allocation of public funds and the terms on which they are made available to the major utilities; it does not have any legal authority over the other sector agencies. Government authority over the sector is exercised by an agency of the Ministry of Mines and Energy, the National Department of Water and Electric Energy (DNAEE), established in 1967. Its control over rates and other tariff matters has already been described (chapter 2); it also participates in national energy planning and is responsible for the development of procedures and standards for the industry, including those for load forecasting, and for a study of ways to increase service to low-income rural and urban populations.

In 1973, some years after the establishment of ELETROBRAS and DNAEE, Coordinating Groups for Interconnected Operations were authorized, of which there are now two. These groups bring together all utilities in a given system and are responsible for maximizing the efficiency of the generating plants and transmission system of the whole group. They have developed effective procedures for preparing operations plans, establishing operating criteria, and reviewing system performance, but with the increasing complexity of the Brazilian system and the prospect of very large hydro projects soon coming on stream these procedures will have to be strengthened. Consequently, the government recently started to set up a National System of Supervision and Control of Interconnected Operations. It will consist of a National Center for Supervision and Coordination and System Operations Centers at eight of the major utilities. By means of computers and telecommunications these will form a hier-archical control system for the operation of the Brazilian interconnected power network. The Bank made a loan to assist in establishing this system in December 1980.

Between 1965 and 1981, in addition to making twenty-three loans for a total of $1,350 million for the expansion of Brazil's power sector, the Bank was concerned with two aspects of the integration of the system. Its concern with financial matters and the procedure for determining rates has already been described. It was also much concerned with the desirability of more comprehensive investment planning over a long time horizon. The first major step of this kind was in 1963–65 when the so-called Canambra plan was prepared. This was an investment program for the South-Central region to meet the expected demand in 1970. It was prepared by a group of consultants financed by the United Nations Special Fund, and the Bank served as executing agency. Much more recently the Bank and ELETROBRAS have discussed the objectives and methodology of investment planning in view of Brazil's rapidly expanding and increasingly integrated system. These discussions have centered around the preparation by ELETROBRAS of an investment plan extending to the year 2000.

The electric power sector in Brazil, although the largest and most complex of all developing countries, is now well organized and most of the major agencies are efficiently operated. The effective organization combines the legal authority of DNAEE over licensing, the final approval of expansion, and particularly the setting of tariffs; the influence of ELETROBRAS in planning and investment and its control over the allocation of public funds for investment; and the coordination of operations through the Coordinating Groups and new National System for the Supervision and Control of Interconnected Operations. This does not, of course, mean that all sectoral problems have been solved, but the organization of the sector does not act as a constraint.

INDIA. The size of the power sector in India, as measured by installed capacity, is very much the same as that in Brazil: in 1979 both were around 29,000 megawatts. In Brazil 85 percent of the capacity is hydro, but in India 60 percent is thermal and only 37 percent hydro, the remainder being nuclear. The Brazilian system, however, is largely concentrated in the more developed south and east of the country, and the process of making it into an interconnected system is well advanced. In India, the capacity is spread over a much wider area, with concentrations around the Punjab in the north, Calcutta in the east, and Bombay in the west, and smaller developments around Madras and in the south. The linking together of these various generating centers has only recently begun. Similarly, although the process of establishing and adapting the institutions necessary for the efficient planning and operation of an interconnected network is now essentially complete in Brazil, it is at a much earlier stage in India.

As already noted, under India's Constitution electric power is a concurrent subject, that is, one on which both the central and the state governments can pass legislation. This division of responsibility was reflected in the Electricity (Supply) Act of 1948 which established State Electricity Boards (SEBS) and a Central Electricity Authority (CEA). The functions of the CEA were to develop national power policy, to report the progress of the electricity supply industry, to provide technical assistance, to train personnel, to promote research, and in general to facilitate efficient power supply. It was responsible, in consultation with state governments, for planning, coordination, design, and construction of schemes for power generation and water utilization. It was, however, limited to an advisory role, and for many years its responsibilities were carried out by the Central Water and Power Commission, the technical arm of the Ministry of Irrigation and Power.

In 1951 there were about 270 power undertakings operated by state governments and municipalities and over 300 private ones. Since then the SEBS have taken over most of these, so that by 1976–77 only 47 private undertakings and 21 municipal ones remained, of which only 12 had any generating capacity. The public sector accounted for 86 percent of total electricity sales. As installed capacity grew it became clear, in India as elsewhere, that there were economies to be gained from an interconnected system. The first institutional response to this need came in the first half of the 1960s with the establishment, by common resolution of the state and central governments, of five Regional Electricity Boards (REBS). The REBS were to coordinate planning and operation of the SEBS in their region, review the progress of projects, coordinate maintenance schedules, and determine the availability of power for interstate transfer and a suitable tariff for such transfers. The effectiveness of the REBS has, however, been limited, chiefly because India's periodic power shortages have reduced the potential incentives and gains from coordination.

Another step toward more coordination came in 1976 when the 1948 Electricity (Supply) Act was amended to strengthen the CEA and provide for new generating companies in the public sector. The CEA was given the authority to approve all investments costing Rs10 million or more. (Virtually all generation and transmission schemes do cost more than this.) It can also modify schemes or require them to be postponed or moved forward. In principle, these provisions lay the legal foundation for coordinated planning for an interconnected system, although only a little progress has so far been made. The CEA has, however, made some progress in financial matters. It has advised state governments on the implementation of the financial provisions of the amendments to the 1948 act, and it has been able to persuade all SEBs to adopt a uniform system of financial accounting, an essential prerequisite for coordinated operation in the long run.

Perhaps the most significant development for the long term was the establishment in 1975 of the National Thermal Power Corporation (NTPC) and the National Hydro Power Corporation (NHPC). Owned by the central government, they were set up to exploit natural resources on a scale and in a way that would not be possible if done by the states. To exploit India's large resources of coal to maximum advantage requires the construction of very large plants capable of supplying more than one state. The harnessing of hydro resources, most of which are in the Himalayas, presents a similar problem.[4] The investment program of NTPC, begun in 1977, consists of four large thermal power stations which will eventually have a combined capacity of 7,300 megawatts. This will increase the total capacity in India, as of 1979, by 25 percent. Because of the much longer time required to study and prepare hydro projects, the program of NHPC has not yet got under way. The growth of these two corporations will mean that a substantial proportion of India's generating capacity and key parts of its transmission system will come under the control of the central government.

As these new large thermal and hydro plants are built and the interconnected system expands, the institutional arrangements for coordinating the growth and operation of the system will need to be strengthened. At the moment, the authority and influence are much less centralized than is the case in Brazil. The CEA in India does not have the authority that the DNAEE does in Brazil. Through its power of financial supervision and audit over the power utilities and its control of the Global Guarantee Fund, DNAEE is able to secure a uniform policy on rates for the whole country; in India rates are under the control of state governments. In India there is no organization similar to ELETROBRAS with control over a substantial volume of public funds to be allocated for power investment and with responsibility for preparing investment plans for the whole system. In India all funds for power investment, other than those for the two central corporations, are channeled through state governments. These differences reflect the provisions of the Indian Constitution, which mean

---

4. In Brazil the nature of the physical resources also made it necessary to coordinate the operation of hydro plants situated in cascade on major rivers.

that the central and the state governments have to agree on the plans and policies of the SEBs.

The recent report of the Committee on Power recommended that by 2000 the central government should own and operate at least 45 percent of the total generating capacity in the country and all the transmission lines necessary for the flow of power between different regions of the country. While the committee recognized that a single all-India corporation would theoretically be the most appropriate form of organization, it thought that such a large undertaking would tend to become over-centralized and too bureaucratic. Instead, it recommended a Regional Electricity Authority and a Regional Electricity Generating Corporation for each of the five regions in the country. The Regional Electricity Authorities would replace the old Regional Electricity Boards, but the new authorities would be full-time statutory bodies with a much wider range of responsibilities. They would operate regional load dispatch centers and interstate transmission lines so that they would have effective control of the generation and movement of power within their regions. They would be responsible to the CEA, which would thereby have greatly increased ability to influence the planning, contribution, and operations of the power sector. It would be involved in project appraisal, the evolution of planning methodologies, the monitoring and evaluation of projects and of the financial performance of power agencies, and would advise on tariffs and numerous other matters.

As the problems of coordination emerged in India, the Bank emphasized strengthening the institutions required to deal with it. It favored giving greater authority to the CEA. It helped finance the cost of consultants to study the technical, economic, and financial aspects of a long-term national plan for the sector. The Bank suggested terms of reference for such a study, and after considerable discussion with CEA, NTPC, and NHPC the suggestion was approved. In 1979 the Bank itself prepared a report, "Economic Issues in the Power Sector," which reviewed the prospective supply and demand for electric power. It concluded that the proposed volume of investment in power, even though it was larger than in previous plans, should be increased further if the shortages which have characterized the power situation for the past several years are to be overcome.

The Bank has been participating in the financing of all four thermal plants being constructed by NTPC and expects to be involved with the forthcoming hydro plants to be built by NHPC. It will therefore be in close contact with those institutions during a period when many crucial problems about sectoral organization will have to be solved.

*Organizational Change in Smaller Countries*

A somewhat similar kind of organizational change has occurred in several smaller countries. In Chile, Guatemala, Costa Rica, and El Salvador no large separate systems had to be linked, but in each country the power supply in the capital city was originally provided by a private foreign company. In the first three countries the government acquired the private company, and it had to be integrated into the system with the government's principal power agency.

In Chile, El Salvador, and Costa Rica the problems of coordinating the two agencies were reasonably well overcome. In Chile the government acquired control of Chilectra, the subsidiary of American and Foreign Power which held a concession covering Santiago and Valparaiso, in 1970. Cooperation between Chilectra and ENDESA, the chief government utility, has not been a problem. Similarly, in El Salvador the private company serving San Salvador is almost entirely for distribution. This simplifies the division of responsibility and facilitates coordination between the company (which remains private) and the main government agency, CEL.

In Costa Rica the government agency, ICE, purchased CNFL (which operated in San José) from American and Foreign Power in 1968. The Bank's fourth loan to ICE, made in 1972, provided for a study of sectoral organization, and the consultants who conducted this study recommended that ICE absorb CNFL and other private and municipal power companies over a five-year period. The government of Costa Rica did not disagree that a unified power sector would be more efficient, but because of political and organizational difficulties it preferred to encourage cooperation between ICE and CNFL and have ICE absorb the other companies gradually and voluntarily.

Events in Guatemala were very similar. EEG, which supplied power to Guatemala City, was financially stronger and more efficient than the government's agency, INDE, which was responsible for generation and transmission elsewhere in the country. Relations between the two agencies had been marked by periodic conflict even after the government became the owner of EEG in 1972. There was no coordinated load forecasting or sector-wide financial planning, nor was there any unified policy on tariffs to final consumers. In 1976 a special government commission recommended that only one entity be responsible for public electricity supply and that INDE absorb EEG's operations as well as those of other private and municipal utilities. Among the many obstacles, however, was the fact that EEG's unionized employees had higher pay scales than those of INDE. After reviewing the matter, the government decided not to merge EEG and INDE, at least for the time being, but to transfer all EEG's generating plants to

INDE. It also appointed a new committee to study the advisability of establishing a regulatory commission for the power sector.

Two countries which had a different solution to this kind of problem were Panama and the Philippines. In both countries the Bank was drawn into institutional conflicts within the sector. In Panama, the Bank's borrower was the Instituto de Recursos Hidráulicos y Electrificación (IRHE), an agency established in 1961 to provide power to four so-called Central Provinces, which were among Panama's least developed. In 1969 IRHE was given responsibility for developing all new sources of generation in the country. It sold part of its output to the Compañía Panamania de Fuerza y Luz (FYL), a private company which supplied power to Panama City and Colon. According to a 1958 Panamanian law, FYL was supposed to return to the government any earnings above a certain figure, but this was not enforced until 1969, when a new government passed a decree reactivating a Regulatory Commission with the authority to enforce the old law. The new government was intent on recovering what it regarded as the excess profit retained by FYL in the years when the law was not enforced. The Bank, however, was about to make a substantial loan to IRHE and was anxious to have the dispute between the government and FYL settled. Since IRHE's earnings depended partly on its sale of power to FYL, the Bank also had, indirectly, a financial interest in FYL. The Bank wanted assurance that FYL would not be seriously weakened by the application of the new decree, but the government appeared to feel that the Bank was taking the part of FYL. Eventually the Bank proceeded with its loan on the understanding that the relevant provisions of the 1969 decree would not be applied retroactively. In 1972 the government mandated a substantial tariff reduction for FYL on the ground that investments resulting from previous earnings in excess of those permitted by the law should be excluded from the rate base. FYL thereupon stated that it would not proceed with its expansion program, and it withheld payments for all supplies. The government then nationalized FYL and its properties were later transferred to IRHE.

In the Philippines, the competition between NPC and MERALCO (see chapter 2) created, on one occasion, a different kind of problem for the Bank. In 1963 NPC first requested a loan from the Bank for a 75 megawatt thermal power plant at Bataan. NPC claimed the plant was needed to meet its future load and to supplement the generation from its hydro plants with firm power. At that time NPC's capacity was entirely hydro, whereas MERALCO's was very largely thermal. After studying this proposal the Bank concluded that there would be little need for the Bataan plant if the facilities of NPC and MERALCO were operated as an integrated system. But it was also clear that there was virtually no prospect, at that time, that the system would be operated on an integrated basis. Specifically, MERALCO was not prepared to provide an assurance that it would supply the thermal power necessary to firm up NPC's capacity; indeed, MERALCO wanted to be independent of NPC and was planning to expand its capacity for that reason. NPC was similarly determined to reduce its dependence on MERALCO, and when the Bank had reservations about the Bataan project, it began to explore the possibility of other financing. It was also apparent that the government was not in a position to force the two agencies to cooperate.

This situation gave rise to prolonged discussion within the Bank. Could the Bank properly regard the project solely from the point of view of NPC's system? This could be defended on the ground that the Bank would be accepting the reality of a situation it could not change. Nevertheless, the project was for that very reason a second-best solution. In the end the Bank did make the loan. It was concerned to continue its support of NPC and to proceed with certain institutional improvements which NPC had agreed to carry out. All this could have been jeopardized and whatever influence the Bank had with NPC greatly reduced if the loan had been refused on the principle that projects should be justified in the context of the whole sector. This decision does seem to have been warranted, since some improvement was made in NPC's management and internal financial reporting systems and, as noted in chapter 2, MERALCO was later reduced to a distribution agency and NPC became responsible for all generation.

As these examples show, it is advisable to give one agency the overall responsibility for operating, or coordinating the operation of, an inter-connected power system and for determining the investment program for its expansion. The desirability of such an institutional arrangement is apparent to outside experts, whether foreign consultants or national commissions. But institutions resist being consolidated or dismantled, and governments are therefore reluctant to attempt such measures unless the institution becomes sufficiently powerless or unpopular that it loses its political support.

## Two Specific Cases

The development of an efficient institutional structure for the power sectors in Argentina and in Colombia has been slow and difficult, and much remains to be done. The reasons are partly political—in the broadest sense—and partly physical in that they stem from the nature of the countries and their resources. But the problems differ markedly in the two countries.

ARGENTINA. Bank lending to Argentina did not begin until June 1961, six years after the end of the Perón regime. The Bank's first power loan, in

January 1962, came after a great deal of preparatory planning, discussion, and negotiation with the new Argentine government.

In the late 1950s when these discussions began, generation and consumption of power in Argentina were heavily concentrated in Buenos Aires and its surrounding area. It was entirely thermal power supplied by two privately owned utilities, CADE (Compañia Argentina de Electricidad) which was owned by SOFINA, a Belgian holding company, and CIAE (Compañia Italo Argentina de Electricidad), which was controlled by Swiss financial interests. During the early 1950s many foreign-owned power companies in Argentina were refused permission to expand their plant or to charge rates in accordance with their concessions. The concessions of CADE and CIAE were canceled in 1957, and in 1958 CADE's distribution system in about half the Buenos Aires area was taken over by AYEE (Agua y Energía Eléctrica), the government's principal power agency. The generating plants and the remaining distribution system were to be bought by the government over a ten-year period. These assets were still operated by CADE, but the name of the company was changed to SEGBA (Servicios Eléctricos del Gran Buenos Aires).

These arrangements had, not unnaturally, adversely affected the operations of the two utilities during the 1950s and had led to serious power shortages in Buenos Aires. The controversies prevented the two utilities from expanding their capacity, and AYEE was planning to build new and more expensive capacity to overcome the shortages. Because of this complicated and unsatisfactory situation, the government in late 1959 undertook a study of the major power problems in the country. This study was carried out under the direction of the Bank and was the first operation financed by the newly established United Nations Special Fund. The study produced a ten-year investment program for the Buenos Aires area, but it also emphasized that the government should eliminate the conflicts between the various entities and ensure proper coordination between them.

Power shortages, the need for funds to overcome them, and institutional conflict in the sector formed the background of the discussions for the first Bank loan. Since a comprehensive solution to the power problem in Buenos Aires area was essential, the so-called Pinedo Plan was formulated under the direction of Dr. Federico Pinedo, an eminent Argentine lawyer and former minister of finance. This plan formed the basis for the first Bank loan. Under the plan the government was to purchase all the shares of SEGBA that were still privately held, and the power generation and distribution facilities in Buenos Aires which had been transferred to AYEE were to be transferred back to SEGBA. Among these assets was the GBA (Gran Buenos Aires) power station then under construction, the completion of which was an important part of the proposed Bank project. This meant that the whole of Buenos Aires would be served by SEGBA except for the comparatively small area served by CIAE. At that time CIAE had an installed capacity of 246 megawatts compared with about 870 megawatts for SEGBA. Although the expectation was that CIAE would eventually be consolidated with SEGBA, this did not happen until almost twenty years later, at the end of 1980.

SEGBA was also given new by-laws and a new concession. The by-laws provided for a board of directors and an executive committee that had wide authority, including control over planning and budgeting, the award of contracts, and all responsibilities for labor relations including wages and salaries. Specific provisions for the salaries of the executive committee ensured that the corporation could attract high-caliber staff. These arrangements were intended to protect the corporation from political interference and were discussed at length with the Bank before the loan was made.

The consolidation of the power facilities under SEGBA and the new concession and by-laws represented a major institutional reform. On the basis of this reform the Bank made a loan for $95 million, at that time (1962) one of the largest it had ever made. Evidence of flexibility is that the loan was for a project already under construction, and a substantial portion of it was disbursed to meet local expenditure, since SEGBA had already arranged a number of borrowings to meet most of the foreign exchange needs.

This institutional reform did lay a sound basis for the power supply for the Buenos Aires area. For many years after 1962, however, the history of SEGBA was marked by difficulties arising from serious inflation and changing government attitudes toward the company. (For a description of these financial problems, see chapter 2.) Another factor which affected the company itself and the Bank's relations with Argentina was that, according to the original plan, SEGBA was to sell shares to the public and eventually regain a substantial private ownership. This was an explicit reversal of the policies pursued by the Perón regime, and it added to the company's problems when a new government came into office in 1963. In March 1964, after the new government had refused a rate increase for SEGBA, the whole executive committee resigned. A new executive vice president was not appointed until January 1965. The efficiency of SEGBA's operations then declined, and labor costs rose substantially because of an unfavorable labor contract inherited from the Peronist period and arrangements made with the union by subsequent governments. In 1965 SEGBA employed more than 25,000 persons, and its management consultants believed that perhaps as many as 6,000 were unnecessary.

The problems of SEGBA's finances and efficiency delayed the conclusion of a further loan which the government requested in early 1965. The Bank was also concerned about the general economic situation at the time and in fact did not lend at all to Argentina between the first SEGBA loan in January 1962 and the second one six years later in January 1968. Another power loan for the El Chocon project was made in December 1968 and a third loan for SEGBA in October 1969. After that the economic situation began to deteriorate again, and there was a second lengthy gap in Bank activity in Argentina from March 1971 until the fourth SEGBA loan in September 1976. This was about six months after the military authorities took over the government when inflation had reached an annual rate of 1,000 percent and the economy seemed on the edge of chaos.

These events made Bank power lending much more spasmodic than it has usually been in other major borrowing countries. This, together with the Bank's interest in SEGBA and the Buenos Aires area—the most important part of the power sector—explains why there was less emphasis than usual on the sector as a whole. Sectoral organization became more urgent as power began to be generated at new hydro stations (and some nuclear ones) at a distance from Buenos Aires. One of the first was El Chocon, a hydro station on the Limay river about 625 miles southwest of Buenos Aires. A new agency, HIDRONOR (Hidroeléctrica Norpatagonia), was set up to build and operate this station, and the Bank made a loan of $82 million for it. Since power from the new project was not expected to be available for five years, when the loan was made it was not possible to make detailed arrangements for the sale of power to SEGBA. There was only an agreement in principle that HIDRONOR would be reimbursed by SEGBA on the basis of its costs of production, which would include an 8 percent return on its assets in accordance with its concession.

After 1968 other new organizations were established in the power sector, but coordination between them was not very effective—in fact, a 1976 appraisal report described the sector as "fragmented." SEGBA, HIDRONOR, CIAE, and AYEE were under the supervision of the Secretariat of Energy, which was responsible for approving tariffs, planning investments, and granting concessions. A separate organization known as CONCAP (Comisión Nacional de la Cuenca del Plata) coordinated Argentina's participation in international projects on the river borders with Brazil, Paraguay, Uruguay, and Bolivia. CONCAP operated under the auspices of the Ministry of Foreign Affairs, and its decisions were greatly influenced by foreign policy considerations. There was also a nuclear power commission, which was responsible for construction and operation of nuclear power plants and which reported directly to the president of

Argentina. And there were two major utilities operated by provincial governments. No overall government authority had even nominal responsibility for coordination of the whole sector. As a result, some investment decisions had been made on noneconomic grounds. To improve the situation the government which came to power in 1976 agreed to study the organization of the power sector and prepare an expansion plan for generation and transmission. These studies became part of the fourth SEGBA power project, and funds were provided in the loan to carry them out. By mid-1980 some further progress had been made: the Secretariat of Energy was made responsible for planning and financing the major generation and transmission works, and the subtransmission and distribution networks of AYEE were transferred to provincial agencies. AYEE and HIDRONOR became responsible for building and operating major generation and transmission projects.

COLOMBIA. The Bank has committed more funds for electric power in Colombia than in any country except India and Brazil. The first loan was made in 1950, and by the end of FY1981 the Bank had made twenty-eight loans for a total of $1,374 million.

The development of the power industry in Colombia was heavily influenced by the geography of the country. The Andean mountains provide a good source of hydroelectric power, and they also divide the country into well-defined regions in which economic and institutional development proceeded with considerable independence. The three largest cities, Bogotá, Medellín, and Cali, became the center for economic development in their surrounding regions, and the most important power utilities were largely owned and operated by the municipal authorities in these cities.

Three of the Bank's first five power loans to Colombia were made to CHIDRAL (Central Hidroeléctrica del Rio Anchicaya Ltd.), a power utility supplying the city of Cali. In 1959 and 1961 the Bank made loans to Empresa Pública de Medellín (EPM), and in 1960 and 1962 loans were made to Empresa Energía Eléctrica de Bogotá (EEEB).

Thus, by the early 1960s the Bank had made loans to three of the major utilities in Colombia's largest cities. It was becoming clear that power development in the central part of Colombia would be most economic if these three systems were linked up and the expansion of the integrated network were planned and developed as a whole. An appraisal report issued early in 1964 on the Nare project, to be carried out by EPM, described the benefits of connecting the network. It reported "full agreement among the three companies and the Bank that interconnection should be made as soon as possible." Consultants were to prepare recommendations on the organization and business aspects of inter-connection. "Questions such as how costs should be allocated, whether a new transmission undertaking should be formed and, if so, how capitalized and what sort of rate structure to use, and others, will have to be answered. These questions are likely to be much more difficult to answer than those of a strictly technical nature." This turned out to be very much the case. The physical interconnection was actually completed and in operation by December 1971, but important issues concerning organization, planning, future least-cost operation, and financing were the subject of controversy through the 1970s.

To prepare plans for the interconnection, the three utilities formed a Comité de Interconexión, which was later joined by ELECTRAGUAS, a government water and power development agency. ELECTRAGUAS was the owner of CHEC, an agency supplying power to the state of Caldas and its capital, Manizales, which was also to be part of the interconnected system. In mid-1965 the consultants employed to study the problems of organization recommended that the power agencies concerned form a new jointly owned company to construct, own, and operate not only the inter-connecting transmission system itself but also future power-generating facilities. The new company, Interconexión Eléctrica, S.A. (ISA), was eventually formed two years later.

It had been hoped to reach agreement on power sales and on an outline for operating all four systems so as to achieve maximum economy. This was not possible, however, and ISA was set up and work on the transmission system was started with these matters still unsettled. The basic statutes of ISA provided that it should purchase power from some utilities and sell it to others at cost, but it was clear that such a simple concept would soon encounter practical difficulties. The appraisal report for the first ISA loan stated: "For example, there is a lack of uniformity of accounting methods among the sponsors,[5] and the question of comparable costs of power production by each has yet to be clarified. Moreover, such pricing policies may prove to be inequitable in the future since they fail to discriminate among the values of different classes of energy, such as firm, dump hydro, economy interchange, emergency, etc." The Bank received assurances from the sponsors that these matters would be studied by consultants and the statutes would be reviewed and revised if neces-sary.

The Bank loan for the interconnection project was made in November

5. The four utilities which owned ISA, namely, EEEB. EPM. CHIDRAL, and ICEL, formerly ELECTRAGUAS (with CHEC).

1968 for $18 million. A much larger loan for $52.3 million was made to ISA in May 1970 for the Chivor hydro project, the first generation project to be owned and operated by ISA for the benefit of the sponsors as a group. An important element in financing the project was the equity and debt capital provided by the sponsors. Although the interconnection itself was completed by December 1971, the Chivor project was not completed until September 1977. This period included the years following the first rise in petroleum prices when inflation in Colombia reached, for example, 25 percent in 1974. The government's attempts to cope with inflation led, as in many other countries, to power utilities being squeezed between rising costs and controlled rates, which in turn led to delays in the construction of Chivor because the sponsors did not provide the necessary funds on time. This situation became so serious that the Bank "informally" suspended disbursements in September 1974 in an effort to persuade the sponsors to fulfill their financial obligations. Disbursements were resumed in March 1975.

During this period there were lengthy discussions among the sponsors themselves and between them and the Bank concerning the arrangements for operating ISA and ISA's role in the planning and development of the integrated network. These discussions were difficult because they had to overcome regional rivalries and some suspicion by the sponsors of intervention by the central authorities. Moreover, the attitude of each sponsor naturally reflected its own situation. EPM, for example, was a financially strong company that produced low-cost power and stood to gain little, at least at first, from the interconnection. At one stage EPM expressed its reluctance to give responsibility to ISA by proposing that future generation projects be implemented by new satellite companies. CHIDRAL had suffered from power shortages and tended to believe it would be better to expand its own capacity rather than rely on power from outside its own region. A major issue which had to be settled was the proposal to include CORELCA, which operated the Atlantic Coast system, in ISA and connect the two systems.

By the time the Chivor project entered into operation in September 1977, there was still no long-term contractual agreement for the sale of Chivor power, and provisional short-term arrangements had to be used instead. The Bank then insisted that long-term arrangements be concluded before it would approve new loans for ISA's San Carlos project and for the 500 kilovolt (kV) connection to the Atlantic Coast. These loans were made in May 1978, and the appraisal report commented:

> Throughout these negotiations the Bank continued to support the concept of centralized planning, construction and operation of the national grid and has resisted proposals that would weaken ISA.

Because of the time required by the shareholders to arrive at decisions on these fundamental issues, Bank consideration of San Carlos I, the 500-kV interconnection and EEEB's proposed Mesitas hydroelectric project, all of them urgently needed to avoid power rationing in Colombia, suffered considerable delays. A compromise solution was evolved in extensive discussions between Bank staff, the Government and the shareholders over the past eighteen months.

In addition to the financial and pricing agreements it was agreed that ISA would define the future generation expansion program for the inter-connected system and would own plants whose construction and opera-tion would require the cooperation of all its shareholders. Hence ISA became responsible for regulation and planning in an important part of the power sector. However, its voting arrangements were changed to require the concurrence of four of its five shareholders in all important decisions. After further discussions in 1979 and 1980, the government, ISA, and the Bank agreed that ISA would, in the long run, own 33 percent of the total generation capacity in the sector and would operate all the trunk transmission lines in the interconnected system. It would also serve as the national dispatch agency to ensure that the system operated at minimum cost.

This account of the institutional evolution in Colombia illustrates the difficulties and delays, particularly when progress has to be achieved largely by mutual agreement between parties whose interests may conflict. For example, the principle of interconnection was accepted in 1963 and planning began in 1964. It was originally hoped that arrangements for the purchase and sale of power might be agreed on by the time the Bank made its first loan for ISA in November 1968. In fact, this agreement was not reached until ten years later when the first San Carlos loan was made. Now the institutional framework for integrated planning, development, and operation of the system does exist, but the extent of central influence which can be brought to bear is still modest. Although the Electric Energy Division of Colombia's Ministry of Mines and Energy is responsible for coordinating and supervising power planning, it does not have the authority that similar agencies, such as DNAEE in Brazil, have to issue licenses, set tariffs, and approve expansion plans. Similarly, ELETROBRAS in Brazil is a government holding company which owns shares in the major generating utilities and exercises influence on the state power agencies through its control of the public funds. In Colombia this situation is reversed: ISA does not own the regional generating companies, it is owned by them and depends on them for a major part of its finance. For this reason, to obtain the maximum benefits from the system, the concept of integrated planning and operation is likely to need continued support.

# 4. Investment Planning and Project Implementation

WHEN THE BANK MADE its first loans for power in the early 1950s it was not difficult to provide an economic justification for the projects. There was, in fact, hardly any problem to solve. All that was required was to estimate the future demand for power and then to decide whether to expand some power plant or add a new one. Frequently there was no alternative to the proposed project or, if there was, the choice was obvious. If there is no choice, there is, of course, no economic problem. Largely for this reason, the Bank's attention in the early loans was devoted, first, to the financial position of the borrower, which was often a serious problem, and then, as described in chapter 3, to its ability to construct the project efficiently.

## The Evolution of Project Appraisal in Electric Power

The issue of economic justification first presented itself in connection with the financing of large hydro projects, such as the first Yanhee project in Thailand and several projects in Austria. The question was how to be sure that the large capital investment was worthwhile when compared with some alternative, normally a thermal project, which required less capital. An internal memorandum prepared in 1956 set out the principle that the savings in operating costs arising from a hydro project could be regarded as a return on the additional investment required for it. The memorandum also dealt with whether the resulting return should be compared with the actual, or nominal, cost of capital to the utility concerned, or with the economic, or opportunity, cost of capital. Since the economic allocation of both the government's and the Bank's funds was an important consideration, it was concluded that the proper comparison should be with the return on capital that could be obtained from alternative investments in the economy concerned. The memorandum pointed out that an estimate of such a return would have to be based on a general knowledge of the economy. Nevertheless, it suggested that, as a starting point, a return exceeding 12 percent should generally be regarded as sufficient while one of less than 6 percent would be clearly inadequate; rates in the intervening range would be subject to specific analysis and decision. This analysis—comparing the return on additional investment with an assumed cost of capital—was nothing more than a particular application of the type of cost-benefit and investment analysis generally used by governments and private business at that time.

A comparison of two possible projects is sufficient when there are, in fact, only two alternatives. As a power system becomes larger, however, there may be many ways to expand it. During the 1950s, engineers and economists working in the power field began to develop analytical techniques which could handle a large number of possible investment programs. This type of analysis has to allow for the fact that a power system may consist of many different sources of energy, each with its own characteristics. There may be single or multipurpose hydro projects of widely different power and energy storage capacities; projects using fossil fuels, such as coal, oil, or gas; nuclear reactors and special-purpose peaking plants such as gas turbines or pumped storage. Moreover, the optimal investment program, which will consist of some selection of these projects, will also be influenced by the nature of the existing power system. To estimate the operating costs of future projects it is necessary to know whether they will be operated as base load or peak load plants or somewhere in between, and the future mode of operation will depend on how the existing system is operated. To handle all these variables, mathematical models and computer technology are employed.[1]

With these methods, the analyst can determine how to meet an estimated future demand for power at the least possible cost, allowing for both operating costs and some assumed cost of capital. Some estimate of future demand must first be made, and it is then assumed that this demand must be met. The analysis does not, in other words, produce any economic evaluation of the benefit of meeting this assumed demand or the costs of not doing so. Nor does it produce an estimate of the economic return on the investment necessary to meet the future demand—a return that could, in theory, be compared with the return on other investments.

The calculation of an economic return on investment in power is made difficult by the problem of measuring the benefits. In many other types of projects the benefits can be measured by the value of the output at market

---

1. For a further explanation, see Ralph Turvey and Dennis Anderson, *Electricity Economics: Essays and Case Studies* (Baltimore, Md.: Johns Hopkins University Press, 1977), chap. 13, "Investment Planning Models."

prices, but for electric power there is no competitively determined price; indeed, the price at which power is sold is frequently below its real economic cost. By using the prevailing power tariff, it is of course relatively easy to calculate the additional revenue that would result from a new project, and this can be expressed as a return on the new investment. This so-called incremental financial return is normally presented in Bank appraisal reports, but it is accompanied, particularly when it turns out to be on the low side, by a warning that it may not be a measure of the economic value of the project but may merely indicate that the price charged for power is too low. Only when electricity tariffs do reflect economic costs—that is, when they are efficiency prices—can revenues be used as a measure of benefits. Then the incremental financial return would be a true economic return.[2]

For most nonpower projects, the analysis of economic justification takes the form of a comparison of the situation with and without the project. But when it is a question of adding capacity to meet a growing demand on an existing power system, such a comparison is hardly meaningful since ceasing to expand the system altogether is not a realistic option. As the demand on the system increases, its capacity must be expanded; otherwise power outages would occur and the sytem would eventually collapse. The cost and disruption caused by power outages is substantial, sometimes as much as $2 or $3 per lost kilowatt-hour, or even more.[3] An electric power system cannot simply decline to meet rising demand as if it were an industry producing clothes or automobiles. This is a crucial point that all development plans should—but do not always— take into account.

The real economic decision which faces power utilities is not whether to expand but how fast to expand. To make this decision requires, first, an estimate of future demand and, second, an agreed standard of security or reliability of the system—that is, the amount of reserve capacity necessary to take care of maintenance, breakdowns, variations in water flow, and so on. In principle, it is possible to calculate a rate of return that would indicate the optimal rate of expansion by comparing costs and revenues if

2. The concept of an economic return in this sense (and that of the incremental financial return, which can be regarded as a kind of approximation—generally a lower limit—for it) is quite distinct from the financial return on average net fixed assets discussed in chapter 3. The former is designed to indicate whether an investment proposal is worthwhile; the latter indicates the financial position of a power agency.

3. See Mohan Munasinghe, *The Economics of Power System Reliability and Planning: Theory and Case Studies* (Baltimore, Md.: Johns Hopkins University Press, 1980), particularly tables E.1 and E.2.

the project were implemented one year later than some given target year. If this resulting "first-year return" is low, and if tariffs are based on economic costs, it means that the project should be delayed until the future demand has risen somewhat more. Of course, if the tariffs are not based on costs, a low return, just as in the use of the incremental financial return, may indicate that tariffs should be increased.

In practice, first-year returns are rarely calculated because data are not often available and, more important, a decision on how fast to expand can usually be made, with sufficient precision to be practical, without such a calculation. If, for example, the supply of power falls sufficiently short of demand to cause load shedding, the resulting costs to the economy rapidly become very large indeed. In other words, on any investment necessary to avoid such costs the rate of return is very high. On the other hand, if expansion moves ahead of demand, there is the cost of capacity not optimally used. But this cost is normally nowhere near as high as the cost of shortages, and it can often be easily offset by postponing some other new power investment. It is therefore preferable to err on the side of overestimation when preparing forecasts of future demand.

To sum up, the proper planning of electric power investment must provide answers to two related questions: what should the rate of expansion be and what is the least-cost method of achieving it? A decision on the rate of expansion is necessary before a least-cost investment program can be prepared because the construction period will differ for different types of projects and the program will be affected by how soon new capacity is needed. The decision on the rate of expansion is derived from an estimate of future demand, or load forecast. There are various ways of forecasting the future load, but whichever method is used the available data necessarily reflect the prevailing power tariffs. If these tariffs reflect the real economic cost of power then the forecast should give rise to an optimal rate of expansion. However, power tariffs, particularly at present, can be significantly below economic costs, so that a load forecast based on them would be an overestimate, the amount of which would depend on the long-run price elasticity of the demand for power. Unfortunately, it is difficult to determine this elasticity at all accurately. In practice, therefore, the only way to take account of this point is to adjust the tariffs so that they do reflect economic costs and then to meet the resulting demand.

Once tariffs are set and the load forecast is estimated, the derivation of the least-cost investment program is predominantly a technical matter. It depends on the characteristics of the existing system, the resource potential (fuels and hydro power sites) of the economy, and the physical location of the resources and the markets.

The economic justification of power projects and the proper planning of investment have obvious implications for the postevaluation or performance auditing of these projects. It is clearly of little value to measure the actual incremental financial return of the project and compare it with that expected at appraisal. Any change in tariffs in relation to costs would affect this comparison. The questions which need an answer follow directly from those just discussed. Did the system expand at the right speed and thus avoid shortages of power and unnecessary reserves of capacity? Was the project or investment, in retrospect, the least costly method of producing the required output? If either or both of these questions are answered in the negative it would be of interest to know which of the original data or assumptions turned out to have been unjustified. If there seems to be some pattern in these errors there is a possibility of learning from experience. Hindsight often reveals where errors were made—but it is quite another matter to know whether they could have been avoided.

Quite obviously, some "errors" are impossible to avoid. All project appraisal depends in some degree on an assumption that the future will resemble the past, even given techniques that allow for some uncertainty. But if some wholly unexpected event occurs, the conclusions of project appraisal may be simply invalidated. In the field of energy two such events have occurred in the recent past: the rise in the price of oil in 1973 and again in 1979. These large changes in the price of one of the world's most widely used resources are bringing about profound structural changes in the world economy, and power systems have been greatly affected. For example, in the mid-1960s a general rule of thumb was that hydroelectric plants with a cost per installed kilowatt exceeding $800 equivalent (in 1981 dollars) would be unlikely to be economic. In 1981, however, several hydro plants under construction were estimated to cost between $2,000 and $3,000 per kilowatt, and some had costs per kilowatt up to $7,000. This change reflects the extent to which the balance of economic advantage has been tilted toward hydro plants and away from plants using fossil fuels, particularly oil. Had it been possible to foresee the rise in oil prices, more hydro plants would have been built since the late 1960s. Countries that did possess and develop their hydro potential benefited correspondingly—or, strictly speaking, they avoided some of the costs they would otherwise have had to bear.

## Extensions of the System: Rural Electrification

As pointed out above, the economic justification for expanding an existing network cannot be based on a with- and without-project comparison because it is not realistic to do without the project entirely. When the question is whether to extend the network to new areas, however, the situation is different. In these circumstances the potential market is already doing without the project, whether by doing without electric power altogether or by using small-scale auto-generators. Hence the method of appraising projects to extend the power supply to new markets, whether urban or rural, more closely resembles normal cost-benefit analysis. Some special aspects deserve mention, however.

Estimating the future demand in an area not yet connected to the main network is obviously more difficult than estimating the future demand on the network itself. In some areas a little power may be supplied by auto-generation. Usually such generation is started by a small business that uses electricity for refrigeration, heating and lighting, or sometimes motive power. If there are a number of such demands in an area, it may develop a micro-grid and serve private households. In this situation there will be some basis for an estimate of future demand. If there has been no power supply, it may be possible to obtain evidence from similar projects elsewhere in the country or in other countries. This can be supplemented by an investigation of the economic conditions of the specific locality to take account, for example, of the prospects for agricultural or industrial growth, the quality of existing public services such as roads and water supply, or possible migration into the area.

Because of the initial high capital costs of extending power lines to new areas and the low demand in rural areas, rural or village electrification schemes generally operate at a financial loss for a number of years. Even when the financial estimates are modified to take account of economic factors—for example, by introducing shadow prices for capital, labor, and foreign exchange and by including consumers' surplus benefits[4]—the resulting economic return in the early years may still be lower than the opportunity cost of capital.

Despite the low initial financial and economic returns, rural electrification can sometimes be justified because of its social and indirect economic benefits. It may, for example, improve the situation of the rural poor or slow migration to urban centers; economic and employment opportunities may increase as a result of irrigation pumping, food processing, artisan-scale manufacturing, and similar activities. These benefits are difficult to estimate, however, and do not follow automatically from a rural electrification program. The direct benefits of household electricity consumption generally go to the better-off among the rural

---

4. The difference between what consumers would be prepared to pay for the service and the lower amount they actually do pay.

population, although the poor may benefit from public uses of electricity such as village health clinics and street lighting.[5] The poor, along with others, will also benefit if employment opportunities are created, but this may not occur unless rural electrification is part of a larger program of rural development. In a successful rural electrification program in the Philippines, the agency in charge also established programs to develop irrigation and industrial cooperatives.

Although a number of projects financed by the Bank in its earlier years contained elements of rural electrification, it was not until 1972 that the Bank began to explore the special problems of rural electrification and to finance projects explicitly for this purpose. The first research was on the effects of introducing electricity on the development of villages. A World Bank Paper, *Rural Electrification* (Washington, D.C., October 1975), assessed the prospects for successful investment in rural electrification and described the various economic, financial, and technical problems involved. Later work dealt with appropriate design standards for rural electrification, because the lack of such standards had forced engineers to borrow those of other countries or urban areas—often unsuitable models. One conclusion was that the design should be flexible because the needs of rural consumers tend to change rapidly; another was that the quality of the supply must be constant because poor voltage damages consumer's appliances and seriously hampers the growth of demand.

Through these and other studies more is being learned about the economic, financial, and institutional conditions which contribute to the success of rural electrification—success in the sense that the system is established and maintained in operation at the lowest possible cost. The extent to which prospective economic returns lower than the estimated cost of capital should be accepted remains a matter of judgment, however. It depends on the general economic prospects of the area concerned, which determine the growth of power demand.

## Forecasting Demand

The starting point of all appraisals for power projects is an estimate of future demand. The usual way of making such forecasts is to examine past trends and then to modify them, if necessary, for any ways the future is

---

5. Judith Tendler, *Rural Electrification: Linkages and Justifications*, A.I.D. Program Evaluation Discussion Paper no. 3 (Washington, D.C.: U.S. Agency for International Development, April 1979).

likely to differ from the past. Separate analyses are often prepared for industrial, commercial, and residential loads. The industrial load forecast may be adjusted to take account of any large plants, such as a steel mill, which may be planned or under construction. Expected changes in population, urbanization, and increased income per capita are also considered.

It is often alleged that load forecasts tend to have an optimistic bias, with the result that the actual load often falls short of the appraisal estimates. It seems reasonable to expect such a tendency, since a higher load forecast would usually make it easier to justify a particular project, and the more optimistic financial outlook would ease the problem of putting together a financing plan. To discover whether there was any substance to this allegation, the Bank did an internal study of the load forecasts used in the appraisal reports for 75 loans in 46 countries.[6] The data yielded 287 comparisons of actual and forecast data. The estimate for any year was compared with the actual for that year so that if an appraisal report contained a forecast for ten years ahead, and the data for the actual increases were available, the forecast yielded ten observations. For each observation the measure of the error used was

$$R = \left(\frac{\text{Forecast change in demand}}{\text{Actual change in demand}}\right) 100 \text{ percent.}$$

Thus an $R$ of over 100 represented an overestimate of demand and vice versa.

The distribution of the forecasting errors was very close to normal, with a mean value of 109. However, this value was affected by a relatively small number (22) of observations for which $R$ was over 200; that is, the forecast was more than double the actual figure. If these were omitted the average was 102, which indicated no significant upward bias in the forecasts. There was, however, a wide range of errors in individual cases. In over 60 percent of the observations the error exceeded 20 percent ($R$ was more than 120 or less than 80) and in 30 percent of them it was over 40 percent ($R$ more than 140 or less than 60). The study also investigated whether the accuracy of the forecasts was affected by certain characteristics of the countries or power systems concerned. The data were analyzed with reference to the size of the network, since large systems

6. Dennis Anderson and Vilma Villaflores, "Ex-Post Evaluation of Electricity Demand Forecasts," World Bank Economics Department Working Paper no. 79 (Washington, D.C., June 18, 1970).

might be thought to exhibit more regular behavior than small ones. Another analysis compared rapidly growing systems with slow-growing ones to see whether the forecasts for the former had a downward bias. Finally, the countries were divided into those in which the Bank had made a relatively large number of loans and those in which it had made only one or two. None of these analyses yielded anything significant. As far as could be ascertained, forecasting accuracy was not affected by the size of the system, the rate of its growth, or the degree of familiarity of the Bank with the country concerned.

Since this study was carried out in 1970, the Operations Evaluation Department of the Bank has prepared audit reports on some 68 power projects in 38 countries. A comparison of the load forecasts and actual results in these reports, using the same method as in the 1970 report, reveals a rather similar situation. The average of $R$ was 130, but again this was not the result of systematic overestimating; it reflected a limited number (21) of $R$'s over 200. Without these extreme values the average of $R$ was 104, hardly different from the 1970 result (102). The range of errors was somewhat smaller, however; only 46 percent were off by more than 20 and only 23 percent were off by more than 40.

Most of the audit reports offer some explanation of the forecasting errors, particularly when they are large. It is therefore possible to make a rough classification of those cases in which demand was substantially overestimated. Whatever the reason for the error, it was almost always unforeseeable. In some countries the estimates allowed for some specific new load which was either delayed or never arose. In the Philippines, for example, a power station on Mindanao was expanded in part to meet the demands of a proposed integrated steel mill, but the steel mill project was subsequently altered and only a rolling mill was built, which required much less power. One reason for an overestimated forecast in Honduras was a protracted negotiation over tariffs with certain fruit companies; other unexpected events that affected this case were a hurricane and a war with El Salvador.

Other circumstances involved the unexpected deterioration of general economic or political conditions. Political uncertainty acts as a brake on investment, and in Ghana it led to the closing of a number of foreign firms and this reduced power demand. A similar situation occurred in Sierra Leone. After the energy crisis, reductions in power demand in countries such as Papua New Guinea and Liberia came as a result of depressed economic conditions or higher prices for power. In Iran a government policy of decentralizing industrial development caused a slowdown of power demand in Tehran.

A fairly common reason for an overestimate of demand is that the actual demand is constrained by insufficient supply. This is quite a different situation from those just discussed, and it could well be argued that it does not constitute a real overestimate at all. But it certainly accounts for some statistical "overestimates" in India, Venezuela, and Uruguay. In Liberia droughts reduced the availability of hydro power and made it necessary to use oil-consuming units instead. The higher prices that had to be charged then reduced demand. In Sierra Leone the demand estimate assumed that the distribution network in Freetown would be expanded, but this was not done.

The conclusion seems to be that there is no general bias in the load forecasts in Bank appraisals, but that a relatively small number of forecasts turn out to be far in excess of the actual demand because of unforeseen economic or political events. Such events almost always have the effect of reducing demand rather than increasing it. There does, however, appear to be quite a wide spread of forecasting errors on either side of the average.[7] But before concluding that much would be gained by more accurate forecasts, it would be desirable to know whether inaccurate forecasts have really led to faulty decisions. The only reason for making a forecast of the demand for power is to arrange to have a supply of power available when it is needed. This means that the necessary new generation, transmission, and distribution capacity must be constructed on schedule. This often does not happen; projects get delayed. There might not be much advantage in refining load forecasts if there were no corresponding improvement in the ability to provide supply on time.

## The Execution of Projects

When carrying out an investment program, the immediate objective of any power agency is to construct the project within the original cost estimate and in accordance with the planned time schedule. An agency's

---

7. In the 1970 study the standard deviation of the errors (excluding the extreme values) was 38; in the audit reports it was 30. By comparison, forecasts in Europe and the United States, as given in a 1964 United Nations study, had a standard deviation of 19. The Bank's 1970 study suggested that the smaller errors in the U.N. study might be the result of the larger effort put into forecasting, less erratic economic growth and less marked structural changes, and the smaller impact of political, social, and other random factors in Europe and the United States.

experience in these two respects is therefore a significant test of its success.

## Estimated and Actual Costs

The cost estimate serves two purposes. The first is to determine whether the project being considered is part of the optimal least-cost expansion program. The second is to provide the basis for the analysis of the financial future of the agency and thus to indicate the amount of finance that needs to be obtained, either by cash generation, borrowing, or capital subscriptions, to construct the project. If a project turns out to be costing substantially more than expected, the question of economic justification may or may not come up, but some kind of financing problem will almost certainly be present.

A considerable amount of data comparing the estimated and actual costs of projects is available, particularly in project completion reports of the World Bank. There are, however, serious pitfalls in any attempt to summarize this evidence. One problem is that the definition of "project" can differ greatly from one loan to another. The word "project," as used by the Bank, is a "term of art"; it means whatever the Bank defines it as being for the purposes of a specific lending operation. Although the term "power plant" tends to bring to mind some clearly defined physical object, this image is really the exception. Most Bank power projects consist of some generation and associated transmission and substation equipment and often include training or consultants' services. Some consist only of transmission or distribution. Although there is obviously some minimum of investment necessary to build a power plant, most projects have some degree of elasticity in the sense that elements can be added or subtracted from them if necessary. For example, a project might consist of the expansion of a distribution system, which can easily be expanded or contracted in accordance with the availability of funds.

In practice, if a cost overrun shows signs of developing, the borrower attempts to reduce the project in some way to conform to the original amount of funding envisaged, unless additional financing is easily available. Conversely, if there is a cost underrun the borrower will usually ask the Bank to permit the unused part of its loan to be used for some additional investment associated with the project. The Bank will often agree to such a request, although it will not permit its funds to be used for some quite different investment which could not be regarded as having been covered by the original appraisal report. The result is that the completed project may be significantly different from the project envisaged at appraisal, so that a simple cost comparison between them is misleading. The comparison of estimated and actual costs is therefore only the starting point for an interpretation of what has happened.

The overall record of the Bank's projects in all sectors is summarized in the "Annual Reviews of Project Performance Audit Reports."[8] The data for the four reviews from 1977 to 1980 show that about 45 percent of all projects are completed with less than a 10 percent cost overrun, about 35 percent have cost overruns exceeding 25 percent, and 17 percent have overruns exceeding 50 percent. The cost overruns for power projects are somewhat greater; 40 percent have overruns exceeding 25 percent, and 22 percent have overruns exceeding 50 percent. This should not be surprising since the group of all projects will contain a large number that are easy to reduce to avoid an overrun. Many agricultural and development finance company projects are of this type.

Some idea of the causes of large cost overruns can be obtained from the audit reports. Of sixty-six power projects, seventeen had cost overruns exceeding 50 percent. In four of these, however, the project had been so much enlarged that the comparison is not meaningful. In the remaining thirteen geological and technical factors were mentioned in six cases, inflation or higher unit costs in eleven, delays in construction and changes in foreign exchange rates in two each. In some instances one factor can be singled out as the principal cause of a rise in cost. The third power project in Costa Rica, for example, required a tunnel 14.5 kilometers long; because the rock conditions changed during the course of the tunnel, a great deal of additional time, material, and equipment was needed, and the eventual cost of the tunnel was three times the estimate. For the wastewater canal which was a part of the Ahuachapan geothermal project in El Salvador, the original design had to be abandoned because the rock conditions turned out to be unsuitable for tunnels. The route for the canal had to be redesigned, and the eventual cost was $13.9 million as compared with the estimate of $1.95 million (in 1972 prices).[9]

8. Since 1977, these annual reviews can be obtained from the World Bank Publications Sales Unit.

9. Partly because of the experience with this and other tunnels and underground structures, in 1974 the Bank prepared an internal directive to its staff in which it emphasized the need to make use of geologists and engineers with extensive experience in tunnelling when appraising projects that involve this kind of work. It also recommended that contingency allowances of from 25 to 50 percent be used. The problem is that it may become expensive to find out exactly what the relevant rock conditions are. A firm of consultants employed to assist with the tunnel problem in Costa Rica concluded that it was doubtful whether it would have been possible to ascertain the rock conditions in advance; further, if the conditions had been known it might not have been possible to find a contractor to carry out the project at all.

Most cost overruns, however, are the combined result of a number of causes. Some of these may be interrelated, as when a technical problem not only increases costs directly but also causes some delay in the project, which in turn increases costs for engineering supervision, interest during construction, and, in periods of inflation, price escalation.[10] One of the most pervasive causes of cost overruns listed in the audits is inflation, since many of the projects were carried out at a time when inflation was increasing. Cost overruns that result from inflation reflect changes in the measuring rod of money rather than real cost increases (although they do create real financial problems). Cost overruns resulting from inflation declined in the later 1970s, not because inflation declined but because it was built into the original estimates.

## Timing

Projects financed by the Bank, like many other human enterprises, tend to take longer than expected to complete. It is not difficult to understand why this common experience is also shared by major investment projects. The estimated completion date for a project is often the result of a detailed schedule covering all aspects of construction. Thus the schedule inevitably becomes a target rather than an objective forecast. It assumes that all the various operations required to complete the project will take no longer than necessary; it does not, in other words, allow for random disturbances or Murphy's law. Any construction schedule which did allow for such things might be regarded as an invitation to project managers to take things easy. The fact that a reasonably random selection of Bank-financed projects took 42 percent more time to complete than estimated is not, therefore, necessarily an indication of inefficiency. It may reflect a kind of norm for the degree of optimism incorporated into the estimated schedules.

10. In one completion report the causes of a cost overrun were analyzed as follows:

|  | *Percent* |
|---|---|
| Changes in scope, design, and increased qualities | 26 |
| Additional preliminary work at dam site | 9 |
| Price escalation and other contractor's claims | 34 |
| Increased engineering costs | 6 |
| Use of tied loan instead of international bidding | 9 |
| Bidding for one contract | 11 |
| Change in foreign exchange rate | 5 |
| Total | 100 |

The Bank has devoted considerable attention to the extent of and the reasons for project "delays." Not only is this matter intrinsically important since it appears to reflect on the efficiency of the investment process, but it also has a direct effect on the Bank's financial operations. It affects the lag between the Bank's commitments—the value of the loans the Bank has signed—and its disbursements, which depend on how fast these loans are drawn down by borrowers. Consequently, considerable data are available on the time taken to disburse different kinds of loans, and these data were analyzed in a 1980 study by the Operations Evaluation Department.

According to this study, which was based partly on audit reports and partly on a study of loans made between 1970 and 1974, the average project took five years from the time the loan became effective to the date of the final disbursement and, as noted above, the amount of time required was 42 percent greater than estimated. Although there were substantial variations between the loans to different sectors and subsectors, power loans were close to the average, both in total time required for disbursement and in the amount of time overrun over the appraisal estimate.

One significant finding was that the time required to disburse loans was greatly influenced by the initial period of disbursement—that is, by the time required to disburse 25 percent of the total loan. This initial disbursement period was both relatively longer and more variable than the remaining disbursement periods. For all projects the average time required to disburse 25 percent of the loan was nine quarters (two years and three months), but the time required to disburse the balance (actually, to reach 95 percent of the loan) was also nine quarters. This reflects the fact that various start-up activities have to be completed before any funds can be disbursed. The most common are the preparation of tender documents, evaluation of bids, and award of contracts. But special conditions agreed on at loan negotiations may have to be met before effectiveness: some legislation affecting the borrower may have to be enacted, a new agency established, or power or railway tariffs increased. It seems likely that the amount of time required for these start-up activities varies because the specific characteristics of each subsector influence the time at which loans are signed and then made effective. For example, water supply and telecommunications loans appear to take longer to disburse (20 quarters) than hydropower projects (17 quarters), and education loans take even longer (23 quarters). On the one hand, 15 of the 23 quarters taken by education loans are needed to reach the 25 percent disbursement mark, and only 8 quarters (or one quarter less than the average of all projects) are needed to disburse the balance. On the other hand, hydro power projects take less than the average (only 7 quarters) to reach 25 percent of disbursements and then require 10 quarters (as do loans for water supply and telecommunications) to complete disbursement. Hydro projects, however, usually require several years of investigation and preparatory work before a loan can be made. The relatively rapid start-up in disbursement thus reflects the fact that these loans are made only when preparation has reached an advanced stage. Altogether, therefore, the record of power projects as regards the speed of execution does not differ in any significant way from that of most other projects.

The audit reports include sixteen power projects that were delayed by more than 50 percent over the original time estimate. An examination of these shows that two types of explanations for delay stand out. The first consists of unforeseen events generally beyond the control of the executing agency. These include geological problems with tunneling such as occurred in Costa Rica (Tapanti scheme), Chile (Alto Polcura diversion), and Turkey (Kadincik), a change in the siting of a power plant as the result of a flood (Guatemala, Escuintla project), and delays in the delivery of equipment (Malaysia). The second source of delay is the procurement process. In the Philippines (Bataan and Maria Cristina project) and Uruguay (Battl extension), the borrowers had to follow lengthy legal procedures to award contracts; in the first case a year and in the second eight months elapsed between the opening of bids and the award of contracts. In Venezuela (Guri extension) the only bid received was regarded as too high, and the contract was then divided into two parts. Other delays were caused by a shortage of finance (Colombia, ISA and Chivor projects) and labor problems (Chile, Alto Polcura project).

Appendix table 10 sets out the sixteen projects with the principal causes of delay classified either as exogenous or endogenous to the borrowing agency or the country concerned. Of the sixteen cases, five were largely due to external events, six were mainly the responsibility either of the agency or the government, while in the remaining five both types of factor played a role. Although these projects were delayed the most, it is likely that small delays in other projects had similar causes.

Although the Bank can do little about external causes, it has taken some steps to reduce delays that can be affected by the borrower or by the Bank itself. In 1975 the Bank introduced a form of lending known as a Project Preparation Facility. This made a financial advance for the preparation of projects, with provision for the amount advanced to be refunded from the proceeds of any subsequent loan made for the project itself. The Bank also established an internal procedure for producing memoranda known as project briefs during the preparation stage in an effort to ensure that any problems could be dealt with as early as possible. It also expanded its staff concerned with procurement matters and instituted short courses on procurement in borrowing countries.

## Effects of Cost and Time Overruns

The effects of cost and time overruns on power agencies are of two kinds. There are, first, the immediate financial consequences for the agency itself and, second, the consequences for the quality and cost of power supply to the economy.

### Financial Consequences

The most obvious financial consequence of a cost overrun is that the agency has to find additional capital. Sometimes it may be able to obtain funds from the government or elsewhere on reasonable terms. However, neither the Bank nor other international or official lending agencies are anxious to make supplementary loans to meet cost overruns on projects for which they have already made a loan. This attitude is intended to encourage "cost consciousness" on the part of the borrower, since if supplementary loans were readily available some financial discipline would be lost. As a result, a power agency faced with a cost overrun may be forced to borrow from private sources at whatever terms are available. Borrowing for a fairly short term can be regarded as in anticipation of future cash generation. If, after the project is completed, expenditure on investment is reduced for a time, the agency may be able to restore its financial position, particularly if rates can be increased as the new project is added to the rate base. But in some cases the burden of debt on power agencies has become a major problem.

During the first half of the 1970s there were several examples of this kind. Moreover, the financial pressure of cost overruns was sometimes accentuated by the rise in oil prices which reduced the agencies' internal cash generation. In Central America at that time, El Salvador, Panama, and Nicaragua were constructing major projects and Costa Rica was also carrying out a large investment program. In all these cases, cash generation was reduced at the same time that large sums had to be borrowed on fairly onerous terms. ICE in Costa Rica found its cash generation in the early 1970s was less than half the expected figure and had to borrow $32 million more than planned, largely from commercial banks. Nicaragua's situation was even more serious because of the 1972 earthquake in Managua. ENALUF's earnings were so reduced that its net cash generation was negative from 1972 to 1974. It had to borrow an additional $16 million from the Venezuela Investment Fund to complete the project being financed by the Bank. Panama and El Salvador also had to borrow substantial amounts from commercial banks for similar reasons.

In a number of instances, however, the Bank was prepared to make supplementary loans. In principle, the policy was that the Bank would be prepared to make a supplementary loan if the need arose because of a decline in the value of the dollar or if the project could not be economically reduced in scale and the borrower were unable to obtain the additional finance from any other source. The former situation was quite common in the early 1970s after the regime of fixed exchange rates came to an end. By itself, however, it did not ordinarily cause a problem serious enough to justify a supplementary loan. In practice, it was the second consideration—the borrower's inability to find funds elsewhere—that lay behind most of the Bank's supplementary loans. Altogether the Bank has made only ten supplementary lending operations for power projects.[11] The first was made in 1958 for a hydro project in Austria before any special policy on supplementary lending had evolved. The causes of the cost overrun were typical: higher wage costs than estimated and unexpected geological problems. Six of the other cases were for projects in Africa,[12] one was in Nepal, and two in Pakistan.[13] The countries concerned were, with one exception, low-income countries that were not able to obtain other financing and could not reasonably be expected to raise the funds from their own resources. The exception was Zambia, a middle-income country, but the project was unusual—the Kariba North project on the Zambesi river which forms the border between Zambia and what was then Rhodesia.

The small number of supplementary lending operations makes it clear that the Bank has pursued a very restrictive policy in this respect. It has sometimes been argued that the Bank should have been more forthcoming, since usually the need for additional funds was in no way the fault of the borrower. It is easy to find cases, such as those in Central America, where the borrower would have been better-off with a long-term loan from the Bank, if one could have been obtained, but instead had to borrow on harder terms elsewhere. Moreover, the Bank was in the odd position of including a debt limitation covenant in its loans to prevent the borrower from borrowing on inappropriate terms, yet at the same time it was

11. One of which, for Kidatu, Stage II, in Tanzania, was a Special Action Credit; see appendix, "Country Summaries."

12. Liberia, Madagascar, Nigeria, Tanzania, and Zambia.

13. Both for the Tarbela project; see appendix, "Country Summaries."

unwilling to help the borrower avoid such action by making a further loan itself. Cost overruns were very numerous during the years inflation was accelerating, however, and there was a real danger that a less restrictive policy would open the door to even more. It was found preferable to provide larger contingencies and more realistic allowance for inflation, and this is what the Bank did.

## Economic Consequences

Information on the results of Bank-financed projects is now provided in the Project Performance Audit Reports prepared by the Operations Evaluation Department. Reports on sixty-six power projects were issued between 1974, when the system was first introduced, and June 30, 1980. These projects can be classified in various ways to try to answer the central economic questions about power investment, namely, whether the projects were part of the least-cost path of expansion and whether they were completed at the proper time in view of the demand for power. In any attempt to classify project results there will be problems and borderline cases; for example, a project might consist of some parts that were completed on schedule and others that were not. Nevertheless, the analysis which follows does shed some light on the diverse results of this group of projects.

Of the sixty-six projects subjected to performance audit, forty-two could fairly be described as having gone according to plan or as having achieved their objectives (those in categories 1 and 2 as shown in appendix tables 8 and 9). This is not, of course, necessarily the same thing. Some projects may not have gone according to plan but nevertheless achieved their objectives, in the sense that even if those responsible for the project had been able to foresee the actual course of events, they would still have proceeded as they did. Two such situations were fairly common. In hydro projects started before 1973, although accelerating inflation or other factors caused cost overruns, because of the rise in oil prices the projects turned out to be even more worthwhile than had been expected. Other projects were delayed for one reason or another but without adverse consequences because the need for them did not appear as soon as expected.

In category 1 were thirty-one projects that were generally in line with expectations. They include nineteen hydro projects (seven of which had cost overruns of more than 25 percent) that were completed without significant delays and regarded as clearly least-cost projects. In addition, there were five gas turbine or diesel projects, four other thermal plants, and three distribution projects also regarded by the audit reports as least-cost projects.

In category 2 were nine projects delayed without significant consequences. In most cases (such as Colombia, Sierra Leone, and Sudan) the load did not grow as expected. In addition, the Keban transmission project in Turkey was delayed two years, but so was the main generation project which the transmission line was to serve.

Of the twenty-six projects that did not work out entirely according to plan, four were completed too early, in the sense that the demand for power was less than expected. In the case of the Maria Cristina project in the Philippines, the plan to build an integrated steel mill was changed, while in Ethiopia (Finchaa hydro project), Thailand (South Bangkok thermal project), and Ghana (first distribution project), economic growth was slower than expected. In Thailand and Ghana the demand soon caught up with capacity, but in Ethiopia it took some six years before the plant was utilized as planned.

There were eighteen projects in which delays in completion did produce adverse results of one form or another. Of these, five were distribution or transmission projects. Distribution projects differ significantly from generation projects in that they usually consist of a large number of additions to the system, the benefits of which are obtained as soon as a specific addition is made. To say that a distribution project is "delayed" therefore means only that it took longer to carry out a certain program of investment than was expected. However, consumers scheduled to be connected at the start of the program do not suffer if those at the end have to wait longer. It would, of course, be desirable if investment in distribution could be carried out more rapidly, but this is true of investment anywhere in the economy.

Generation projects are a different matter. They do not yield any benefits until they are completed. The consequences of delay depend partly on the length of the delay and partly on the situation of the power system as a whole. If the delay is fairly short and the system has sufficient reserve capacity, the only consequences may be the greater use and the higher costs of that capacity, which usually consists of older and less efficient equipment. If the delay is long enough, it may be necessary to resort to load shedding. Of the eleven generation projects in which delays led to additional costs, six resulted in some load shedding. These included the Port Dickson plant expansions in Malaysia, which were delayed entirely by the late delivery of equipment by the foreign supplier, and the ISA and Chivor projects in Colombia, which were delayed largely by financial problems arising from inflation and lagging rate increases. In the other five cases the additional costs were of a different kind. In Costa Rica (Tapanti project) and Taiwan (Tachien project) it was possible to accelerate the installation of gas turbines which had been planned for later. In Turkey (Kadincik project) and Guatemala (Escuintla project) the principal consequence was greater use of more expensive plant. In the case of the Xavantes hydro project in Brazil, however, it is difficult to trace the precise consequences of the delay since the project is part of a substantially larger system.

The last two projects in the group of sixty-six are difficult to classify. One was the Turlough Hill pumped storage plant in Ireland. The operating cost of this plant was severely affected by the rise in fuel prices, and the audit report concluded that it would have been better to install a base-load steam plant instead. The Electricity Supply Board of Ireland did not wholly agree with this conclusion, however, and emphasized the flexibility provided by the plant. Since it has, in fact, been used to a greater extent than expected, there must have been unquantified benefits, as the appraisal report had pointed out. The plant has provided spinning reserve for the systems in both the Republic of Ireland and Northern Ireland. It has also enabled the use of larger, more economical units to provide base-load power than would otherwise have been possible.

The second case is that of Liberia where, in 1970 and 1971, the Bank financed the expansion of the Mount Coffee power station, a run-of-river plant on the St. Paul river, as well as additional gas turbines for the Bushrod station in Monrovia. When the Mount Coffee dam and power station were built in the first half of the 1960s, it was known that some upstream storage would be necessary if the power plant were to be fully utilized, although no detailed study of the cost of providing this storage had been made. In 1968–69 a study by consultants concluded that the construction of upstream storage in Liberia would not be economic and that the least-cost solution would be to expand the Mount Coffee plant and add two gas turbines at Bushrod. Unfortunately, this solution was made much more expensive by the rise in the oil prices and by the droughts in the Sahel in 1972, 1973, and 1974, which reduced the output at Mount Coffee and increased the load on the gas turbines. In addition, the gas turbines were subject to frequent breakdowns. As a result, further studies of upstream storage were started and diesel capacity was added to the system.

As noted above, numerous hydro projects, despite sometimes substantial cost overruns, were judged to be even more worthwhile than originally expected because of the rise in oil prices, and it may at first appear surprising that very few thermal projects could in retrospect be said not to have been least-cost alternatives. The reason lies largely in the difference in lead time between hydro and thermal projects. Although they may be regarded as alternatives in a mathematical model concerned only with the structure of their capital and operating costs and period of construction, there are much greater differences in practice. Construction of a thermal power plant, like that of a factory, is a fairly routine procedure once the site is selected and the type of equipment determined. A hydroelectric project is quite different. A great deal of information has to be collected and analyzed about water flows and geological conditions before any estimate of the probable costs and output of the project can be made. This circumstance, together with the longer construction period, often means that thermal capacity of some kind has to be installed because not enough is known about possible hydro alternatives. In other words, a given thermal project may accurately be judged to be least-cost, but only in terms of the amount of knowledge and time available when the decision was made. Different decisions might well have been made if more investigation and planning had been done. In retrospect, there are many hydroelectric plants that should have been built earlier than they were, even without the rise in fuel prices. But the events of 1973 certainly gave a strong impetus to the study and preparation of hydro projects in many countries.

The tendency for long-term planning to suffer from the urgency of day-to-day problems is not uncommon. From the beginning of its power lending, the Bank has therefore emphasized the importance of studies and plans for future investment and has been prepared to include funds in its loans to assist borrowers with these tasks. In its early years this assistance was mainly for feasibility studies for specific projects, but later it was extended to investment plans for the whole of the borrower's system. The Bank has also consistently urged its borrowers to stretch their planning horizons. As power systems grow larger and more complex it becomes important to plan further ahead, and in the larger developing countries twenty-year plans are now necessary.

Very few, if indeed any, of the sixty-six audited projects could be said to be "errors" or to have failed to reach their intended objectives. Several were delayed, and some involved losses to the economy which might otherwise have been avoided. But on the whole the record is a good one.

A project-by-project investigation, however, does not necessarily reveal the entire story. Although the Keban transmission project in Turkey, considered on its own, certainly successfully achieved its objective, it cannot be said that the main power system in Turkey has provided an adequate and reliable supply of power for the economy in recent years. In other countries, too, such as India, Nigeria, and Colombia, the power supply has been insufficient to meet the demand, not just occasionally, but as a more or less chronic condition lasting several years. This does not appear to have been the result of incorrect decisionmaking, poor planning or appraisal techniques, or inaccurate load forecasting. It has been the result of a shortage of financial resources and institutional problems that have hampered the operation and maintenance of the system and the construction of projects. In Turkey, for example, TEK's cash generation has been low, and investment in the power sector has had to rely heavily on an overstrained government budget. In addition, a serious shortage of experienced staff has hampered the physical execution of projects and made it extremely difficult to introduce modern management practices.

India has suffered from shortages of power beginning in the late 1960s and continuing to a greater or lesser degree through the 1970s. Electricity consumption in India increased at over 10 percent a year between 1960–61 and 1975–76, a period in which economic growth was a little less than 3.5 percent a year. This difference is unusually large, and the increase in the economy's reliance on electricity is exceptional. Part of the explanation seems to be that power-intensive industries in India have grown particularly rapidly. Another contributory factor is probably that tariffs have been significantly below long-run marginal costs. In 1975 a Bank study of tariffs in Andhra Pradesh concluded that actual tariffs ranged from about 60 percent less than marginal costs for agricultural consumers to about 20 percent less for domestic bulk consumers. Similar results have been found in other states.

The immediate reasons that the supply of power has lagged behind the rapid rise in demand have been inadequate maintenance and substantial delays in the construction of most projects, arising largely from difficulties with civil works, the flow of equipment, and of course the availability of funds. During the fifth plan (1974–75 to 1978–79) a central government monitoring system was established and the situation has since improved. Furthermore, the large thermal plants now being constructed by the National Thermal Power Corporation (NTPC) with financial assistance from the Bank are in much closer accord with their schedules. Contributing to both the maintenance problems and the delays in construction was the shortage of finance. Not enough resources were allocated to power in the Indian economic planning process. Even though the proportion of total plan outlays allocated to power increased steadily from 12 percent in the first plan (1951–56) to 23 percent in the current plan (1979–83), actual expenditure on power always exceeded the planned amount. The shortage of financial resources was compounded by the low earnings of the State Electricity Boards.

Nigeria has also suffered from serious power shortages during the past decade. In this case the unusually rapid increase in demand, averaging 20 percent a year over many years preceding 1979, and severe droughts after 1976 were important causes. In addition, an acute shortage of experienced staff caused institutional difficulties in the National Electric Power Authority (NEPA) that led to delays in project construction and many interruptions in the transmission and distribution of power. In Colombia, too, demand has exceeded the installation of new capacity because of planning delays and a shortage of capital. The resulting power shortages and interruptions to the supply were aggravated by unusually long dry seasons in 1980 and 1981.

# 5. The Bank's Role in Power Development: Past and Future

THE BANK'S LENDING for electric power must be assessed against the background of the Bank's concept of economic development as a process and of its own role in it. The evolution of this concept has affected and been affected by the experience of power lending. As a consequence, power lending can provide specific illustrations of, and perhaps lessons about, the effectiveness of the Bank's changing approach to its operations.

## Changing Approaches to Development

The gradual broadening of the Bank's view of the development process has often been noted, and its own role has sometimes been described as evolving from that of a bank to that of development agency.[1] In its early years the Bank regarded itself primarily as a provider of capital for investment in public services, particularly power and transport. There was some lending for agriculture and industry, but it was much less important than that for the public services. Not only was it thought that, given adequate public services, private sources would provide the necessary investment in the directly productive sectors, but also industrial and agricultural projects were difficult to prepare and execute. At that time it was believed, with some justification, that "absorptive capacity" set rather strict limits to the volume of projects suitable for Bank lending, and these limits appeared narrower for industry and agriculture than for infrastructure. Furthermore, since many potential projects in these sectors were small, the Bank had to devise a technique for lending for them. Hence a considerable proportion of early lending for these sectors was

---

1. Edward S. Mason and Robert E. Asher, *The World Bank since Bretton Woods* (Washington, D.C.: Brookings Institution, 1973), chap. 19, provides a more detailed discussion of this question.

through intermediary credit institutions, the industrial and agricultural banks.

As pointed out by Mason and Asher, the notion of limited absorptive capacity was discussed as early as 1949 and was put forward as an explanation for the slow increase in the volume of bank lending.[2] In the words of the Bank's 1949 annual report, absorptive capacity was limited by the low level of education and health in most developing countries and in the economic and financial insecurity often arising from frequent changes in government. The result was that "money alone is no solution" and there was a "gap . . . between the concept of development potentialities and the formulation of practical propositions designed for the realisation of these potentialities."

One measure that was seen as a solution was the provision of technical assistance. At first, technical assistance was primarily for engineering studies, market surveys, and the economic analysis of costs and benefits to help with the preparation of projects. The 1949 annual report did point out, however, that an organization must be created to carry out the project and competent management must be obtained. This is probably the first public reference to what later became known as institution building. Five years later, the annual report included a chapter on "Collaboration in Project Preparation and Execution," in which the Bank observed that many undertakings financed by the Bank were of a kind or on a scale new to the organization carrying them out. The organization might not therefore be fully equipped to deal with all the problems that could arise: "indeed, regardless of the stage of development reached by the country concerned, consultant services or other outside assistance may be required by any organization embarking on a new project. In cases where assistance is needed the Bank is willing, and conceives it to be an integral part of its function, to see that this assistance is provided—either through members of its own staff or through help to the borrower in obtaining expert assistance elsewhere." By this time, as described in the foregoing chapters, experience with serious delays and other problems with projects had led the Bank to stress the importance of institution building.

A section on "Administration and Management" in the 1954 annual report discussed the various problems that might arise and the measures

2. Ibid., pp. 460–62. Mason and Asher imply that the idea of limited absorptive capacity was not an explanation but an excuse for a modest lending volume. They do not refer to another significant factor limiting the volume of projects financed in any year, namely, the size of the Bank's staff. For obvious reasons, there has been a close correlation between the number of projects financed and the size of the staff.

needed to cope with them, among which are many that subsequently became central elements in the notion of institution building:

> Progress may be impeded by inadequate accountancy standards and inventory controls, cumbersome procurement procedures, or ill-advised personnel policies. It is often necessary to take positive steps towards making a career in the new enterprise attractive to the best-qualified people; this may, for instance, require measures to ensure that salary standards are adequate, that tenure of employment is reasonably secure and that promotion will be by merit. The Bank studies these matters and may suggest ways of improving the conditions under which management has to operate.
>
> In governmental enterprises, even though management possesses the necessary qualifications, it cannot be fully effective if its actions are hampered by outside interventions and pressures. As a protection against this, the Bank has sometimes recommended the establishment of an autonomous body to run the project.

The report then went on to emphasize the importance of good management for the operation of completed projects and noted some of the qualities required, including those of leadership, the ability to look beyond the immediate task and to handle personnel, and relations with labor and government. For this reason, "the Bank may arrange that the management of a project must be acceptable to the Bank as well as to the borrower."

Experience since 1954 clearly shows the importance of these matters. Problems such as improving accounting systems, rationalizing procurement procedures, and fixing salaries at an adequate level have been continuing concerns. The caliber of senior management personnel also obviously retains its importance, even though the attempt to make the staffing of specific posts subject to the Bank's approval has had only mixed success. Some other aspects of institution building have emerged since this early exposition. Although the lack of education was mentioned in a general way, specific training programs did not become an explicit part of Bank lending operations until some ten to fifteen years later, after the Bank had itself entered into lending for education. Furthermore, building a successful autonomous agency turned out to be much more difficult than would appear from the simple sentence quoted above. An appropriate legal basis was not enough. The agency needed to be efficiently operated and, most important, financially sound, which in turn required more than a legal statement or concession to the effect that it should earn some minimum financial return. The legal establishment of an autonomous agency is only the initial step toward achieving real independence.

The early Bank lending for infrastructure, particularly electric power and transportation, thus reflected the then prevailing view of how foreign financial assistance could most effectively promote economic development. But through this lending the Bank was able to formulate its first objectives and policies that went beyond the provision of finance and concern with creditworthiness. These policies, suitably modified, were later applied to most other areas of Bank lending.

In 1958 Bank operations entered a new phase characterized by a substantially higher volume of lending and a shift in emphasis from infrastructure to agriculture, industry, and, after the establishment of IDA in 1961, education. The power sector participated in the general increase in lending despite the new emphasis on agriculture; in fact, it was not until 1973 that the annual value of agricultural loans exceeded that for power. This general broadening of the kinds of project regarded as suitable for Bank lending—which came to embrace not only education but also water supply, tourism, population control, and urban improvement—was followed by the Bank's response to the issues of development policy that came to the forefront in the 1970s: namely, who was receiving the benefit of economic growth and what could be done to ensure that the lowest income groups shared in this benefit? This new phase emphasized projects explicitly designed to bring the rural and urban poor into the developing economy.

These changes affected mainly Bank lending other than for power. As other sectors were emphasized, however, power was necessarily de-emphasized, and there was some tendency to regard power lending as a rather routine activity, which might well be left to others. As noted in chapter 1, power lending measured in real terms declined slightly from 1964 to 1978, but as rising oil prices took their toll in developing countries, power lending began to receive more priority.

Rural electrification received greater attention, as did making power available to the urban poor by such methods as lifeline rates—especially low residential tariffs for limited amounts consumed. In 1975 an analysis of the problems of rural electrification was published as a World Bank Paper, and more loans were made expressly for rural electrification. Even before this, projects financed by the Bank probably contributed to rural electrification since many of them included transmission lines which facilitated the linking up of nearby villages. But it is not possible to say how much rural electrification was financed because any items that might be regarded as such would have been included with other parts of the project. There had been, however, some reluctance to finance rural electrification projects, mainly because of the difficulty of making a reliable economic appraisal of them. In the 1960s there was almost no evidence on the economic impact of rural electrification, and even now there is not much.[3] In addition, rural electrification normally involves financial losses during the period before the load builds up. In some countries, however, the load growth in rural areas could be quite rapid and thus limit the financial losses incurred.

Beginning in 1975 the Bank made a number of loans specifically for rural electrification projects. By June 1981, $676 million, or 8 percent of total power lending, had been committed for these projects in fourteen countries, the largest amounts being for India, Thailand, and the Philippines. In these operations special attention was given to the economic appraisal in order to ensure that the areas with the highest potential were given priority. The calculation of the economic return was based on estimates not only of the direct revenues from sales but also of the additional savings arising from the use of electricity rather than other forms of fuel. In some areas where income per capita was significantly below the average for the whole country, a social rate of return was also calculated, which gave a greater weight to benefits received by the poorer sections of the population.[4]

One of the most important changes of the past two decades to affect attitudes toward economic growth has been concern for the environment. Most economic activities affect the environment in one way or another, and some can have significantly detrimental effects unless specific measures, which usually cost money, are taken to avoid them. The possible environmental effects of development projects are now investigated as part of the Bank's appraisal, and an Office of Environmental Affairs is responsible for providing expertise and devising guidelines for handling environmental problems.

The economic activities which have the most impact on the environment are industrial and mining development and urbanization. Power projects, however, can also have environmental effects: thermal power stations can cause air pollution, and the water from the cooling process can affect life in the bodies of water into which it is discharged. These can normally be taken care of without too great a cost. Hydro projects are often fairly "clean," although the reservoirs they sometimes create can

3. Judith Tendler, *Rural Electrification: Linkages and Justifications*, A.I.D. Program Evaluation Discussion Paper no. 3 (Washington, D.C.: U.S. Agency for International Development, April 1979), is an example. It contains a bibliography.

4. Lyn Squire and Herman van der Tak, *Economic Analysis of Projects* (Baltimore, Md.: Johns Hopkins University Press, 1975).

contribute to the spread of water-borne diseases if preventive measures are not taken.

One potentially serious problem is the necessity to relocate the inhabitants of areas which will be inundated by a hydro project. The involuntary resettlement of people can give rise to many socioeconomic problems, particularly if whole communities are to be relocated in unfamiliar surroundings. In some of the Bank's early operations these problems were not well foreseen or planned for and created a great deal of difficulty. Since then the problems of resettlement have been the subject of sociological research, and the implications are better understood. In the past decade resettlement has been handled effectively in many instances with a minimum of danger to the well-being of the people concerned. One of the first was the Paulo Alfonso hydro project in Brazil, which involved the relocation of some 10,000 people. Detailed plans for resettlement were an integral part of the design of the project, and the Bank's agricultural staff reviewed the progress of this program. A great deal was learned from this experience which was used to good effect in other cases such as a water supply project in Ghana and a hydro project in Thailand. In 1980 the Bank prepared an operational memorandum for its staff covering all aspects of involuntary resettlement programs.

## Electric Power and the Energy Sector

The "energy crisis"—that is, the rise in price of petroleum from around $2 or $3 a barrel in 1973 to $18 to $20 and then the further rise in 1979 to more than $30 a barrel—has resulted in a number of measures and proposals for new policies by the Bank, some of which have implications for electric power lending. A report, "Energy in the Developing Countries," published by the Bank in August 1980, analyzed the issues and indicated desirable directions for the Bank to follow. The first and most obvious departure was the financing of projects for the exploration and development of oil and natural gas in developing countries. Early in 1979 the Bank adopted an accelerated program for this new type of lending.[5] The preparatory work on which this program was based showed that many developing countries probably did have petroleum resources

5. *A Program to Accelerate Petroleum Production in the Developing Countries* (Washington, D.C.: World Bank, January 1979).

not yet discovered, but it also revealed a serious lack of information about potential energy resources. Many oil-importing countries appeared to need some assistance in devising policies and programs for energy development.

In an effort to meet this need the Bank started to organize reviews of the energy sector in many oil-importing countries. Among other purposes, they were to assess potential energy resources, identify energy policy issues, and provide impartial advice. A central issue facing many countries is the formulation of a policy for pricing the various types of energy. The Bank's concern with the price of electric power is long-standing, and its emphasis on basing prices on economic costs began in the early 1970s. Much of the effectiveness of cost-related pricing in electric power, however, depends on the existence of similar cost-related prices for other sources of energy. Hence the energy sector reviews have as one of their principal concerns the establishment of a rational system of prices for the whole sector.

In addition, the reviews set the role of electric power in the wider context of the production and use of all forms of energy. Electricity is both a primary and a secondary source of energy; power from hydro, nuclear, and geothermal sources is considered primary energy while that produced from fossil fuels is secondary energy. A significant effect of the rise in the price of oil was to increase the economic role of primary power as against most kinds of secondary power, particularly that produced from oil and gas. One consequence for hydro development already mentioned is that it is now economic to build hydro plants, even though they cost as much as $2,000 to $3,000 per kilowatt as against only $800 per kilowatt in the 1960s. Consequently, a great deal of work has been put into the preparation of feasibility studies for major hydro projects.

With the increase in the priority of hydro power small projects may become economic. Particularly in view of the long construction periods for large hydro projects, it may well turn out that plants as small as 5 megawatts might be economically worthwhile in some countries. Some even smaller projects ("mini" hydro, that is, 50 kilowatts to 2 megawatts) might also be economic, but the cost of feasibility studies necessary to build a large enough number of such projects to have a significant impact on the energy situation in a country is a serious obstacle. The Bank and other development agencies are financing demonstration mini hydro projects in several countries, and the Bank has commissioned a study to investigate methods whereby feasibility studies of a large number of small projects might be done at a reasonable cost.

So far the Bank has done virtually no financing of nuclear power. In

1959 a loan was made for a nuclear plant in Italy, and at the time this was thought to be the forerunner of many others in developing countries. Nuclear plants have a minimum economic capacity of about 600 megawatts, however, and the systems in many developing countries are too small for them. The fall in the cost of conventional thermal plants during the 1950s and 1960s and the rise in the cost of nuclear power meant that the latter expanded much more slowly in developing countries than had been expected. Those countries that did build nuclear plants had no difficulty in finding the required finance from bilateral sources, and it seems likely that this situation will continue. The chance of the Bank being asked to finance nuclear power thus appears remote.

Conservation and increased efficiency are of course among the most important strategies for overcoming the energy crisis. Conservation is largely a problem for consumers of electric power; the main contribution the power industry can make in this respect is to ensure that its tariffs reflect economic costs so as not to give an incorrect signal to consumers. But increasing the efficiency of the process whereby power is generated, transmitted, and distributed could bring substantial savings. Studies have shown that large returns can be made on investment in rehabilitation, load management, plant efficiency, and better operating procedures. From the point of view of a foreign aid agency, these kinds of investment are not easy to handle because they do not readily form an "investment project" and generally require some form of management assistance. Moreover, by their very nature, they are often not able to command priority in the eyes of planning ministries.

The Bank, however, has actively encouraged its borrowers to reduce the proportion of energy that is lost or unaccounted for. Losses occur for two reasons. The first is that theft and inefficient metering and billing procedures reduce the revenue of the agency. The corresponding power is used by the consumers, however, even though it is not paid for, which offsets to some extent the loss to the economy. The second type of loss is caused by technical deficiencies such as insufficient distribution facilities. Savings from improvements in this respect can be substantial. For example, using reasonable assumptions about capacity and fuel costs in one major developing country it was estimated that the potential savings from reducing losses would amount to $50 million a year. In the fiscal years 1978–80, twenty-eight power projects out of sixty-two financed by the Bank included components which should improve system efficiency, and five projects included efficiency as a specific objective. The Bank is attempting to persuade power agencies and planning ministries to pay more attention to this problem.

## Investment Requirements for Electric Power

All countries of whatever level of development have to carry through the profound economic adjustments made necessary by the changed energy situation. These changes, together with the demand for additional energy to sustain future economic growth, require an amount of capital substantially larger than has been necessary in the past.

The Bank's report, *The Energy Transition in Developing Countries*, includes an estimate of the investment needs for electric power in the 1982–92 period. This estimate is part of an analysis of investment requirements concerning all the major sources of energy—electric power, oil, natural gas, and coal—with an allowance for investment in refineries. The estimate for electric power is based on an analysis of country studies which show that electricity consumption in developing countries is likely to grow at 6 to 7 percent a year over the period, which is slightly less than its rate of growth from 1973 to 1978. It means that the total electricity supply in developing countries would increase from about 1,320 tetrawatt-hours by the end of 1980 to about 2,850 tetrawatt-hours by 1992.[6] Based on current costs per kilowatt of the type of capacity likely to be needed, the resulting investment requirements, together with those of other types of energy, is as shown in table 3.

Two obvious points emerge from these figures. First, they represent a large increase in investment in real terms. It is estimated that in 1980 these countries invested about $25 billion in energy development, whereas the table implies an investment of $130 billion a year by 1992.

Second, almost half of the capital required is for investment in electric power. This high proportion requires some explanation. A large part of it is that a substantial amount of the energy derived from other sources has to be converted into electricity in order to meet the pattern of commercial demand. Despite the low mechanical efficiency of this conversion, it is economically beneficial because of the high convenience and efficiency of electricity when it is finally consumed. For example, the efficiency of an electric motor is about 85 percent, whereas that of a diesel engine is only 15 to 20 percent. Electric cookers and water heaters may be twice as efficient as oil or gas units, and electric lighting is several times more efficient than other forms. A second reason is the familiar one that electric power is a capital-intensive activity, and this applies both to the development of primary electricity and to the conversion of other forms of

6. A tetrawatt is equal to 1 billion kilowatts.

Table 3. *Investment Requirements for Energy in Developing Countries, 1982–92*
(billions of 1982 U.S. dollars)

| Energy source | Low-income countries | Middle-income countries | | All developing countries |
| | | Oil importers | Oil exporters[a] | |
| --- | --- | --- | --- | --- |
| Electric power | 173.9 | 354.9 | 129.6 | 658.4 |
| Oil | 66.9 | 87.3 | 311.7 | 465.9 |
| Gas | 21.8 | 24.5 | 43.8 | 90.1 |
| Coal | 55.2 | 27.2 | 6.3 | 88.7 |
| Refineries[b] | 30.8 | 52.8 | 39.7 | 123.3 |
| Total | 348.6 | 546.7 | 531.1 | 1,426.4 |

*Note:* Estimates do not include investments in fuel storage and retail distribution (except for pipelines for domestic distribution of natural gas) or for infrastructure needed for energy imports.

a. Excludes capital surplus oil exporters.

b. May vary by as much as 20 percent, depending on the refinery mix in China and the extent of trade in refined products.

*Source:* World Bank, *The Energy Transition in Developing Countries* (Washington, D.C., 1983), table 5.1.

energy into electricity. Furthermore, the degree of capital intensity is increasing. Although in many smaller developing countries the expansion of the power network may bring economies of scale, many of the larger ones face the prospect of higher average costs as capacity expands—for example, when less favorable hydro sites have to be developed.

The high prices of oil and gas are also leading to some substitution of primary electricity as an energy source. In the 1960s primary electricity accounted for only 7 percent of the increments to the world energy supply; in the 1970s this share rose to 17.5 percent, and in the 1980s it is expected to be 18.5 percent. Furthermore, the "energy intensity" in developing countries—that is, energy consumption as a proportion of GDP—is increasing.[7] Consequently, the probable demand for power in developing countries rises faster than GDP; hence the expectation underlying table 3 that power demand will increase by 6 to 7 percent a year.

A rapid increase in demand for an increasingly capital-intensive public

7. See *World Development Report 1981* (New York: Oxford University Press, 1981), pp. 37–39.

service leads to the great increase in financial requirements for power shown in the table. The size of the increase is likely to raise the question of whether it is firmly justified—whether or not there is some less costly alternative. Because an investment program is capital-intensive, however, does not mean that it is uneconomic. It means only that a high proportion of the cost of final output is represented by capital charges, but this final cost may still be lower than less capital-intensive alternatives. Nevertheless, the possibility obviously arises that the large financial requirements of the developing countries for power investment may not be met, even with a major effort on their own part.

If capital is short, then in principle a high shadow price should be applied to capital for the purpose of determining the price of power, and this should in turn reduce demand. How effective this rationing by price would be and what consequences it would have for economic development is impossible to say, since there is very little prior experience to learn from. In practice, however, it seems highly unlikely that electricity prices would be increased to a level sufficient to reduce demand significantly. The price of electricity is much more rigid than, for example, the price of petroleum and its products. When oil prices rose many governments attempted to moderate the effect of the increase on consumers by methods such as price control or a reduction in excise taxes. But market forces were strong enough to overcome these obstacles, and most consumers (except in some oil-producing countries) have had to pay prices reflecting economic costs. There is, however, no comparable free-market mechanism for forcing up the price of electricity. Indeed, as the account of the financial problems of power agencies in chapter 2 made clear, the price of power is frequently held down by governments in an attempt to control inflation so that power prices tend to lag behind other prices. Hence it seems quite unlikely that high power prices could be used to bring about any shift to other forms of energy, even if any other forms were to be of lower economic cost. Much more probable is that power prices will be held below real economic costs, which will encourage demand and reduce the financial resources available for investment by power agencies. It may therefore turn out that shortages of electric power become more common toward the end of the 1980s and act as a serious brake on economic growth.

## The Role of the Bank

As pointed out in chapter 1, during the late 1960s and the 1970s increased lending in other sectors, particularly agriculture, meant that power lending, when measured in constant dollars, showed a slight declining trend. Since disbursements are mainly determined by commitments made in previous years, it would take some years of increasing loan commitments to reverse this trend. According to present lending plans, which envisage lending for power of about $7.6 billion (in current dollars) for 1981–85, loan disbursements for power would be about $3.9 billion (in 1980 dollars), about the same as for the past five years. Unless there is a substantial increase in power lending, therefore, and in view of the rising investment needs of developing countries, the role of the Bank, at least in the purely financial sense, will decline.

Whether or not this will occur depends on the decisions concerning both the overall scale of operations of the Bank and IDA and the relative priority to be accorded electric power. In making its case for a continuation or expansion of its operations, the Bank has always stressed the significance of its nonfinancial or institution-building role, since Bank operations alone are inevitably a modest part of total investment in developing countries. All the same, it is a well-known but often overlooked phenomenon that large aggregates are made up of many small parts, each of which, when viewed in isolation, could be dismissed as unimportant. To emphasize the institutional aspects of Bank operations is not to detract from its financial role. Moreover, there is a close connection between them. The question sometimes raised, rather rhetorically, is why, if its strength lies in institutional improvement, the Bank does not devote most of its efforts to providing technical assistance for this purpose and leave finance to others. But this, of course, could not be done because the technical assistance—in its widest sense—and the financial assistance are very closely bound together. This leads to the question of the methods used by the Bank to encourage institutional improvement.

The institutional role that the Bank has played, and the role that it could play, should be seen against the background of the increasing financial requirements of the power industry and the changing institutional demands that its expansion create. The remainder of this chapter sets forth this role under three headings: the Bank's objectives, the methods it employs to further them, and the results. It presents at the same time a summary of the preceding analysis and some conclusions that may be drawn from it.

## Objectives

The Bank's financial objectives originated in its concern over the creditworthiness of its borrowers. To ensure that its borrowers charged adequate rates for power therefore became one of its earliest and, as it turned out, one of its most enduring objectives. It was supplemented by other financial objectives such as the improvement of internal financial management, the reduction of accounts receivable, and independent audits of borrowers' accounts. These objectives, which related to particular agencies, paralleled efforts to ensure that whenever various power agencies in a country become linked into an integrated network, the financial and accounting systems were adapted to the new requirements. This involved the collection of information, the unification of accounting systems, and agreement on the terms on which power was to be exchanged between agencies. All these were steps toward dealing with the financial problems of the whole network as a unified system.

The Bank's first purely institutional objective in the power field was the establishment of autonomous agencies to operate the power system. At the start, this was regarded as largely a legal problem having to do with the statutes or concession of the power agency. It gradually became apparent that real as opposed to nominal autonomy required more than this; the agency had to have the necessary strength to resist pressures, and it therefore had to have some degree of financial soundness and operational efficiency. Thus the Bank was led into a concern with the quality of the senior management, the internal organization and management systems, and problems of staff employment, salary policy, and training. It also endeavoured to ensure that the agency had the responsibility for procurement and the award of construction contracts.

To ensure that projects reached proper standards of engineering efficiency and economic justification, the Bank began to assist in the process of project preparation. Its loans soon began to include funds for feasibility studies, and its engineering staff began to participate in discussions of future projects at an early stage. This led in turn to a wider concern for investment planning, and the Bank pushed its borrowers to prepare investment plans stretching over longer periods as systems grew, projects became larger, and hence lead times longer. When the analysis of investment programs indicated that economies could be obtained by linking utilities together rather than by separate development, the Bank urged its borrowers to follow this course even if it meant overcoming organizational and political rivalries. Other objectives associated with project and investment appraisal that have gained in importance are the protection of the environment, the use of marginal cost pricing, and the economic analysis of rural electrification schemes.

## Methods

The Bank has a number of instruments or "weapons" which it can use to further its objectives. The most obvious is the use of its funds, but there are other means at its disposal. Bank staff visit a project regularly during its construction. These so-called supervision missions not only review the projects and keep the Bank informed but also assist the borrower with any current problems. Since in many sectors, of which electric power is one, projects follow each other at intervals, the technical staff concerned with a country acquire a close knowledge of its situation and problems.

In early 1980 the Bank's Operations Evaluation Department reviewed the supervisory process, particularly in view of the larger number of projects and the trend toward greater complexity of projects in such fields as rural and urban development and education. It also assessed the efficiency of supervision from the point of view of both the Bank and the borrower. Despite the occasional suspicion that developing countries suffer from too many visitors from numerous aid agencies, the great majority of those questioned thought that the missions came with about the right frequency—normally twice a year—and stayed for about the right length of time. Furthermore the respondents, with few exceptions, rated the missions' performance either "good" or "fair" in helping overcome various problems. The review described some of the ways in which these missions appeared to be helpful to the borrowers. The visit of a mission often served as a catalyst for discussion and decisionmaking. Missions also brought together other agencies and government departments involved with the project and focused their attention on its problems. Discussions on power tariffs and future financing plans for the agency are examples.

The periodic supervision missions are also vehicles for a virtually continuous interchange between the agency staff and the Bank's engineers on the numerous technical aspects of the projects. Because this book has focused on the economic, financial, and institutional aspects of power development, there has been no detailed description of the numerous technical problems inseparable from the construction and expansion of power systems. This does not properly reflect the contribution of the Bank's power engineers. It should be stressed that all the major technical decisions and issues of project formulation and engineering design are reviewed and discussed by the Bank's staff. Two specific illustrations can be given. The first, already mentioned, is the attention given to the cost of tunneling and the problem of how much test drilling is worthwhile. The second concerns the safety of dams. In the late 1960s and early 1970s there were a number of disastrous dam failures. Consequently all engineers, including those in the Bank, began to look more closely into problems of the design and construction of large dams. The Bank made it a normal practice to require that, for any large dam or one with unusual features, the design should be reviewed by a panel of independent experts.

It also included in its loan agreements a covenant that borrowers should carry out a program of regular monitoring and inspection of the dam after it had been completed.

The Bank also exercises some influence through its written reports, particularly its appraisal reports. These reports contain not only a description and economic justification of the project but also an analysis of the financial situation and prospects of the power agency, its institutional and operational problems, and the power sector as a whole. They are intended primarily for the Bank's senior management and Executive Directors, but since they contain the Bank's views on the strengths and weaknesses of the agency and on the problems of the sector, they are often read with some care by those about whom they are written. Sometimes they are used as supporting evidence by those seeking solutions to the problems discussed.

The most powerful influence the Bank can exercise derives, of course, from its power to make or withhold loans. This enables it to participate in the planning and preparation of the projects to ensure that the finished proposal is acceptable. The loan documents contain not only the kind of protective financial covenants that most lenders to commercial enterprises employ, but also covenants concerning the way in which the project is to be constructed and operated. The agreements also include the standard remedies under which, if the borrower does not observe the agreement, the Bank may suspend disbursements and, eventually, declare the loan in default.

Despite having made more than 2,000 loans and 1,200 IDA credits, the number of occasions on which the Bank has made use of its remedies is relatively modest. By mid-1982 they numbered between twenty and thirty. For example, in six cases all loans to a country were temporarily suspended because of civil war or similar disturbances. In two cases all loans to a country were suspended because of delays in repayments to the Bank. There have been less than a dozen cases in which disbursements were suspended because of difficulties with the project, and six of these suspensions were informal. Only two involved power loans, both of which were caused by financial problems.

On other occasions the Bank has informed the borrowers that, unless some remedial action is taken, it will feel compelled to suspend disbursements and this may precipitate a discussion of the issue and an agreement on measures to be taken. How many such instances there have been is not known, but they are not likely to be numerous. Threatening to suspend disbursements is not something the Bank does lightly. Nor is it difficult to see why. To suspend disbursements is a measure of last resort to be taken only after other efforts have failed. Suspension involves a cost not only to the borrower but also to the Bank. It places a strain on relations between the Bank and the borrower and it precludes progress on the project. Since the main purpose of the loan is to complete the project, suspension is a confession of failure. In many cases in which disbursements were suspended because of project difficulties—rather than for external reasons such as civil disruption—work on the project had already come to a halt. The Bank could then suspend disbursements at much less "cost." But to suspend disbursements when the project is going ahead is a very different proposition, and in practice the Bank does so only when it concludes that there is no alternative.

Because the Bank's resort to its legal remedies is comparatively rare—none of the more than 350 loans for power projects has been formally suspended (other than as part of a general suspension on nonproject grounds) and only two have been informally suspended—it might be thought that the Bank is a kind of paper tiger whose agreements can be ignored with impunity. In practice, however, borrowers do not act on this assumption; when borrowers' representatives visit Washington for the purpose of concluding negotiations for a loan they study the proposed loan agreements with great care, and particular phrases and numbers may be determinedly contested until a compromise is reached. At the end of the process there is little doubt that both sides have a clear understanding of what has been agreed and how the agreements are to be carried out and that the borrowers do intend to carry them out to the best of their ability.

Apart from the obvious fact that it takes an exceptional human being to sign an official document with no intention of abiding by it, one important reason for adherence to Bank agreements is that very few loans are one-shot operations. In almost all cases the borrower is likely to want another loan for a successor project after the present one is completed. In any case, the government of the country concerned is always involved, either as direct borrower or as guarantor. The prospect of a subsequent loan is enhanced if good progress has been made with the previous one. In fact, an important part of most loan negotiations is a discussion of what has happened to the previous loan and, if it has encountered problems, to agree on what should be done about them. The Bank is naturally reluctant to approve a new loan to a borrower who has not observed the terms of a previous loan agreement. If the matter cannot be put right without delay, the Bank wishes to have some agreed timetable of measures to deal with it.

The Bank's ability to use a new loan to improve the situation with regard to a previous project, or some related factor such as the borrower's financial position, is much the most important way it uses its command over money to make progress toward its objectives. If the problems are major, loans may be delayed, even at the cost of delays in the project. Alternatively, the Bank may proceed to sign the loan documents but may make their effectiveness subject to some measures being taken by the borrower. In extreme cases the legal effectiveness of a loan may be delayed for a year or more. There are no data on how frequently this sort of delay occurs, but in any case such data would be virtually impossible to interpret since the degree to which the procedure produces results does not depend on a loan's being delayed at all. In all loans that are part of a series the process is at work, even if it leaves few explicit traces in the documents.

One other use of the Bank's funds often plays a significant role in its operations. This is the use of a part of the loan for some specific purpose, such as paying for consultants' services to prepare a feasibility study, an investment program, or a training program or covering the costs of training staff abroad. These amounts are frequently quite modest, and in many cases the allocation may not even increase the size of the loan itself. Nevertheless, the practice is clearly effective; the Bank's willingness to provide funds for a specific purpose demonstrates its belief in its importance and can be used by the borrower to counter any criticism that might otherwise arise. In some cases the provision of foreign exchange by the Bank may eliminate the problem some borrowers encounter in obtaining foreign exchange from domestic authorities.

## The Bank's Objectives: A Brief Digression

The preceding paragraphs assume that it is legitimate for the Bank to have objectives and to use whatever influence it has to achieve them. These assumptions are sometimes challenged. Should the Bank have objectives which are in any way different from the borrower's objectives?[8] Is not the Bank's task to assist the borrower to achieve its objectives whatever they may be? Is it acceptable for the Bank to exercise leverage in order to pressure a borrower into doing something it might not otherwise do? Critics of the Bank demand to know why, for example, borrowers should accept the Bank's view of what the price of electricity should be or, in other sectors, what the interest rate on industrial loans or the procurement price of wheat should be. Are these not the internal

8. The major policies and objectives of the Bank are determined by its Executive Directors. Although directors representing developing countries do not control a majority of the voting power, they can and do ensure that the views of borrowers are fairly taken into account.

affairs of the country concerned? The Bank could reply that all borrowers are entirely free to set any power rates they choose provided they do not expect the Bank to lend to them if it finds the rates unacceptable. This kind of interchange leads nowhere and tends to obscure the real issue.

It is a commonplace within the Bank that no project can succeed unless it has the support of the government and other relevant authorities in the country. Although the term "Bank project" is frequently used, all projects are the borrower's projects. Equally, such objectives as providing a reliable source of power at the lowest possible cost, carrying out the project efficiently, and ensuring that the power agency is in a sound financial situation are clearly shared by the borrower and the Bank. The problems arise when these objectives have to be set out in specific terms and the precise methods of achieving them have to be agreed. It is one thing to agree that power revenues should enable an agency to be financially sound, but it is a different matter to agree that they should average ten cents a kilowatt-hour and should be raised to this figure over a period of two years. Almost all the issues which arise between the Bank and its borrowers are questions of method and of degree. Is, for example, the financial situation of the agency really as bad as the Bank thinks or is it only as bad as the agency is prepared to admit? How much is required to remedy the situation and how long will it take? Will the future load really increase at this rate or is the estimate optimistic? Does the agency require an infusion of equity capital and if so how can it be obtained? Does the long-term investment program need updating and should the methodology be improved? The chief executive of one power agency described discussions of this kind with a felicitous, if slightly mixed, metaphor: "The Bank always wants the moon, and we always have to bring it down to earth."

The inevitability of argument and compromise over such issues arises directly from the nature of any agency whose function is to provide aid in accordance with stipulated criteria. If, as in the Bank's case, it provides aid for "productive" projects and to "creditworthy" borrowers or, as in the case of the International Monetary Fund, to borrowers who must have a program for overcoming a balance of payments problem, the agency concerned has to determine whether any specific project or program is acceptable under the relevant criteria. If for some reason it finds some project or program not acceptable, it must give its reasons with sufficient precision to enable the potential borrower to make the project acceptable if the borrower so desires. Since the agency's criteria are well known, the borrower may take issue with its decision and argue that the proposal really is acceptable. The agency will put up counterarguments and eventually a compromise is worked out. In the case of the Bank, this process could be described as exercising leverage over the borrower for the purpose of meeting the Bank's criteria. Or it could be described as two parties arguing over whether a specific situation accords with certain general criteria. It could even be described as the borrower exercising leverage over the Bank to compel it to stretch its criteria and make a loan. For in an important sense the Bank "needs" projects if any of its objectives are to be met, and only borrowers can provide them. For this reason, borrowers are far from without bargaining power. But whatever form of words is chosen to describe it, the reality remains the same.

## The Results

How far can the Bank claim to have succeeded in achieving its objectives? Since the Bank is essentially an aid agency, that is, an agency that helps recipients carry out their projects, there is no way in which the contribution of the Bank can be unambiguously separated from the actions of the borrowers themselves. It is not possible to know what would have happened if the Bank had not existed. Nor is it possible to make any meaningful statistical comparisons between countries in which the Bank has been heavily engaged in power lending and those in which it has been involved only slightly or not at all. The other factors involved are too numerous and the course of events too complex. In this area, therefore, conclusive proof is impossible. What can be done is to set the Bank's objectives and methods against the background of what has happened, but conclusions as to cause and effect must remain to some extent subjective.

The most reliable data are those concerning the results of specific projects which were summarized in chapter 4. It was clear that few, if any, projects could be called uneconomic. Given the steady increase in demand for power, however, avoiding uneconomic projects is not difficult. More important are, first, the preparation of investment plans for a long enough period to enable major projects to be constructed by the time they are needed and thus avoid pressure to install expensive emergency capacity; and second, the ability to construct the projects without delays and thus avoid power shortages. The planning process has made a great deal of progress, and many countries now plan for much longer periods than formerly. There is, however, little general evidence on whether implementation has improved. In some well-known instances, such as India, there was considerable success in speeding up the construction of new super thermal plants. An important contribution to the efficiency of implementation, which is associated with all Bank lending, is the economies that arise from international competitive bidding on projects.

The Bank has encouraged this practice by familiarizing borrowers with it and by conducting seminars on procurement in many developing countries.

Any judgment about the success of the Bank's efforts to strengthen the financial situation and earnings of its borrowing power agencies has to be seen in the context of a changing set of world economic circumstances. During the 1950s and most of the 1960s inflation was fairly modest, and many power agencies made good progress in improving their finances. As shown in appendix table 6, in the early 1970s before the first rise in oil prices, many agencies were earning reasonable returns. After 1973, rising oil prices and mounting inflation together with the efforts of many governments to hold down inflation put great pressure on power agencies, and even the stronger ones were affected; any agency which succeeded in running hard enough to stay in the same place could feel well pleased. It was also in this period that the Bank began systematically urging its borrowers to study and put into practice the principles of efficiency or marginal cost pricing as a basis for electricity tariffs.

Although in the 1950s and early 1960s it could plausibly have been argued that the Bank's approach to power tariffs was based only on some very general accounting notions plus a general belief that it was a sound idea to increase public savings in developing countries, this is certainly no longer true. Because of the rising real costs of power in the 1970s and the associated rise in investment requirements, basing prices on a proper economic analysis of costs has become crucial, for without it there will be little hope of supply keeping pace with demand. The Bank has played a significant role as an intermediary transmitting these new ideas to the developing countries. There is still a long way to go before it can be said that the ideas have been translated into practice in most countries, but there is a marked contrast between present attitudes to them and those of ten years ago.

The influence of financial factors on the overall efficiency and autonomy of an agency is not difficult to see. In many countries during the 1950s and early 1960s the cost of power was falling owing to economies of scale and technical progress. Power agencies were frequently able to lower their tariffs by less than the fall in costs, or even to keep them constant and hence build a strong financial position. When this situation occurred in a politically stable country, the result was an efficient and independent agency which was then better able to obtain permission to increase its rates when power costs began to rise in the 1970s. The opposite situation is also not uncommon: an agency whose earnings are controlled at too low a level finds that it cannot raise the funds necessary for its expansion so that power shortages develop which reinforce the difficulty of raising tariffs.

There is no objective way in which one can measure the efficiency of an agency or that of a whole power system. In the past few years the Bank has been collecting data on various performance indicators for power agencies such as growth of capacity and generation, energy sales, system losses, load factor, outages, kilowatt-hours sold per employee, consumers per employee, as well as financial indicators such as rate of return and debt service coverage. However, there is little in the way of systematic analysis of the data so far. Even when data of this kind are available they reflect not only the performance of the agency but also all the external factors which act upon it. For this reason, such statistics have to be interpreted; they provide only a starting point, not a conclusion.

Statements about such concepts as efficiency, good management, or financial viability inevitably have a subjective element. Furthermore, it is obvious that an agency's quality and the course of its development depend as much on the political and economic environment in which it operates as on its own internal attributes. Thus, all agencies start from a different point and travel a different route, marked to some extent by different obstacles. In some countries—for example, Argentina, Chile, Ghana, Indonesia, Nigeria, Turkey, and Uruguay—political changes or instability have created serious problems for the power agencies. In Indonesia, with the end of the Sukarno regime, the government power agency PLN was able to begin a steady process of improvement; similarly, ENDESA, the chief government utility in Chile, has strengthened its position since the severe inflation of the early 1970s. Political instability can affect power agencies not only directly—for example, by causing numerous changes in the top management—but also through financial pressures, since in periods of political instability governments are less able to withstand the consequences of increasing prices. In contrast, countries with a record of political stability frequently have strong and efficient power agencies as in Brazil, Kenya, Malaysia, Thailand, Tunisia, and until recently Tanzania, Costa Rica, and El Salvador.

The factors which determine whether a rational organization of the sector as a whole can be established seem to be more complex and more dependent on historical accident than those affecting individual agencies. One of the largest countries, Brazil, has been one of the most successful in bringing about coordinated and efficient systems throughout the sector. The authority of the central government was sufficiently greater than that of the states and the individual utilities to ensure the necessary coordination by means of legislation and control of investment resources.

Colombia is a smaller country but is more clearly divided into regions, each of which developed its own power agencies. When it became necessary to construct an interconnected network, the central government did not find it easy to bring about the necessary agreements, and the central organizations still have difficulty ensuring sufficiently coordinated planning and operation. In India, sector organization seems likely to be the most important question the central government and the states will have to deal with in the coming decade. In most smaller countries sector coordination is much easier, but in quite a few, relations between agencies have been marked as much by conflict as by cooperation.

For the sake of exposition the financial issues, the more strictly institutional problems, and the questions of investment planning, appraisal, and execution have been dealt with separately, but all these matters are closely interrelated in practice. They interact with and reenforce each other either for good or for ill, and this process determines the nature and quality of the institution. The formula for ruining a power agency is not difficult to devise. It should be kept in a state of acute financial stringency so that it is unable to expand capacity in line with demand or carry out essential maintenance. The deterioration in the quality of supply will then provide an excuse for not relieving the financial problems. An attempt can then be made to cure the problem by changing the senior management at frequent intervals, and the inexperience of the management can be used as an excuse for running the day-to-day affairs of the agency by a government committee. This will lower morale within the agency, a process which can be helped along by a low limit on salaries. The failing reputation of the agency will encourage staff to leave and make it difficult to recruit replacements so that the agency will be forced to operate with far fewer experienced engineers than it needs. After a few years of this sort of thing one can be reasonably confident that the system will be in a parlous state. The main element in the formula for institution building is therefore to refrain from doing these things; the various vicious circles can then eventually be slowed down and reversed.

The experience of institutional change as it has emerged in these chapters illustrates two familiar themes. The first is that such change is generally far more time-consuming than is initially expected. Most Bank appraisal reports contain specific dates by which the borrower hopes, or even is obligated, to make certain changes or prepare a certain study, for example. These dates are rarely met. In some degree, this is natural since the dates are deliberately chosen as targets rather than forecasts; they do not contain much by way of a contingency allowance for wholly unexpected events or even for normal human procrastination. But even allowing for this, there seems to be a strong tendency by all the parties involved—for the borrowers agree to the various dates and time schedules—to overestimate the speed at which changes can be made. Of course, the opposite occurs in some cases, such as the unexpected rapid financial recovery of PLN in Indonesia, but these are notable because they are exceptions. More typical is the time taken to establish ISA, a jointly owned company in Colombia where various parties with different interests had to reach agreement. Sometimes political changes cause substantial delays, as in Sri Lanka where the proposal for an autonomous electricity board, after having received government approval, then had to receive a second approval after a change of government. Major organizational changes are always difficult and sometimes not possible at all; it may be necessary to wait a long time before a favorable political climate develops and makes such a change possible. Institutional improvements internal to the agency generally do not take so long, but still the time can be substantial between the preparation of a study or report on some problem, the implementation of recommendations, and the appearance of tangible results. Granted that the Bank's appraisal reports and implementation schedules for projects must contain an element of ambition, the contrast between what is expected and what actually happens is large enough to create a false impression of failure. The institutional objectives set forth in appraisal reports and loan documents are rarely met in the short run. Thus almost every loan, considered in isolation, appears in this respect to have failed. But if the achievements of, say, loan five are set against the objectives of loan two and so on, the record looks considerably different.

By the time loan five is reached, however, the objectives of loan two may have been superseded. This reflects another important characteristic of institution building, which is that institutions are never completely "built"; all the objectives—financial, institutional, operational, and economic—are open-ended. Some forms of infrastructure such as roads or railways may reach a stage at which the major elements might be said to be in place, but an electric power system in a growing economy is always expanding. Larger plants and longer and higher voltage transmission lines have to be built, and the planning of investment becomes more complex as the system grows; all this demands greater expertise from the engineers and other personnel. The financial objectives also change; in the next decade they seem likely to be even more difficult to achieve than they have been in the past one. This open-ended nature of all aspects of the development of a power system is the main reason the need for more financial and operational efficiency, better sector organization, and system planning—that is, the need for improvement in the whole spectrum of institutional problems—remains and is even increasing.

The moving nature of the objectives of all power utilities and hence of the Bank's efforts to assist them, together with changing economic and political conditions which can help or hinder the utilities' attempts to meet their goals, also explain why the effectiveness of the Bank's lending operations is not capable of conclusive proof. It is hard to believe, however, that the Colombian interconnection, the rehabilitation of PLN in Indonesia, and the frequency unification in Mexico were not significantly accelerated by the Bank's intervention. The Bank has consistently urged its borrowers to permit their power agencies to maintain a strong financial position and to rationalize the organization of their power systems. It has used its ability to lend to persuade power agencies to improve their planning methods and to plan for longer periods, to strengthen their internal organization and personnel, and, more recently, to take economic factors into account in devising their tariff structures. In some countries it appears that all this pressure has produced little effect because the general political or economic situation has been too unstable. But the vast development of electric power in most of the developing world could not have occurred unless the financial and institutional bases of the systems had been greatly improved.

Many representatives of power agencies readily acknowledge the benefits, and not merely the financial contribution, they have obtained from the Bank. The number of countries borrowing from the Bank for power continues to increase. In 1980–83 seven countries received power loans for the first time. Obviously the need for capital is a preeminent reason for borrowing, but, perhaps more significant, the largest countries, such as Brazil, India, and Yugoslavia, where Bank lending is only a small percentage of power investment, still continue to borrow.

The purely financial contribution of the Bank through its lending for power development is straightforward and obvious. The nonmonetary contribution is more subtle; it is not a simple transfer of expertise from the Bank staff to that of its borrowers. The Bank's power staff does constitute a pool of experience, but most developing countries now have a considerable, if not sufficient, number of well-qualified power engineers. It is the fact that Bank lending takes place in the context of a continuous dialogue in which the staff, as objective and experienced observers, can concentrate attention on the long-term underlying tasks ahead—they can, in fact, "demand the moon" and provide some incentive to reach out for it.

At the outset of the 1980s, the constraints which may affect all external aid, including the role of the Bank and IDA, have still to be determined. Hence the extent to which the Bank will be able to continue or expand its power operations remains to be seen. Only the need is clear.

# *Appendix. Country Summaries*

THE FOLLOWING SUMMARIES of lending in selected countries are intended to provide additional illustrations of the points made in the main text, to furnish some background information on countries referred to, and to complete the coverage of the Bank's major borrowers.

## Asia

### Pakistan

The principal power agency in Pakistan is the Water and Power Development Authority (WAPDA), established in 1958. It is responsible for the construction and operation of all the major power generation, transmission, and distribution facilities in the country except for those in Karachi, which are the responsibility of the Karachi Electricity Supply Corporation (KESC). WAPDA is also responsible for the development of the Indus basin irrigation system, the largest and most complex in the world. A major transmission line connecting the WAPDA system in the center and north of the country with the KESC system in Karachi will soon be completed. It will then be possible to meet the needs of Karachi with surplus energy during the flood season from WAPDA's hydro plants on the upper reaches of the Indus and Jhelum rivers, while the generating capacity in Karachi can be used to meet some of the needs of the rest of the country during the dry season.

The Bank's power operations in Pakistan fall into three distinct categories. First, there were four loans made to KESC between 1955 and 1967. KESC is a well-managed and financially strong agency, and lending was not continued only because KESC met its borrowing needs primarily from the Asian Development Bank. Second, there was the Bank's role in the Indus Basin Development Fund and the Tarbela Development Fund, the first of which included funds for the Mangla dam on the Jhelum while the second was solely to finance the Tarbela project on the Indus. Third, the Bank made three power loans to WAPDA between 1971 and 1980.

The Bank's involvement in the Indus Basin and Tarbela Development Funds arose out of its well-known role in mediating the dispute between India and Pakistan over the division of the Indus waters. This long mediation process and the Bank's role in administering the two development funds was a unique experience.[1] After some nine years of negotiations the governments of India and Pakistan signed the Indus Waters Treaty in September 1960, under which, after a transition period, India was to have full use of the water of the three eastern tributaries of the Indus, and Pakistan would have the use of the Indus itself and its two western tributaries. An essential part of the solution was that Pakistan would receive financial assistance to build the necessary dams, barrages, and canals to implement the division of water and to develop new sources of water to replace those lost to India. The necessary assistance, amounting initially to $895 million equivalent, was contributed by the governments of Australia, Canada, the Federal Republic of Germany, New Zealand, the United Kingdom, the United States, India, and Pakistan and by the Bank. The Bank acted as administrator of the Indus Basin Development Fund into which these funds were paid as needed for expenditure on the works.

It was originally thought that there would be enough money from the initial contributions to build not only the barrages and canals but also the Mangla dam and the Tarbela dam. But it was soon clear that this was not the case. The program of works had to be reduced, the Tarbela project was postponed, and an additional $315 million was provided by the contributing governments and the Bank. At the same time, the Bank arranged to carry out a comprehensive study of the water and power sector in what was then West Pakistan. This study endorsed the feasibility and high priority of the Tarbela dam, and eventually the Tarbela Development Fund was established in 1968, with contributions from Canada, France, Italy, the United Kingdom, and the United States as well as the Bank amounting to $174 million. This amount, in addition to a balance of about $324 million available from the Indus Basin Fund, was expected to be sufficient to meet the foreign exchange cost of Tarbela.

Tarbela is the largest earth and rock-fill dam ever constructed. The powerhouse will eventually have twelve generators for a total capacity of 2,100 megawatts. The project was essentially completed in 1975 and

---

1. A brief acccount of it appears in Edward S. Mason and Robert E. Asher, *The World Bank since Bretton Woods* (Washington, D.C.: Brookings Institution, 1973), pp. 610–27. A more detailed account is given in N. D. Gulhati, *Indus Waters Treaty: An Exercise in International Mediation* (New Delhi: Allied Publishers, 1973).

power became available in 1977. However, there was a series of mishaps as the project was put into operation. At the first attempt to fill the reservoir in 1974 one of the gates on an intake tunnel could not be fully closed, and serious damage to the tunnel entrance resulted. To make the necessary repairs an additional $40 million was raised from contributors to the Tarbela Fund, with the Bank contributing $8 million, and the filling of the reservoir was postponed until 1975. Unfortunately, further problems arose. The force of the water removed parts of the concrete floor of one stilling basin, and the underlying rock eroded. Rock fell into the plunge pool at the bottom of the main spillway, and the pool sides eroded from the movement of the water. In 1978 it was estimated that the necessary remedial work would cost about $150 million. The Bank contributed a further $35 million, which brought the total amount provided by the Bank for Tarbela to $216.5 million. The balance of the $150 million required was raised from other contributors and some OPEC countries. The experience of the Tarbela project illustrates what can happen when an unprecedentedly large project—one near or at the state of the art—is constructed on a less than ideal site. It generally increased the caution with which engineers regard large projects, and within the Bank it led to renewed emphasis on the importance of design and procedures to ensure and monitor the safety of dams.

The third element in the Bank's power operations in Pakistan was three loans to WAPDA in 1971, 1976, and 1980 for the development of its transmission and distribution system. For several years after it was set up WAPDA was heavily engaged in the construction of the works resulting from the Indus Waters Treaty, but its operational role as a supplier of power grew gradually until it became a major responsibility. This required much more emphasis on financial and accounting matters, and the task of strengthening WAPDA's capability in this respect was one of the major concerns of the Bank. In addition, high losses plagued the system, partly because of long and overloaded transmission and distribution lines and partly as a result of inefficient metering and theft. When losses were identified as a problem in the first loan in 1971, they amounted to 31 percent of generation, but they continued to rise until they reached 37 percent in 1977, after which they began to decline. This continued rise in system losses was partly because the distribution investments financed by the 1971 loan were not installed as fast as planned.

The growing losses, together with insufficient tariff increases and the agency's inability to meet all the demand on the system—which in turn was the result of a shortage of funds to expand capacity—kept WAPDA's finances in a difficult state for much of the 1970s. The Bank's second and third loans were made in the context of agreements on specific tariff increases and rate covenants based on contributions to investment of 35 and 40 percent. By 1979 there was a substantial improvement, and WAPDA was able to meet 35 percent of its investment program by self-financing.

Only after 1975 was there any significant progress in reforming the financial, accounting, and managerial systems. WAPDA agreed to engage full-time consultants, and a concentrated effort was made to analyze and make recommendations to improve the operations of the Power Wing. By 1981, though substantial progress had been made in moving the Power Wing toward an efficient commercially oriented operation, considerable work remained to be done and was being continued with assistance from the loan made in 1980.

## *Singapore*

The Bank made four power loans for the Public Utilities Board of Singapore (PUB) in 1963, 1966, 1967, and 1969. PUB was established in 1963 to take over the electricity, water, and gas supply operations of Singapore City Council. The organization, responsibilities, and powers of PUB were all discussed with the Bank before the first loan was made.

The appraisal report for the final loan described PUB as "presently operating in a reasonably satisfactory manner," although it had difficulty in recruiting experienced staff to replace departing expatriates. A specific issue concerned the position of general manager. The first permanent general manager was appointed in 1966, but the Bank felt that the chairman and the board continued to perform managerial functions, a situation it regarded as unsatisfactory. When the first general manager's term expired in 1969, PUB advertised internationally for a replacement. No appointment was made, however, until PUB appointed its own chief water engineer to be general manager in 1973. During this interregnum a fifth loan was negotiated, but the Bank was not prepared to proceed with it in the absence of a general manager and it was eventually dropped.

Despite its difficulties in obtaining a general manager and other senior staff, PUB did make progress in improving its organization, particularly its financial management and accounting. With the assistance of external auditors appointed in accordance with the first loan, PUB's accounting system was established on a commercial basis, and its management reporting system was greatly improved. Power lending to Singapore was not resumed because all Bank lending to Singapore came to an end in June 1975, when Singapore became able to obtain the external capital it needed without recourse to the Bank.

## Taiwan

The Bank has made three loans to the Taiwan Power Company (Taipower), the first in 1968, the second in 1970, and the third in 1971. Taipower is government-owned and was established in 1946; it is responsible for all generating and transmission facilities within the country. Taipower is an efficient and well-managed agency, and the only institution-building aspect of the Bank loans was that funds were provided for consultants to assist with financial planning and management systems. The consultants were first engaged for this purpose in 1969, but they have been employed ever since even though, after the Bank's second loan, the foreign exchange costs were financed by the U.S. Eximbank.

# Africa

## Ghana

The first Bank loan to Ghana was in 1961 when it provided $47 million for the Volta river power project. This large project was made feasible by the simultaneous construction of an aluminum smelter by the Volta Aluminum Company (VALCO), a subsidiary of Kaiser Aluminum. The power project and the smelter formed a closely related package based on a long-term "take-or-pay" contract for the purchase of power by the aluminum company at a determined price. Since the power project and smelter together gave rise directly to substantial foreign exchange earnings, the additional external debt service required for the borrowings for the project did not place any net burden on the balance of payments. Consequently, it was possible for lenders, including the Bank, to lend substantially more for the project than they otherwise would. The Bank's loan of $47 million was unusually large for an economy the size of Ghana at that time.

When this loan was made, the Ghana government agreed to establish two new power agencies, the first, the Volta River Authority (VRA) would be responsible for the operation of the project and would sell power to the smelter, certain mining companies, and the local township at Akosombo, the site of the dam. It would also sell power to the second agency, the Electricity Corporation of Ghana (ECG), which would distribute it to all other customers in the country. ECG was also responsible for generation from diesel units in areas not connected to the main grid. Power from the Akosombo dam was sufficient to supply the smelter and to meet the entire requirements of the economy, apart from isolated diesel units, for almost two decades.

Both VRA and ECG found it difficult to recruit experienced staff, particularly for senior management positions. The Bank's second loan to VRA, made in 1969, provided for a review of the authority's organization and staffing as well as for its accounting system and cost allocation and depreciation practices. These problems were eventually largely overcome, and VRA developed into an efficient and well-managed agency.

ECG's staffing difficulties have been more persistent, and since about 1972 they have been compounded by financial problems. Because of an unexpected decline in the rate of growth of energy sales and substantial increases in salary and wage costs and in the cost of fuel, ECG's financial return declined from over 7 percent in 1973 to 3.3 percent in 1975.

The problem of electricity tariffs in Ghana is complicated by two different but related issues. The first is the long-term power sales contract between VRA and VALCO. The original contract, signed in 1962, was valid for thirty years and had no provision for adjustment. Nevertheless, VALCO did agree to certain rate increases after a tariff study was completed in 1976 by consultants jointly engaged by VRA and VALCO. The second complicating factor is that the low-cost power from Akosombo has now been fully utilized and additional power costs much more. Once the full capacity of Akosombo was reached there was, in effect, a sharp, discontinuous increase in the real economic cost of additional power. A study of the tariffs required to make the price of power reflect economic costs was completed in 1981. It concluded that ECG's rates to low-voltage consumers should be increased from 3.3 *cents* per kilowatt-hour to 10.6 cents, and VRA's rate to VALCO should be increased from 4.75 *mills* per kilowatt-hour to about 13.6 mills, in both cases an approximate tripling. Therefore, despite its relatively light dependence on oil for power generation, Ghana faces much the same problem of rising costs in the long run as do many oil-importing developing countries.

When the decision was originally made to establish two power agencies in Ghana, the Bank hoped they could eventually be consolidated. The appraisal report on the second loan to ECG in October 1970 stated that the need for two separate power organizations had been and was still under consideration by the government. It noted that VRA would have completed the Akosombo project by 1971–72 and that ECG should by then have "no serious problems in coping with its distribution expansion program," and concluded that a merger would have "appreciable advantages." The advantages noted, particularly the better utilization of qualified staff, were similar to those put forward in the rather similar case of Nigeria. Under the loan a study was made of the benefits from a merger, but no merger has taken place, largely because of opposition from VRA.

*Kenya*

The organization of the power sector in Kenya is unusual. It consists of three companies, the East Africa Power and Lighting Company (EAP&L), the Kenya Power Company (KPC), and the Tana River Development Company (TRDC). The latter two companies were created by EAP&L and, though legally and financially separate, they are managed, staffed, and operated by EAP&L.

The reasons for this are historical. EAP&L was originally a private company established in 1922, and it operated in the former U.K. dependencies of Kenya, Tanganyika, and Uganda. When these territories became independent, the latter two took over power facilities in their own territories and EAP&L's operations were confined to Kenya. KPC was established in 1955 for the purpose of constructing and operating a transmission line to connect with the Uganda power system and make use of power produced by the Owen Falls project at the source of the Nile. At that time it was financially and politically impracticable for a private company to obtain finance in the amount needed. KPC was therefore set up with a nominal equity and substantial government ownership; the project was financed almost wholly by borrowed funds. In 1964 TRDC was set up in much the same way and for essentially similar reasons to develop the hydroelectric resources of the Tana river. In 1970 the Kenya government made a bid for all the outstanding shares of EAP&L and succeeded in acquiring a controlling interest in the company. It has continued to purchase shares as they become available in the market. Eventually, after the bulk of the remaining shares have been obtained by the government, it may be advantageous to integrate all three companies. Because of the unified control by EAP&L, however, the usual problems of coordination between power agencies do not arise.

The Bank made its first power loan in 1971 shortly after the government had acquired control of EAP&L. At that time the Bank clearly felt that consolidation of the three companies was desirable, but it was equally clear that any consolidation would require study and time because of the complex financial and legal situation. The government agreed to have a study prepared on the issue, and the Bank proceeded with its loan. Since then experience has shown that the situation, despite its complications, works quite well, and pressure for consolidation has receded. Since its 1971 loan for a hydro project on the Tana river, the Bank has made a loan in 1975 for a second hydro project and two loans, in 1978 and 1980, for the preparation and construction of a geothermal project.

When Kenya became independent, the management and senior staff of

EAP&L were virtually all expatriates. In 1971 when the Bank's first loan was made, there were 189 expatriates, and the first Kenyan had just been appointed to the position of chairman after the government had acquired control of the company. At the end of 1978 the number of expatriates had been reduced to 56. That this degree of Africanization was possible with little or no decline in efficiency is largely due to the considerable attention EAP&L has given to training. It sponsors students at the local university and provides them with graduate training, usually overseas. It also operates a residential training school for all grades of staff up to technician level.

EAP&L and its associated companies have maintained a satisfactory financial condition for many years. A fuel surcharge was introduced in 1974 to pass on to consumers the higher cost of fuel oil, and a new tariff structure was introduced throughout the country in 1979 to take long-run marginal costs into account. There have been only occasional power shortages as a result of low water flows, a reduction in supplies from Uganda, or other factors beyond the control of the companies.

## Nigeria

Between 1964 and 1982 the Bank made six power loans to Nigeria. The Bank's involvement began essentially with the preparatory work for the large Kainji dam on the river Niger. Studies on the hydroelectric potential of this river began in the early 1950s, and in 1959 the Bank acted as executing agency for a UNDP-financed study of a possible multipurpose project. The study concluded that a dam at Kainji would be the most economic way of developing the power resources of the river.

The government established the Niger Dams Authority (NDA) in 1962 to construct and operate the project, and the Bank loan was made in July 1964. Other external aid was provided by the United States, the United Kingdom, Italy, and the Netherlands. This loan was the second Bank power loan to Nigeria; a few months earlier the Bank had made a loan to the Electricity Corporation of Nigeria (ECN) to assist in financing an interim program to provide power before the Kainji project was completed. ECN had been created in 1950 to consolidate a number of government power undertakings. Since it had been set up as the government's original "chosen instrument" for the power sector, the proposed establishment of NDA clearly presented problems of coordination. The appraisal report for the Kainji loan stated: "Before the start of operations at Kainji a corporate and financial consolidation of ECN and NDA would seem to be in the best interests of Nigeria." In addition to the usual advantages of a single agency the report emphasized that a merger would reduce the need for scarce managerial skills. At that time, however, the government was not willing to proceed with a consolidation and planned to rely on cooperation. In 1968 the Bank made a further loan for Kainji to cover part of an unforeseen increase in its cost, and the Bank again stated that consolidation would be the best long-term solution and hoped that the Nigerian government would reconsider this matter when more stable conditions returned to the country.

The next Bank loan was made in 1972 after the civil war (1967–69) had been brought to an end and when income from oil exports was beginning to have an impact on the economy. The physical and financial condition of ECN and NDA had deteriorated since the Bank's previous loans. Both were extremely short of experienced management personnel, and coordination between them had been "practically nonexistent." Consequently, the government had decided, after all, to merge the two agencies and commissioned a report from a firm of Canadian consultants to make recommendations on the merger and improvements in management. The new agency, the National Electric Power Authority (NEPA) was established in 1972. In 1979 Nigeria adopted a new Constitution which provided that state governments in Nigeria would have concurrent rights with the federal government to generate, transmit, and distribute electricity. In practice, however, it appears that the states will operate only in geographic areas where NEPA does not provide service.

NEPA has had to face very difficult problems, the most serious of which is the shortage of trained and experienced staff. NEPA and its predecessors have had not only to replace the departing expatriate personnel but at the same time to carry out a greatly expanded investment program. After NEPA was set up it appointed a team of consultants to assist it with problems of organization and training. Small amounts had been included in early Bank loans for training, but in the 1979 loan considerable attention was devoted to NEPA's training program and a substantial sum, $2.7 million, was allocated for training purposes. NEPA's staff shortages were rendered much more severe by the fact that it was not authorized to pay salaries competitive with Nigeria's private sector.

Although ECN, NDA, and subsequently NEPA were all obligated to earn an 8 percent financial return, for various reasons they did not do so. Earlier, the main reason was the events culminating in the civil war, but in the 1970s the ready availability of oil revenues enabled the government to provide NEPA with large loans on comparatively easy terms so that it could finance a large investment program without increasing its rates. The proportion of investment financed from NEPA's own resources fell from 30 percent in 1975 to 7 percent in 1978. A major tariff revision increased rates by over 50 percent in August 1979, shortly before the Bank's loan of November 1979. This brought NEPA's rate of return up to 3 percent and its cash generation to about 15 percent of investment.

## Tanzania

The Bank has made four loans and has provided one Special Action Credit[2] for power in Tanzania. The first loan was made in 1967 for a diesel generating plant urgently required to meet a rapidly increasing load in Dar es Salaam. The remaining four operations were for the first and second stages of the Kidatu hydroelectric development on the Greater Ruaha river in southern Tanzania. Both stages of the Kidatu scheme had major cost overruns which had to be met by additional borrowing. Thus the Bank's main loan for Kidatu I was made in 1970 for $30 million and a supplementary loan of $5 million was made in 1974. The loan for Kidatu II was made in 1976, and the Special Action Credit to assist in financing the overrun was made in 1980. The Swedish Development Agency participated in the financing of both these projects, and it also made extra finance available to help meet the cost overruns.

All these loans were made to the Tanzania Electric Supply Company (TANESCO), the government-owned agency which provides all the public power supply. TANESCO was established as a subsidiary of EAP&L, and after independence the government of Tanzania purchased all EAP&L's shares in the company.

As in the case of EAP&L, at independence TANESCO's top management and senior positions were filled by expatriates. In 1970 there were fifty but, in accordance with the government's Africanization policy, by 1975 there were only three. This rapid reduction did create some difficulties for the company. The first Tanzanian general manager took over in 1973, and between 1974 and 1976 TANESCO was reorganized along lines recommended by a firm of management consultants. TANESCO has several programs for staff training and development and operates its own training institute. The Bank loan for Kidatu II included provision for training middle-management and professional staff in power systems planning, design, and operation and in accounting and financial management.

The financing of the two Kidatu projects has been a major effort, and although some liquidity problems occurred in 1974–75, TANESCO has maintained a generally strong financial position. It has not, however, earned the 7 percent return stipulated in the Bank's loan agreements. One

2. Special Action Credits are made from resources provided to the Bank in accordance with an agreement reached in May 1978 with the European Economic Community. Under this agreement the EEC made about $385 million available to the Bank for assistance to low-income countries whose development prospects had been seriously affected by "external factors"—a phrase which in practice meant the energy crisis. The projects for which Special Action Credits were made were appraised and administered in the same way as those for which the Bank provided its own funds.

reason for this was the increase in costs arising from higher oil prices, but another was that the demand for power was significantly less than expected. In the 1960s the demand for power in Tanzania had been rising unusually rapidly, and in the early 1970s the shortage of power had held back industrial development. When the large block of power from Kidatu I became available these shortages disappeared. But in 1975 sales of power were 20 percent less than expected at appraisal.

## Middle East and North Africa

### Egypt

The best-known power project not financed by the Bank is undoubtedly the High dam at Aswan. An account of the Bank's efforts to organize finance for the High dam and its lack of success, for reasons having nothing to do either with the project or with the Bank, can be found in Mason and Asher.[3] After this episode, the first Bank loan to Egypt was made in 1954 for widening the Suez Canal, but Bank lending to Egypt did not really begin until 1970 and the first power project was financed in 1977. By 1980 two more projects had been financed. The Bank's loans were made to the Egyptian Electricity Authority (EEA), which is responsible for all electric power generation and transmission in the country.

Although not a major oil exporter, Egypt has produced an exportable surplus since 1976, and by 1978 petroleum accounted for 50 percent of foreign trade receipts. Egypt's economy is characterized by numerous controls, one facet of which has been to maintain low energy prices in an effort to encourage industrialization. Not only are internal prices for oil kept below international prices, as they are in many oil-producing countries, but there is also an effective financial subsidy on electric power arising from the low earnings of EEA. A study prepared in connection with Bank operations concluded that power prices were about one-fifth of their real value as determined by marginal cost. This policy has been the principal issue between the Bank and the government in connection with the power loans. It did not seem, at least by the time the third loan was made, that the Bank's efforts had met with much success. As the Bank has found in Mexico and elsewhere, it is far from easy to persuade a country with a surplus of energy that it should place the same value on this energy

---

3. *The World Bank since Bretton Woods*, pp. 627–42.

as does the rest of the world, rather than use it up in any way which seems desirable.

### Iran

The Bank has made four power loans to Iran, the first in 1960 and the other three in 1970, 1972, and 1974. The first loan was for the Dez irrigation and power project. The power station which was part of this project, together with other hydro plants and thermal power stations, formed the basis of the interconnected network developed in the 1960s. An Iranian Power Authority was established in 1963 but was replaced in 1964 by a new Ministry of Water and Power. A group of utility executives sponsored by the U.S. Agency for International Development recommended that the power system be operated as a single consolidated company, but this recommendation was not accepted.

The Bank's second loan was made in 1970 to the Tehran Regional Electricity Company (TREC), one of nine regional electricity distribution companies in the sector. At that time the Bank was also concerned about the organization of the sector, and the government agreed that another review of sector organization would be made. But a year later the government withdrew its support for the review and it was never carried out. The government's view was that the power sector should remain decentralized. The appraisal report for the Bank's last loan, made in 1974, commented: "This arrangement is satisfactory for the short term while operations and accounting systems are being corrected, but as a long-term aim the goal of a single national power utility seems desirable."

The Bank's third and fourth loans were made to the Iran Power Generation and Transmission Company (TAVANIR). This agency was the largest in the power sector; it generated power from thermal stations, purchased power from the hydro stations, operated the main transmission network, and sold power to the regional electric companies. In connection with its loan to TREC and its two loans to TAVANIR the Bank sought to obtain some institutional improvement, not only by taking up the issue of sector organization, but also by pushing for the introduction of uniform accounting systems and by trying to establish a training program. But the power sector had great problems. It was decentralized, only loosely coordinated, and expanding rapidly, and it had great difficulty in retaining staff in competition with Iran's booming private sector. Coordination was made more difficult by the different capabilities of the various regional agencies. TREC was strong and financially sound whereas most of the others were much weaker. After 1974 the rise in Iran's oil income brought all Bank lending to an end, and therefore no further attempts could be made to improve the power sector. The Bank's involvement with the power sector in Iran was a comparatively short one; leaving aside the 1960 loan, of which power was not the important part, it lasted only from 1970 to 1974.

## Tunisia

The Bank has made five loans to the Société Tunisienne d'Electricité et du Gaz (STEG), a government-owned corporation created in 1962 when foreign-owned utilities were nationalized. STEG is responsible for the production, transmission, and distribution of both electric power and gas for the entire country. Three of the Bank's five loans were for electric power—made in 1972, 1976, and 1981—and two for gas, one in 1971 and the other in 1980.

STEG had been in existence for eight years when Bank lending began. It was already a well-run utility and had been using consultants' services from Electricité de France for various technical and operational matters, including the development of a training program. The Bank's first power loan included funds to cover studies on system stability and power sites, organization and improvement of management information, reorganization of the accounting system, a transmission and distribution system inventory, the tariff structure, and rural electrification. According to an audit report on this loan, all these studies "had in general the expected positive results." In particular, the tariff study led to a revision of the tariff structure in 1975.

Tunisia is an oil-exporting country and therefore benefited from the oil price rise in 1973. As in many such countries, however, some domestic energy prices, including the price of fuel oil, were not permitted to rise to reflect the higher international prices. Since STEG's generating plant was heavily dependent on fuel oil, it received an implicit subsidy which enabled it to maintain its strong financial position. In connection with the Bank's second power loan in 1976 the government agreed to carry out a study of the problem of the pricing of oil, gas, and electricity. In January 1981 the government made some moves toward reducing the disparity between the domestic and international prices of gas and oil.

However, the most serious of the problems which had to be agreed on before the 1980 loan were the financial and pricing policies applied to both electric power and other forms of energy. The appraisal report remarked that internal prices of petroleum products were among the lowest in the world, with regular gasoline selling for 19 cents a gallon equivalent. It also estimated that electricity tariffs in 1979, in real terms, were lower than they were before the first rise in oil prices in 1973–74.

The 1980 loan included agreements on numerous financial measures such as tariff increases for both electricity and fuel used for power generation, revaluation of assets, preparation of consolidated financial statements, engagement of private auditors, improvement of billing procedures, a system of penalties for late payment, and preparation of a tariff study based on marginal cost.

## Latin America

### Bolivia

The government's power agency, Empresa Nacional de Electricidad (ENDE), was established in 1965 as a direct result of the discussions between the government, the Bank, and the Inter-American Development Bank which preceded the first IDA credit. Before the establishment of ENDE, the major power installations in Bolivia were owned and operated by the Bolivian Power Corporation (BPC), a private subsidiary of the International Power Company of Montreal. COMIBOL, the government-owned mining company, also produced a substantial amount of power for its own use. The remaining capacity consisted of small government or municipally owned installations.

To establish ENDE and bring about a rational organization of the power sector, the Bolivian government had to negotiate a comprehensive agreement with BPC defining the authority and responsibility of ENDE and BPC and settling various financial issues between the government and BPC. In addition, it was agreed that the government would set up an autonomous regulatory agency, the Dirección Nacional de Electricidad (DINE) to formulate policies for the power sector and to approve tariffs for all power utilities in the country. Both the first and second credits for ENDE included funds for consultants to assist in the establishment and initial operations of DINE. In 1968 the government enacted an electricity code to provide a uniform basis for the operation, regulation, and expansion of the electricity industry.

Since ENDE was established, substantial progress has been made toward an integrated power system in Bolivia. The three major systems in the north, center, and south of the country have been interconnected. In the early 1970s the government held some negotiations for purchasing BPC, but they did not lead to an agreement. More recently, ENDE and BPC have signed a preliminary agreement—after several attempts—under which ENDE would take over most of BPC's installations. ENDE has been assisted by management consultants to improve its financial, accounting, and monitoring systems. Because of the familiar policy of government control of rates in an attempt to combat inflation, the financial problems of ENDE and BPC have been the most serious issue in relations with the Bank. The situation has improved since the early 1970s but is still a major problem.

## *Ecuador*

Bank lending for power in Ecuador has been somewhat sporadic; a loan was made in 1956 and another in 1957, but the third loan did not follow until 1972 and the fourth was made in 1981. The first three loans were made to the Empresa Eléctrica Quito (EEQ), a municipally owned utility serving the Quito area. The fourth was made to the Instituto Ecuatoriano de Electrificación (INECEL), the government's principal power agency. It was set up in 1961 to be responsible for assessing power resources, planning power sector expansion, constructing and operating generation and transmission facilities, supervising other utilities, and setting electricity tariffs. At that time the sector consisted essentially of EEQ, EMELEC (a privately owned utility operating in Guayaquil), and a large number of small private and municipal operations. In its early years INECEL was mainly concerned with planning and promoting the integration of small local systems. Its first generating plant was not commissioned until 1976.

The third loan to EEQ provided for a study by management consultants of financial and administrative problems, but their work was discontinued because of a dispute over fees. EEQ's major problems in the early 1970s were lack of continuity of management and serious labor difficulties.

The Bank's involvement with sector problems in Ecuador did not begin until the discussions with INECEL which led to the 1981 loan. By that time, by a process of merger and consolidation, INECEL had reduced the number of power companies from more than a hundred to sixteen; in addition, there were 42 small municipal undertakings. It was preparing a master plan for national electrification with the assistance of consultants financed by a general technical assistance loan the Bank had made to the government in 1977. The 1981 loan reflected agreement on a number of measures for improving sectoral organization, including engaging management consultants, improving the supervision of its subsidiaries, consolidating all power services into nine regional companies, and working out a system for transferring funds between them.

## *Peru*

Between 1960 and 1967 the Bank made four loans to Electrolima (formerly Empresas Eléctricas Asociadas), the largest and best-managed utility in Peru. At that time there were numerous power agencies in Peru, many of them privately owned, and the question of how to rationalize the sector was a controversial one. A 1972 law set up a central state-owned enterprise, Electroperu, to be responsible for planning and constructing all new generating facilities and providing for an interconnected system. Although this law was sound, there were a number of practical problems in its administration. When the Bank made its next loan—also for Electrolima—it provided technical assistance for a study on coordination of the agencies in the sector, the preparation of a master plan for the interconnected system, a tariff study, and the training of personnel. On the basis of these studies the government prepared further legislation to reorganize the sector. Electroperu was made responsible for system planning, the execution of large generation and transmission projects, and the operation of interregional connections. This new law envisages a number of regional utilities to serve as distribution companies and expand their operations into the surrounding regions.

As in many countries, the financial position of Peru's power sector remained reasonably sound during the 1960s but deteriorated seriously in the 1970s. The new law provides that rates be set to earn a 12 percent return on a defined rate base, and a Bank loan made in 1982 established a series of targets leading to the 12 percent return by 1985. The law also provides for an increase in the energy tax from 5 to 25 percent, with the increase being assigned to Electroperu for investment in system expansion. If this tax revenue were regarded as revenue to Electroperu, it would increase the financial return to 16 or 17 percent. This illustrates the effect of the great increase in capital requirements in many middle-income developing countries.

# *Appendix Tables*

 1. Commitments and Number of Lending Operations
    by Economy, June 30, 1982                                         *162*
 2. Commitments and Disbursements for Electric Power               *163*
 3. Disbursements for Power Projects by Region
    and Economy                                                      *164*
 4. Investment in Power and Bank Disbursements                     *168*
 5. Lending Commitments by Sector                                  *172*
 6. Financial Rates of Return: Selected Borrowers                  *173*
 7. India: Financial Rates of Return for State Electricity Boards
    and the Effect of Rural Electrification (RE)                    *178*
 8. Summary of Project Results                                     *178*
 9. Project Results                                                *179*
10. Causes of Delay                                                *182*

*Note*: Data in the appendix tables are all for fiscal years.

Appendix Table 1. *Commitments and Number of Lending Operations by Economy, June 30, 1982*
(millions of current dollars)

| Economy | Commitments | Number of lending operations | Cumulative total |
|---|---|---|---|
| India | 3,059.0 | 25 | |
| Brazil | 1,876.8 | 35 | |
| Colombia | 1,374.2 | 27 | |
| Indonesia | 1,305.0 | 11 | |
| Mexico | 714.8 | 11 | |
| Thailand | 642.1 | 13 | |
| Argentina | 617.0 | 6 | 8,971.9 (50% of total) |
| Turkey | 456.4 | 11 | |
| Nigeria | 402.5 | 6 | |
| Malaysia | 394.3 | 10 | |
| Yugoslavia | 358.0 | 6 | |
| Egypt | 314.0 | 3 | |
| Romania | 305.0 | 4 | |
| Philippines | 281.7 | 8 | |
| Pakistan | 237.7 | 8 | |
| Honduras | 235.6 | 8 | |
| Iran | 211.0 | 4 | |
| Peru | 208.7 | 7 | |
| Zambia | 197.1 | 3 | |
| Japan | 178.2 | 9 | |
| Chile | 167.1 | 6 | 13,369.1 (75% of total) |
| Sri Lanka | 166.7 | 7 | |
| Bangladesh | 160.0 | 3 | |
| Taiwan | 149.5 | 3 | |
| Guatemala | 149.0 | 4 | |
| Syria | 145.6 | 3 | |
| Venezuela | 145.0 | 4 | |
| Panama | 141.0 | 5 | |
| Kenya | 135.0 | 4 | |
| Ghana | 127.1 | 6 | 14,855.1 (83% of total) |
| Costa Rica | 124.3 | 6 | |
| Morocco | 116.0 | 3 | |
| Rhodesia (Zimbabwe) | 115.7 | 3 | |
| Korea | 115.0 | 1 | |
| Sudan | 112.0 | 3 | |
| Algeria | 106.0 | 3 | |
| Uruguay | 106.0 | 5 | |
| Australia | 100.0 | 1 | 15,750.1 (88% of total) |
| Subtotal | | 285 | |
| Other countries (48) | 1,769.4 | 128 | 17,819.5 |
| Total number of projects | | 413 | |

Appendix Table 2. *Commitments and Disbursements for Electric Power*
(millions of current and fiscal 1981 dollars)

| Fiscal year | Commitments | | Disbursements | |
|---|---|---|---|---|
| | *Current* | *Fiscal 1981* | *Current* | *Fiscal 1981* |
| 1963 | 2,373 | — | 1,670 | — |
| 1964 | 375 | 2,027 | 326 | 1,502 |
| 1965 | 360 | 1,915 | 328 | 1,464 |
| 1966 | 254 | 1,316 | 275 | 1,196 |
| 1967 | 347 | 1,718 | 264 | 1,100 |
| 1968 | 277 | 1,248 | 267 | 1,203 |
| 1969 | 370 | 1,468 | 280 | 1,284 |
| 1970 | 527 | 1,836 | 267 | 1,068 |
| 1971 | 506 | 1,543 | 306 | 1,085 |
| 1972 | 521 | 1,386 | 368 | 1,164 |
| 1973 | 321 | 750 | 357 | 973 |
| 1974 | 769 | 1,585 | 427 | 1,024 |
| 1975 | 504 | 923 | 466 | 923 |
| 1976 | 949 | 1,528 | 517 | 961 |
| 1977 | 952 | 1,348 | 513 | 869 |
| 1978 | 1,146 | 1,460 | 601 | 844 |
| 1979 | 1,355 | 1,577 | 643 | 788 |
| 1980 | 2,392 | 2,572 | 770 | 840 |
| 1981 | 1,323 | 1,323 | 946 | 946 |
| 1982 | 2,131 | 1,988 | 1,070 | 1,064 |
| *Annual average* | | | | |
| 1964–68 | 323 | 1,633 | 292 | 1,293 |
| 1969–73 | 449 | 1,397 | 316 | 1,115 |
| 1974–78 | 864 | 1,368 | 505 | 924 |
| 1979–82 | 1,800 | 1,865 | 857 | 903 |

*Note:* To derive data in constant dollars, the Bank's commitment and disbursement deflators have been used. The disbursement deflator is derived from a unit value index of exports of machinery and equipment from developed market economies to developing countries. The commitment deflator is more complicated. Since most of the commitments of any year are not spent until later years, the real value of the commitments made in that year depends on the behavior of export prices during the later years when the funds are disbursed. The average Bank loan is disbursed over a period of seven years, with the largest proportion disbursed in the second and third years after commitment. The commitment deflator is therefore calculated as a weighted average of the disbursement deflators for the relevant following years. This means that in order to calculate the commitment deflators for recent years, the Bank has to make estimates of the disbursement deflator for some future years. If these estimates are inaccurate, the commitment deflators for recent years have to be revised as the actual disbursement deflators become available.

Appendix Table 3.  *Disbursements for Power Projects by Region and Economy*

| Region and economy | 1960 | 1961 | 1962 | 1963 | 1964 | 1965 | 1966 | 1967 | 1968 | 1969 | 1970 |
|---|---|---|---|---|---|---|---|---|---|---|---|
| **Past borrowers** | | | | | | | | | | | |
| Australia | ... | ... | ... | 31.8 | 27.0 | 23.5 | 17.1 | 0.5 | ... | ... | ... |
| Austria | 8.2 | 5.4 | 5.2 | 4.1 | 2.0 | ... | ... | ... | ... | ... | ... |
| Denmark | 5.6 | 6.0 | 3.8 | 1.8 | 8.9 | 9.9 | 4.2 | 2.5 | ... | ... | ... |
| Finland | 2.4 | 1.3 | 1.7 | 3.0 | 9.2 | 6.8 | 4.1 | 1.9 | ... | ... | ... |
| Iceland | ... | ... | ... | ... | ... | ... | ... | 3.3 | 6.6 | 6.9 | 1.0 |
| Ireland | ... | ... | ... | ... | ... | ... | ... | ... | ... | 0.0 | 2.1 |
| Italy | 4.2 | 5.0 | 12.6 | 14.2 | 1.1 | 2.9 | ... | ... | ... | ... | ... |
| Japan | 30.4 | 26.2 | 5.9 | ... | ... | 0.3 | 3.0 | 7.2 | 10.3 | 4.2 | ... |
| Malta | ... | ... | ... | ... | 0.3 | 1.9 | 2.7 | 0.5 | 0.6 | ... | ... |
| New Zealand | ... | ... | ... | ... | ... | 20.0 | 12.5 | 11.8 | 2.7 | 0.9 | 0.3 |
| Norway | 7.9 | 10.6 | 4.6 | 10.8 | 15.8 | 10.2 | 4.9 | 6.7 | 8.2 | 1.7 | ... |
| South Africa | ... | .... | 4.1 | 7.9 | 1.9 | ... | ... | 10.3 | 8.0 | 1.6 | ... |
| Subtotal | 58.7 | 54.6 | 38.0 | 73.8 | 66.1 | 75.5 | 48.4 | 44.8 | 36.5 | 15.3 | 3.3 |
| **Eastern Africa** | | | | | | | | | | | |
| Ethiopia | ... | ... | ... | ... | ... | 4.2 | 7.0 | 5.3 | 3.7 | 2.8 | 2.3 |
| Kenya | ... | ... | ... | ... | ... | ... | ... | ... | ... | ... | ... |
| Madagascar | ... | ... | ... | ... | ... | ... | ... | ... | ... | ... | ... |
| Malawi | ... | ... | ... | ... | ... | ... | ... | ... | ... | ... | 0.2 |
| Mauritius | ... | ... | ... | ... | 3.7 | 2.1 | 1.2 | ... | ... | ... | ... |
| Sudan | ... | ... | ... | ... | ... | ... | ... | ... | ... | 3.4 | 5.2 |
| Swaziland | ... | ... | ... | ... | 2.3 | 1.6 | 0.3 | ... | 0.2 | 1.6 | 0.7 |
| Tanzania | ... | ... | ... | ... | ... | ... | ... | ... | ... | 1.6 | 1.6 |
| Uganda | ... | ... | 4.3 | 2.1 | 1.7 | 0.2 | ... | ... | ... | ... | ... |
| Zambia | ... | ... | ... | ... | ... | ... | ... | ... | ... | ... | ... |
| Zimbabwe | 19.3 | 6.1 | 1.0 | ... | ... | 0.1 | 6.5 | 1.1 | ... | ... | ... |
| Subtotal | 19.3 | 6.1 | 5.3 | 2.1 | 7.7 | 8.3 | 15.0 | 6.4 | 3.9 | 9.4 | 10.0 |
| **Western Africa** | | | | | | | | | | | |
| Ghana | ... | ... | ... | 3.2 | 16.6 | 13.9 | 9.3 | 3.5 | 0.1 | 4.4 | 3.7 |
| Guinea | ... | ... | ... | ... | ... | ... | ... | ... | ... | ... | ... |
| Ivory Coast | ... | ... | ... | ... | ... | ... | ... | ... | ... | ... | ... |
| Liberia | ... | ... | ... | ... | ... | ... | ... | ... | ... | ... | ... |
| Nigeria | ... | ... | ... | ... | ... | 14.7 | 26.5 | 21.7 | 23.5 | 26.0 | 6.2 |
| Senegal | ... | ... | ... | ... | ... | ... | ... | ... | ... | ... | ... |
| Sierra Leone | ... | ... | ... | ... | ... | 2.5 | 0.6 | 0.6 | 0.2 | 0.1 | 1.1 |
| Subtotal | 0.0 | 0.0 | 0.0 | 3.2 | 16.6 | 31.0 | 36.3 | 25.8 | 23.8 | 30.5 | 10.9 |
| **Europe, Middle East, North Africa** | | | | | | | | | | | |
| Afghanistan | ... | ... | ... | ... | ... | ... | ... | ... | ... | ... | ... |
| Algeria | ... | ... | ... | ... | ... | ... | ... | ... | ... | ... | ... |
| Cyprus | ... | ... | ... | ... | 2.2 | 4.3 | 6.0 | 2.6 | 0.1 | 1.9 | 0.2 |
| Egypt | ... | ... | ... | ... | ... | ... | ... | ... | ... | ... | ... |
| Iran | ... | 14.4 | 12.0 | 13.0 | 1.1 | 1.4 | ... | ... | ... | ... | ... |
| Jordan | ... | ... | ... | ... | ... | ... | ... | ... | ... | ... | ... |
| Lebanon | 2.6 | 3.2 | 3.0 | 2.3 | 4.6 | 4.0 | 1.7 | ... | ... | ... | ... |
| Morocco | ... | ... | ... | ... | ... | ... | ... | ... | ... | ... | ... |
| Portugal | ... | ... | ... | ... | 3.3 | 5.8 | 4.8 | 16.4 | 10.3 | 8.7 | 6.1 |
| Romania | ... | ... | ... | ... | ... | ... | ... | ... | ... | ... | ... |
| Syria | ... | ... | ... | ... | ... | ... | ... | ... | ... | ... | ..: |
| Tunisia | ... | ... | ... | ... | ... | ... | ..: | ... | ... | ... | ... |
| Turkey | 0.1 | 0.2 | ... | 0.3 | 0.7 | 1.9 | 5.0 | 2.0 | 3.3 | 9.3 | 9.1 |
| Yemen Arab Republic | ... | ... | ... | ... | ... | ... | ... | ... | ... | ... | ... |
| Yemen, Peoples Dem. Rep. of | ... | ... | ... | ... | ... | ... | ... | ... | ... | ... | ... |
| Yugoslavia | ... | ... | 11.5 | 9.8 | 10.7 | 14.5 | 8.0 | 4.2 | 1.0 | 0.1 | ... |
| Subtotal | 2.6 | 17.9 | 26.6 | 25.4 | 22.6 | 32.0 | 25.5 | 25.3 | 14.8 | 20.0 | 15.5 |

| 1971 | 1972 | 1973 | 1974 | 1975 | 1976 | 1977 | 1978 | 1979 | 1980 | 1981 | 1982 |
|---|---|---|---|---|---|---|---|---|---|---|---|
| ... | ... | ... | ... | ... | ... | ... | ... | ... | ... | ... | ... |
| ... | ... | ... | ... | ... | ... | ... | ... | ... | ... | ... | ... |
| ... | ... | ... | ... | ... | ... | ... | ... | ... | ... | ... | ... |
| ... | ... | ... | ... | ... | ... | ... | ... | ... | ... | ... | ... |
| 0.2 | ... | ... | 0.3 | 2.1 | 4.2 | 3.4 | ... | ... | 0.0 | 0.0 | 0.0 |
| 5.1 | 5.5 | 4.9 | 7.3 | 12.0 | 8.2 | 4.4 | ... | ... | ... | ... | ... |
| ... | ... | ... | ... | ... | ... | ... | ... | ... | ... | ... | ... |
| ... | ... | ... | ... | ... | ... | ... | ... | ... | ... | ... | ... |
| ... | ... | ... | ... | ... | ... | ... | ... | ... | ... | ... | ... |
| ... | ... | ... | ... | ... | ... | ... | ... | ... | ... | ... | ... |
| 5.4 | 5.5 | 4.9 | 7.6 | 14.0 | 12.4 | 7.8 | 0.0 | 0.0 | 0.0 | 0.0 | 0.0 |
|  |  |  |  |  |  |  |  |  |  |  |  |
| 5.2 | 10.1 | 3.9 | 1.1 | 0.9 | 0.0 | ... | ... | ... | ... | ... | ... |
| ... | 3.4 | 8.0 | 7.7 | 2.7 | 15.4 | 15.7 | 12.6 | 13.9 | 4.2 | 31.1 | 4.6 |
| ... | ... | ... | ... | ... | ... | ... | ... | 3.8 | 6.7 | 10.8 | 12.4 |
| 1.3 | 1.7 | 2.0 | ... | 2.2 | 3.1 | 2.2 | 3.3 | 9.1 | 11.9 | 0.7 | ... |
| ... | ... | ... | ... | ... | ... | ... | ... | 0.1 | 0.8 | 1.8 | 2.0 |
| 5.6 | 2.6 | 1.3 | 0.8 | ... | 1.5 | 4.0 | 11.6 | 4.2 | 0.5 | 6.1 | 10.9 |
| 0.2 | ... | ... | ... | ... | ... | ... | ... | ... | ... | ... | 1.9 |
| 1.4 | 11.2 | 7.2 | 10.4 | 4.6 | 1.9 | 0.7 | 4.5 | 8.3 | 10.0 | 6.0 | 0.7 |
| ... | ... | ... | ... | ... | ... | ... | ... | ... | ... | ... | ... |
| 3.3 | 5.1 | 9.6 | 24.8 | 39.0 | 40.9 | 34.1 | 19.9 | 13.3 | 1.6 | 1.1 | 0.1 |
| ... | ... | ... | ... | ... | ... | ... | ... | ... | ... | ... | ... |
| 17.0 | 34.2 | 32.1 | 44.8 | 49.3 | 62.8 | 56.8 | 51.9 | 52.6 | 35.6 | 57.5 | 32.8 |
|  |  |  |  |  |  |  |  |  |  |  |  |
| 3.2 | 8.0 | 2.9 | 1.2 | ... | ... | ... | 15.4 | 6.9 | 12.5 | 14.6 | 5.9 |
| ... | ... | ... | ... | ... | ... | ... | ... | 0.3 | 0.7 | 0.0 | 3.3 |
| ... | ... | ... | ... | ... | ... | ... | ... | ... | ... | ... | 1.9 |
| 0.2 | 2.4 | 7.3 | 3.3 | 1.3 | 0.4 | 0.2 | 0.5 | 4.3 | 4.9 | 1.7 | 0.2 |
| 6.8 | 1.0 | ... | 9.4 | 24.5 | 18.4 | 18.7 | 2.5 | 0.0 | 2.5 | ... | ... |
| ... | ... | ... | ... | ... | ... | ... | ... | ... | ... | 0.3 | 0.5 |
| 2.1 | 0.6 | ... | ... | ... | ... | ... | ... | 7.2 | 0.5 | 0.3 | 0.1 |
| 12.3 | 12.0 | 10.2 | 14.0 | 25.9 | 18.9 | 18.9 | 18.5 | 18.7 | 21.0 | 16.9 | 11.9 |
|  |  |  |  |  |  |  |  |  |  |  |  |
| ... | ... | ... | ... | ... | ... | 1.2 | 8.8 | 0.0 | ... | ... | ... |
| ... | ... | ... | ... | 2.3 | 10.8 | 11.7 | 23.1 | 27.3 | 15.2 | 4.0 | 0.0 |
| 1.4 | 2.6 | 1.1 | 4.6 | 2.9 | 0.6 | 0.5 | 0.3 | ... | ... | 0.9 | 2.7 |
| ... | ... | ... | ... | ... | ... | ... | 0.4 | 7.1 | 12.8 | 17.9 | 20.5 |
| 0.0 | 2.7 | 18.2 | 23.3 | 37.8 | 42.0 | 19.7 | 5.0 | 4.4 | 0.8 | 2.4 | ... |
| ... | ... | ... | 1.2 | 1.3 | 3.8 | 2.5 | 3.5 | 0.8 | 2.4 | 8.1 | 4.3 |
| ... | ... | ... | ... | ... | ... | ... | ... | ... | ... | ... | ... |
| ... | ... | ... | 3.9 | 12.8 | 2.1 | 2.0 | 8.6 | 24.5 | 16.8 | 1.3 | 1.9 |
| 1.9 | 0.3 | ... | ... | ... | ... | ... | 1.3 | 8.6 | 21.2 | 4.9 | ... |
| ... | ... | ... | ... | ... | 28.3 | 21.9 | 28.6 | 14.3 | 11.9 | 24.4 | 116.9 |
| ... | ... | ... | ... | ... | 14.2 | 28.4 | 23.6 | 12.3 | 11.2 | 8.2 | 1.0 |
| ... | ... | 4.1 | 4.4 | 1.6 | 1.4 | 3.1 | 10.2 | 0.8 | 0.2 | 0.0 | 0.5 |
| 14.3 | 7.5 | 15.2 | 11.3 | 10.2 | 3.2 | 22.3 | 44.8 | 47.6 | 28.7 | 31.5 | 41.2 |
| ... | ... | ... | ... | ... | ... | ... | ... | ... | 0.6 | 4.0 | 1.9 |
| ... | ... | ... | ... | ... | ... | ... | ... | ... | 0.3 | 3.0 | 0.4 |
| ... | ... | ... | 6.0 | 27.5 | 21.9 | 8.8 | 5.9 | 29.5 | 33.0 | 28.1 | 24.4 |
| 17.6 | 13.2 | 38.7 | 54.7 | 96.5 | 128.3 | 122.2 | 164.2 | 177.5 | 155.1 | 138.9 | 215.1 |

*(continued on next page)*

## Appendix Table 3 *(continued)*

| Region and economy | 1960 | 1961 | 1962 | 1963 | 1964 | 1965 | 1966 | 1967 | 1968 | 1969 | 1970 |
|---|---|---|---|---|---|---|---|---|---|---|---|
| **Latin America** | | | | | | | | | | | |
| Argentina | ... | ... | 5.1 | 39.8 | 33.1 | 14.9 | 0.5 | ... | 1.9 | 25.0 | 44.0 |
| Bolivia | ... | ... | ... | ... | ... | 2.2 | 5.7 | 5.0 | 0.9 | 0.4 | 0.6 |
| Brazil | 20.7 | 21.7 | 20.2 | 15.1 | 8.2 | 4.0 | 1.7 | 5.1 | 17.8 | 24.9 | 47.4 |
| Chile | 4.1 | 4.1 | 4.5 | 3.9 | 5.1 | 5.3 | 10.0 | 4.9 | 8.7 | 5.7 | 11.4 |
| Colombia | 6.5 | 13.2 | 19.4 | 28.0 | 29.2 | 27.3 | 15.1 | 6.8 | 20.0 | 14.4 | 12.1 |
| Costa Rica | ... | ... | 4.5 | 3.4 | 2.7 | 6.1 | 7.8 | 4.8 | 1.4 | ... | 1.9 |
| Ecuador | 3.5 | 1.8 | 0.0 | ... | ... | ... | ... | ... | ... | ... | ... |
| El Salvador | 1.0 | 1.6 | 1.1 | 1.5 | 1.2 | 3.7 | 1.3 | 0.8 | ... | ... | ... |
| Guatemala | ... | ... | ... | ... | ... | ... | ... | ... | 2.8 | 4.7 | 3.5 |
| Guyana | ... | ... | ... | ... | ... | ... | ... | ... | ... | ... | ... |
| Haiti | ... | ... | ... | ... | ... | ... | ... | ... | ... | ... | ... |
| Honduras | 0.1 | 0.8 | 1.4 | 5.4 | 2.5 | ... | ... | ... | ... | 1.1 | 5.5 |
| Jamaica | ... | ... | ... | ... | ... | ... | ... | 7.1 | 8.0 | 4.1 | 1.2 |
| Mexico | 7.2 | 9.6 | 8.6 | 38.8 | 64.1 | 30.1 | 31.9 | 37.3 | 42.8 | 47.5 | 43.9 |
| Nicaragua | 0.7 | 0.3 | 1.2 | 2.8 | 4.3 | 2.9 | 0.5 | 4.0 | 0.8 | 1.0 | 3.4 |
| Panama | ... | ... | ... | 0.1 | 1.1 | 0.6 | 1.0 | 0.7 | 0.4 | 0.0 | ... |
| Peru | ... | 2.0 | 8.0 | 6.4 | 8.5 | 7.3 | 5.7 | 5.0 | 2.1 | 3.5 | 4.0 |
| Trinidad & Tobago | ... | ... | 1.5 | 4.4 | 6.5 | 3.2 | 2.3 | 1.3 | 2.1 | ... | 0.6 |
| Uruguay | 5.8 | 1.6 | 0.9 | 0.7 | 0.0 | ... | ... | ... | ... | ... | ... |
| Venezuela | ... | ... | ... | ... | 13.1 | 14.8 | 14.7 | 18.5 | 29.5 | 17.5 | 4.2 |
| Subtotal | 49.6 | 56.8 | 76.7 | 150.4 | 179.5 | 122.5 | 98.3 | 101.4 | 139.3 | 150.0 | 183.7 |
| **East Asia and Pacific** | | | | | | | | | | | |
| Taiwan | ... | ... | ... | ... | ... | ... | ... | ... | ... | ... | 3.3 |
| Fiji | ... | ... | ... | ... | ... | ... | ... | ... | ... | ... | ... |
| Indonesia | ... | ... | ... | ... | ... | ... | ... | ... | ... | ... | ... |
| Korea, Rep. of | ... | ... | ... | ... | ... | ... | ... | ... | ... | ... | ... |
| Malaysia | 2.3 | 3.4 | 5.6 | 9.7 | 5.4 | 11.6 | 14.0 | 18.1 | 16.3 | 13.0 | 5.0 |
| Papua New Guinea | ... | ... | ... | ... | ... | ... | ... | ... | ... | ... | ... |
| Philippines | 3.8 | 0.9 | 2.0 | 6.0 | 5.6 | 12.3 | 6.9 | 3.2 | 2.5 | 2.2 | 4.0 |
| Singapore | ... | ... | ... | ... | 2.1 | 7.8 | 1.6 | 11.0 | 4.8 | 9.3 | 11.5 |
| Thailand | 11.7 | 11.7 | 14.7 | 13.7 | 7.9 | 3.2 | 2.8 | 4.1 | 2.8 | 2.5 | 0.8 |
| Subtotal | 17.8 | 15.9 | 22.3 | 29.5 | 21.0 | 34.9 | 25.3 | 36.4 | 26.4 | 27.0 | 24.5 |
| **South Asia** | | | | | | | | | | | |
| Bangladesh | ... | ... | ... | ... | ... | ... | ... | ... | ... | ... | ... |
| India | 10.5 | 10.5 | 3.3 | 3.4 | 7.2 | 19.8 | 23.3 | 21.7 | 20.1 | 17.6 | 15.4 |
| Nepal | ... | ... | ... | ... | ... | ... | ... | ... | ... | ... | ... |
| Pakistan | 2.0 | 4.6 | 3.4 | 2.8 | 1.3 | 1.7 | 0.3 | 0.7 | 2.2 | 10.4 | 3.6 |
| Sri Lanka | 1.8 | 2.3 | 5.3 | 5.2 | 3.8 | 2.3 | 2.0 | 1.3 | 0.2 | ... | 0.1 |
| Subtotal | 14.3 | 17.4 | 12.1 | 11.4 | 12.3 | 23.9 | 25.7 | 23.7 | 22.4 | 28.0 | 19.1 |
| Total | 162.3 | 168.7 | 180.9 | 295.9 | 325.9 | 328.1 | 274.5 | 263.9 | 267.2 | 280.2 | 267.1 |

... Zero or negligible.

| 1971 | 1972 | 1973 | 1974 | 1975 | 1976 | 1977 | 1978 | 1979 | 1980 | 1981 | 1982 |
|---|---|---|---|---|---|---|---|---|---|---|---|
| 26.1 | 33.5 | 40.3 | 12.4 | 9.7 | ... | 0.0 | 5.5 | 16.9 | 22.6 | 26.1 | 25.7 |
| 1.7 | 3.2 | 1.4 | 1.2 | 3.2 | 2.5 | 0.5 | 10.3 | 7.9 | 6.4 | 0.0 | ... |
| 50.9 | 74.5 | 60.3 | 44.5 | 70.8 | 82.3 | 71.0 | 99.1 | 70.6 | 80.6 | 70.6 | 87.7 |
| 20.4 | 11.0 | 4.7 | 7.7 | 0.0 | ... | ... | ... | 2.2 | 1.4 | 7.0 | 1.4 |
| 20.1 | 11.6 | 15.0 | 20.2 | 23.6 | 14.3 | 11.5 | 7.8 | 14.7 | 53.3 | 52.1 | 73.1 |
| 5.5 | 3.6 | 5.0 | 1.9 | 0.3 | 1.8 | 13.8 | 11.6 | 7.7 | 2.2 | 3.8 | 9.8 |
| ... | ... | 2.8 | 0.9 | 0.8 | 0.8 | 0.4 | 1.0 | ... | ... | ... | ... |
| ... | 2.4 | 2.8 | 4.5 | 7.3 | 7.3 | 5.9 | 5.2 | 10.7 | 12.0 | 11.4 | 1.8 |
| 4.7 | 2.7 | 2.9 | 0.2 | 0.4 | ... | ... | 9.5 | 16.8 | 41.5 | 17.1 | 19.1 |
| ... | ... | 0.7 | 0.9 | 2.0 | 1.9 | 0.4 | 0.1 | 0.0 | ... | 0.3 | 2.3 |
| ... | ... | ... | ... | ... | ... | 8.2 | 5.1 | 2.6 | 1.7 | 1.7 | 6.1 |
| 3.8 | 3.7 | 6.2 | 5.8 | 4.1 | 7.7 | 10.6 | 13.3 | 7.1 | 11.4 | 31.0 | 19.9 |
| 0.3 | ... | ... | ... | ... | ... | ... | ... | 0.2 | 6.1 | 4.8 | 6.2 |
| 52.6 | 68.8 | 24.4 | 68.0 | 34.7 | ... | ... | ... | ... | ... | ... | ... |
| 6.4 | 5.0 | 0.5 | 3.6 | 3.2 | 10.8 | 2.8 | 3.2 | 3.6 | 3.9 | 5.7 | 4.5 |
| 0.4 | 6.5 | 7.3 | 13.2 | 9.1 | 18.6 | 11.0 | 3.4 | 1.5 | 4.3 | 8.0 | 24.4 |
| 3.2 | 5.7 | 3.0 | 1.9 | ... | ... | 3.4 | 6.1 | 5.8 | 5.8 | 5.8 | 4.2 |
| 0.5 | 0.8 | ... | ... | ... | ... | ... | ... | ... | ... | ... | ... |
| ... | 1.5 | 1.8 | 7.2 | 7.2 | 0.2 | 0.0 | ... | ... | 0.0 | ... | 3.0 |
| 3.7 | 9.7 | 7.7 | 7.6 | 2.6 | ... | ... | ... | ... | ... | ... | ... |
| 200.5 | 244.3 | 186.9 | 202.0 | 179.1 | 148.2 | 139.6 | 181.5 | 168.5 | 253.2 | 245.6 | 289.1 |
| | | | | | | | | | | | |
| 7.1 | 26.0 | 36.4 | 47.3 | 14.8 | 11.6 | 0.8 | 1.7 | ... | ... | ... | ... |
| ... | ... | ... | ... | ... | ... | ... | ... | 1.1 | 2.4 | 5.7 | 7.7 |
| 0.6 | 1.4 | 6.0 | 5.7 | 13.8 | 34.7 | 37.6 | 55.3 | 46.2 | 74.1 | 87.7 | 110.4 |
| ... | ... | ... | ... | ... | ... | ... | ... | ... | ... | 0.3 | 8.0 |
| 6.1 | 4.5 | 2.5 | 6.8 | 7.3 | 12.6 | 11.7 | 12.2 | 28.6 | 14.0 | 11.7 | 13.2 |
| ... | 0.9 | 3.4 | 7.7 | 11.2 | 5.8 | 2.8 | 1.4 | 0.6 | 0.2 | ... | ... |
| 3.7 | 0.2 | 1.4 | 3.7 | 9.7 | 18.7 | 19.9 | 22.6 | 13.0 | 33.4 | 45.4 | 14.3 |
| 12.1 | 5.5 | 1.6 | 0.0 | ... | ... | ... | ... | ... | ... | ... | ... |
| 4.0 | 14.1 | 23.8 | 16.5 | 16.0 | 9.7 | 17.4 | 22.4 | 21.6 | 32.6 | 48.3 | 73.5 |
| 33.7 | 52.6 | 75.1 | 87.7 | 72.9 | 93.1 | 90.2 | 115.7 | 111.1 | 156.9 | 199.3 | 227.2 |
| | | | | | | | | | | | |
| ... | ... | ... | ... | ... | ... | ... | ... | ... | 0.1 | 0.1 | 0.3 |
| 13.4 | 2.1 | 4.7 | 7.8 | 18.1 | 42.7 | 72.5 | 60.9 | 86.8 | 134.3 | 266.6 | 285.7 |
| ... | ... | ... | ... | ... | ... | ... | 6.0 | 4.9 | 9.3 | 13.2 | 3.7 |
| 4.6 | 0.5 | 1.1 | 3.5 | 6.6 | 6.1 | 3.8 | 1.8 | 21.6 | 4.6 | 7.0 | 3.4 |
| 1.3 | 3.3 | 2.9 | 4.5 | 2.8 | 4.2 | 1.5 | 1.0 | 0.9 | ... | ... | 0.3 |
| 19.3 | 5.9 | 8.7 | 15.8 | 27.5 | 53.0 | 77.9 | 69.7 | 114.3 | 148.2 | 287.0 | 293.4 |
| 305.8 | 367.7 | 356.8 | 426.6 | 465.3 | 516.6 | 513.4 | 601.4 | 642.7 | 770.0 | 945.1 | 1,070.2 |

Appendix Table 4. *Investment in Power and Bank Disbursements*
(millions of U.S. dollars)

| Region and economy | 1967 | 1968 | 1969 | 1970 | 1971 | 1972 |
|---|---|---|---|---|---|---|
| LATIN AMERICA | | | | | | |
| *Brazil* | | | | | | |
| Total investment | 473.65 | 531.57 | 571.24 | 752.57 | 873.98 | 1,087.7 |
| Bank disbursements | 5.10 | 17.80 | 24.80 | 47.50 | 50.90 | 74.5 |
| As percentage of total investment | | | | | | |
| *Colombia* | | | | | | |
| Total investment | n.a. | n.a. | n.a. | 25.17 | 34.49 | 31.97 |
| Bank disbursements | n.a. | n.a. | n.a. | 12.10 | 20.10 | 11.60 |
| As percentage of total investment | | | | | | |
| *Costa Rica* | | | | | | |
| Total investment | n.a. | n.a. | n.a. | 10.58 | 16.20 | 18.88 |
| Bank disbursements | n.a. | n.a. | n.a. | 1.90 | 5.50 | 3.60 |
| As percentage of total investment | | | | | | |
| *Mexico* | | | | | | |
| Total investment | n.a. | n.a. | n.a. | n.a. | 284.00 | 312.00 |
| Bank disbursements | n.a. | n.a. | n.a. | n.a. | 52.60 | 68.80 |
| As percentage of total investment | | | | | | |
| ASIA | | | | | | |
| *India* | | | | | | |
| Total investment | n.a. | n.a. | n.a. | n.a. | 692.50 | 812.2 |
| Bank disbursements | n.a. | n.a. | n.a. | n.a. | 13.4 | 2.1 |
| As percentage of total investment | | | | | | |
| *Indonesia* | | | | | | |
| Total investment | n.a. | n.a. | n.a. | n.a. | 13.98 | 45.78 |
| Bank disbursements | n.a. | n.a. | n.a. | n.a. | 0.6 | 1.4 |
| As percentage of total investment | | | | | | |
| *Philippines* | | | | | | |
| Total investment | n.a. | n.a. | n.a. | n.a. | n.a. | n.a. |
| Bank disbursements | n.a. | n.a. | n.a. | n.a. | n.a. | n.a. |
| As percentage of total investment | | | | | | |
| *Thailand* | | | | | | |
| Total investment | n.a. | n.a. | n.a. | n.a. | 55.6 | 90.6 |
| Bank disbursements | n.a. | n.a. | n.a. | n.a. | 4.0 | 14.1 |
| As percentage of total investment | | | | | | |

| 1973 | 1974 | 1975 | 1976 | 1977 | 1978 | 1979 | Total |
|---|---|---|---|---|---|---|---|
| 1422.4 | 1,746.1 | 2,311.1 | 2,676.3 | 3,280.5 | n.a. | n.a. | 15,727.11 |
| 60.3 | 44.6 | 70.8 | 82.3 | 71.0 | n.a. | n.a. | 549.60 |
| | | | | | | | 3.5 |
| 64.15 | 87.92 | 82.04 | 96.75 | 115.42 | 183.88 | n.a. | 721.79 |
| 15.00 | 20.20 | 23.60 | 14.30 | 11.50 | 7.90 | n.a. | 136.30 |
| | | | | | | | 19.0 |
| 27.59 | 16.22 | 23.80 | 50.41 | 80.40 | n.a. | n.a. | 244.08 |
| 5.00 | 1.90 | 0.30 | 1.80 | 13.80 | n.a. | n.a. | 33.80 |
| | | | | | | | 14.0 |
| 416.00 | 408.00 | 592.00 | n.a. | n.a. | n.a. | n.a. | 1,992.00 |
| 24.50 | 68.00 | 34.70 | n.a. | n.a. | n.a. | n.a. | 248.60 |
| | | | | | | | 12.5 |
| 781.80 | 942.20 | 1,156.1 | 1,423.4 | 1,697.1 | 2,107.8(Est) | n.a. | 9,613.1 |
| 4.7 | 7.8 | 18.1 | 42.7 | 72.5 | 60.9 | n.a. | 222.2 |
| | | | | | | | 2.3 |
| 53.01 | —[a] | 187.95 | 450.6 | 387.95 | 412.80 | 454.55 | 2,006.62 |
| 6.0 | —[a] | 19.5 | 84.8 | 37.6 | 55.3 | 46.2 | 201.4 |
| | | | | | | | 10.0 |
| 12.62 | 37.16 | 142.78 | 277.42 | 497.43 | 507.19 | 853.93 | 2,328.53 |
| 1.4 | 3.7 | 3.2 | 18.7 | 19.9 | 22.6 | 13.0 | 82.5 |
| | | | | | | | 3.5 |
| 113.5 | 86.1 | 105.6 | 137.2 | 175.6 | 317.0 | 197.7 | 1,278.9 |
| 23.8 | 16.5 | 16.0 | 9.7 | 17.4 | 22.4 | 21.6 | 145.5 |
| | | | | | | | 11.4 |

*(continued on next page)*

## Appendix Table 4 *(continued)*

| Region and economy | 1967 | 1968 | 1969 | 1970 | 1971 | 1972 |
|---|---|---|---|---|---|---|
| *Malaysia* | | | | | | |
| Total investment | n.a. | n.a. | n.a. | 15.26 | 20.86 | 27.79 |
| Bank disbursements | n.a. | n.a. | n.a. | 4.9 | 6.1 | 4.5 |
| As percentage of total investment | | | | | | |
| | | | | | | |
| AFRICA | | | | | | |
| *Malawi* | | | | | | |
| Total investment | n.a. | n.a. | n.a. | 3.38 | 5.98 | 5.71 |
| Bank disbursements | n.a. | n.a. | n.a. | 0.20 | 1.30 | 1.70 |
| As percentage of total investment | | | | | | |
| *Sierra Leone* | | | | | | |
| Total investment | n.a. | n.a. | 0.511 | 1.111 | 4.06 | 1.57 |
| Bank disbursements | n.a. | n.a. | 0.1 | 1.1 | 2.10 | 0.60 |
| As percentage of total investment | | | | | | |
| *Sudan* | | | | | | |
| Total investment | n.a. | n.a. | n.a. | n.a. | 15.82 | 9.89 |
| Bank disbursements | n.a. | n.a. | n.a. | n.a. | 5.60 | 2.60 |
| As percentage of total investment | | | | | | |
| *Tanzania* | | | | | | |
| Total investment | n.a. | n.a. | n.a. | 4.15 | 15.04 | 24.63 |
| Bank disbursements | n.a. | n.a. | n.a. | 1.60 | 1.40 | 11.20 |
| As percentage of total investment | | | | | | |
| | | | | | | |
| EUROPE AND MIDDLE EAST | | | | | | |
| *Yugoslavia* | | | | | | |
| Total investment | n.a. | n.a. | n.a. | n.a. | n.a. | n.a. |
| Bank disbursements | n.a. | n.a. | n.a. | n.a. | n.a. | n.a. |
| As percentage of total investment | | | | | | |
| *Tunisia* | | | | | | |
| Total investment | n.a. | n.a. | n.a. | n.a. | n.a. | n.a. |
| Bank disbursements | n.a. | n.a. | n.a. | n.a. | n.a. | n.a. |
| As percentage of total investment | | | | | | |

n.a. Not available.

a. Accounting procedure changed; 1974 data shown in 1975.

*Source:* Data are given only for years in which investment estimates are available.

| 1973 | 1974 | 1975 | 1976 | 1977 | 1978 | 1979 | Total |
|---|---|---|---|---|---|---|---|
| 35.0 | 56.7 | 76.4 | 134.8 | 145.6 | 173.1 | 258.5 | 947.01 |
| 2.5 | 6.8 | 7.3 | 12.6 | 11.7 | 12.2 | 28.6 | 97.2 |
| | | | | | | | 10.3 |
| 3.92 | 5.07 | 7.76 | 12.08 | 14.68 | 20.67 | n.a. | 79.45 |
| 2.00 | n.a. | 2.20 | 3.10 | 2.20 | 3.30 | n.a. | 16.00 |
| | | | | | | | 20.0 |
| n.a. | n.a. | n.a. | n.a. | n.a. | n.a. | n.a. | 7.25 |
| n.a. | n.a. | n.a. | n.a. | n.a. | n.a. | n.a. | 3.90 |
| | | | | | | | 54.0 |
| 5.56 | n.a. | n.a. | n.a. | n.a. | n.a. | n.a. | 94.18 |
| 1.30 | n.a. | n.a. | n.a. | n.a. | n.a. | n.a. | 18.10 |
| | | | | | | | 19.2 |
| 27.54 | 45.67 | 24.06 | 20.74 | n.a. | n.a. | n.a. | 161.83 |
| 7.20 | 10.40 | 5.60 | 1.90 | n.a. | n.a. | n.a. | 38.30 |
| | | | | | | | 24.0 |
| n.a. | 359.71 | 755.86 | 1,166.65 | 1,299.66 | n.a. | n.a. | 3,511.88 |
| n.a. | 6.00 | 27.50 | 21.90 | 8.80 | n.a. | n.a. | 64.20 |
| | | | | | | | 1.2 |
| 24.57 | 32.43 | 79.65 | 82.05 | 99.57 | n.a. | n.a. | 318.27 |
| 4.10 | 4.40 | 1.60 | 1.40 | 3.10 | n.a. | n.a. | 14.6 |
| | | | | | | | 5.0 |

Appendix Table 5. Lending Commitments by Sector

| Sector | Total through 1963 | 1964–68 | 1969–73 | 1974 | 1975 | 1976 | 1977 | 1978 | 1979 | 1980 | 1981 |
|---|---|---|---|---|---|---|---|---|---|---|---|
| | *Millions of current dollars* | | | | | | | | | | |
| Total commitments | 7,617 | 5,633 | 12,849 | 4,314 | 5,896 | 6,632 | 7,067 | 8,411 | 10,011 | 11,482 | 12,291 |
| Infrastructure[a] | 4,882 | 3,699 | 6,673 | 2,008 | 1,757 | 2,669 | 2,440 | 2,835 | 4,388 | 4,599 | 3,249 |
| Electric power | 2,373 | 1,613 | 2,245 | 769 | 504 | 949 | 952 | 1,146 | 1,355 | 2,392 | 1,323 |
| Agriculture | 468 | 621 | 2,585 | 956 | 1,857 | 1,628 | 2,308 | 3,270 | 2,522 | 3,458 | 3,763 |
| Industry[b] | 780 | 701 | 1,822 | 765 | 1,294 | 1,367 | 1,343 | 1,302 | 1,520 | 1,572 | 2,237 |
| Oil and gas | ... | ... | 110 | ... | 80 | 49 | 150 | ... | 112 | 385 | 650 |
| Other[c] | 1,487 | 612 | 1,659 | 585 | 908 | 919 | 826 | 1,004 | 1,469 | 1,468 | 2,392 |
| | *Percentage of total commitments* | | | | | | | | | | |
| Infrastructure[a] | 64 | 66 | 52 | 47 | 30 | 40 | 35 | 34 | 44 | 40 | 26 |
| Electric power | 31 | 29 | 17 | 18 | 9 | 14 | 13 | 14 | 14 | 21 | 11 |
| Agriculture | 6 | 11 | 20 | 22 | 32 | 25 | 33 | 39 | 25 | 30 | 31 |
| Industry[b] | 10 | 12 | 14 | 18 | 22 | 20 | 19 | 15 | 15 | 14 | 18 |
| Oil and gas | ... | ... | 1 | ... | 1 | 1 | 2 | ... | 1 | 3 | 5 |
| Other[c] | 20 | 11 | 13 | 13 | 15 | 14 | 11 | 12 | 15 | 13 | 19 |

... Zero or negligible.

a. Electric power, transport, communications, and water supply.

b. Loans to industrial development finance companies and direct loans to industry.

c. Education, tourism, population, urbanization, program lending, technical assistance, and unallocated.

Appendix Table 6. *Financial Rate of Return: Selected Borrowers*

| Borrower | 1954 | 1955 | 1956 | 1957 | 1958 | 1959 | 1960 | 1961 | 1962 | 1963 | 1964 | 1965 | 1966 |
|---|---|---|---|---|---|---|---|---|---|---|---|---|---|
| *Latin America and Caribbean* | | | | | | | | | | | | | |
| Argentina: SEGBA | n.a. | n.a. | n.a. | n.a. | n.a. | n.a. | n.a. | n.a. | 8.2 | 6.4 | 2.1 | 5.5 | 8.6 |
| Bolivia: ENDE | n.a. | n.a. | n.a. | n.a. | n.a. | n.a. | n.a. | n.a. | n.a. | n.a. | n.a. | n.a. | n.a. |
| Brazil | | | | | | | | | | | | | |
| CEMIG | n.a. | n.a. | n.a. | n.a. | n.a. | n.a. | n.a. | n.a. | n.a. | n.a. | n.a. | n.a. | 12.3 |
| Light | n.a. | n.a. | n.a. | n.a. | n.a. | n.a. | n.a. | n.a. | n.a. | n.a. | n.a. | n.a. | n.a. |
| ELECTROSUL | n.a. | n.a. | n.a. | n.a. | n.a. | n.a. | n.a. | n.a. | n.a. | n.a. | n.a. | n.a. | n.a. |
| Furnas | n.a. | n.a. | n.a. | n.a. | n.a. | n.a. | n.a. | n.a. | n.a. | n.a. | n.a. | n.a. | n.a. |
| CESP | n.a. | n.a. | n.a. | n.a. | n.a. | n.a. | n.a. | n.a. | n.a. | n.a. | n.a. | n.a. | n.a. |
| Chile: ENDESA | n.a. | n.a. | 11.4 | 14.1 | 15.8 | 5.9 | 3.0 | 4.7 | 4.0 | 3.6 | 5.0 | 7.7 | 7.7 |
| Colombia | | | | | | | | | | | | | |
| EEEB | n.a. | n.a. | n.a. | n.a. | n.a. | n.a. | n.a. | n.a. | n.a. | n.a. | n.a. | n.a. | n.a. |
| ISA | n.a. | n.a. | n.a. | n.a. | n.a. | n.a. | n.a. | n.a. | n.a. | n.a. | n.a. | n.a. | n.a. |
| Costa Rica: ICE | n.a. | n.a. | n.a. | n.a. | 0.7 | 3.3 | 3.7 | 5.0 | 7.4 | 6.0 | 6.0 | 8.4 | 9.6 |
| El Salvador: CEL | n.a. | n.a. | n.a. | n.a. | n.a. | 7.4 | 9.1 | 9.6 | 9.7 | n.a. | n.a. | n.a. | n.a. |
| Guatemala: INDE | n.a. | n.a. | n.a. | n.a. | n.a. | n.a. | n.a. | n.a. | n.a. | n.a. | n.a. | n.a. | 5.6 |
| Honduras: ENEE | n.a. | n.a. | n.a. | 16.4 | 13.8 | 21.6 | n.a. | n.a. | 19.4 | 5.6 | 6.9 | 8.3 | 10.6 |
| Mexico: CFE | n.a. | n.a. | n.a. | n.a. | 4.2 | 3.2 | 2.7 | 4.4 | 7.2 | 5.4 | 4.1 | 5.0 | 6.8 |
| Nicaragua: ENALUF | 10.0 | 10.0 | 12.7 | 9.0 | 8.7 | 0 | 9.6 | 6.7 | 8.8 | 13.1 | 16.8 | 12.1 | 10.4 |
| Panama: IRHE | n.a. | n.a. | n.a. | n.a. | n.a. | n.a. | n.a. | n.a. | n.a. | n.a. | n.a. | n.a. | n.a. |
| Peru | | | | | | | | | | | | | |
| EEA | n.a. | n.a. | n.a. | n.a. | n.a. | n.a. | n.a. | n.a. | n.a. | n.a. | n.a. | n.a. | n.a. |
| Electrolima | n.a. | n.a. | n.a. | n.a. | n.a. | n.a. | n.a. | 13.1 | 12.1 | 12.4 | 7.2 | 8.2 | n.a. |
| Trinidad & Tobago: T&TEC | n.a. | n.a. | n.a. | n.a. | n.a. | n.a. | n.a. | 4.4 | 6.1 | 4.4 | 7.8 | 8.0 | 8.2 |
| Uruguay: UTE | n.a. | n.a. | n.a. | n.a. | n.a. | n.a. | n.a. | n.a. | n.a. | n.a. | n.a. | n.a. | n.a. |
| Venezuela: EDELCA | n.a. | n.a. | n.a. | n.a. | n.a. | n.a. | n.a. | n.a. | n.a. | n.a. | n.a. | n.a. | n.a. |

(continued on next page)

173

Appendix Table 6 *(continued)*

| Borrower | 1954 | 1955 | 1956 | 1957 | 1958 | 1959 | 1960 | 1961 | 1962 | 1963 | 1964 | 1965 | 1966 |
|---|---|---|---|---|---|---|---|---|---|---|---|---|---|
| *Africa* | | | | | | | | | | | | | |
| Ghana | | | | | | | | | | | | | |
| ECG | n.a. | n.a. | n.a. | n.a. | n.a. | n.a. | n.a. | n.a. | n.a. | n.a. | n.a. | n.a. | n.a. |
| VRA | n.a. | n.a. | n.a. | n.a. | n.a. | n.a. | n.a. | n.a. | n.a. | n.a. | n.a. | n.a. | n.a. |
| Kenya: EAPL, TRDC, and KPC | n.a. | n.a. | n.a. | n.a. | n.a. | n.a. | n.a. | n.a. | n.a. | n.a. | n.a. | n.a. | n.a. |
| Liberia: PCA and LEC | n.a. | n.a. | n.a. | n.a. | n.a. | n.a. | n.a. | n.a. | n.a. | n.a. | n.a. | n.a. | 5.5 |
| Malawi: ESCOM | n.a. | n.a. | n.a. | n.a. | n.a. | n.a. | n.a. | n.a. | n.a. | n.a. | n.a. | n.a. | n.a. |
| Nigeria | | | | | | | | | | | | | |
| NEPA[e] | n.a. | n.a. | n.a. | n.a. | n.a. | n.a. | n.a. | n.a. | n.a. | n.a. | n.a. | n.a. | n.a. |
| NEPA[f] | n.a. | n.a. | n.a. | n.a. | n.a. | n.a. | n.a. | n.a. | n.a. | n.a. | n.a. | n.a. | n.a. |
| Sierra Leone: SLEC | n.a. | n.a. | n.a. | n.a. | n.a. | n.a. | n.a. | n.a. | n.a. | n.a. | n.a. | n.a. | n.a. |
| Tanzania: TANESCO | n.a. | n.a. | n.a. | n.a. | n.a. | n.a. | n.a. | n.a. | n.a. | n.a. | n.a. | n.a. | n.a. |
| *Asia* | | | | | | | | | | | | | |
| Malaysia: NEB | n.a. | n.a. | n.a. | n.a. | 7.7 | 7.1 | 8.2 | 9.0 | 10.0 | 8.6 | 7.7 | 9.0 | 10.5 |
| Papua New Guinea: ELCOM | n.a. | n.a. | n.a. | n.a. | n.a. | n.a. | n.a. | n.a. | n.a. | n.a. | n.a. | n.a. | n.a. |
| Philippines | | | | | | | | | | | | | |
| MERALCO | n.a. | n.a. | n.a. | n.a. | n.a. | n.a. | n.a. | 11.0 | 9.1 | 8.3 | 8.2 | 7.5 | 8.8 |
| NPC | n.a. | n.a. | n.a. | n.a. | 4.6 | 6.1 | 5.6 | 6.2 | n.a. | n.a. | 6.7 | 8.7 | 8.6 |
| Sector[g] | n.a. | n.a. | n.a. | n.a. | n.a. | n.a. | n.a. | n.a. | n.a. | n.a. | n.a. | n.a. | n.a. |
| Singapore: PUB | n.a. | n.a. | n.a. | n.a. | n.a. | n.a. | n.a. | n.a. | n.a. | n.a. | n.a. | n.a. | n.a. |
| Taiwan: Taipower | n.a. | n.a. | n.a. | n.a. | n.a. | n.a. | n.a. | n.a. | n.a. | n.a. | n.a. | n.a. | n.a. |
| Thailand: EGAT | n.a. | n.a. | n.a. | n.a. | n.a. | n.a. | n.a. | 5.3 | 8.2 | 7.3 | 2.8 | 4.8 | 6.8 |
| *Others* | | | | | | | | | | | | | |
| Cyprus: EAC | n.a. | n.a. | n.a. | n.a. | n.a. | n.a. | n.a. | n.a. | n.a. | n.a. | n.a. | n.a. | n.a. |
| Ireland: ESB | n.a. | n.a. | n.a. | n.a. | n.a. | n.a. | n.a. | n.a. | n.a. | n.a. | n.a. | n.a. | n.a. |
| Tunisia: STEG | n.a. | n.a. | n.a. | n.a. | n.a. | n.a. | n.a. | n.a. | n.a. | n.a. | n.a. | n.a. | n.a. |
| Turkey | | | | | | | | | | | | | |
| TEK | n.a. | n.a. | n.a. | n.a. | n.a. | n.a. | n.a. | n.a. | n.a. | n.a. | n.a. | n.a. | n.a. |

| Borrower | 1967 | 1968 | 1969 | 1970 | 1971 | 1972 | 1973 | 1974 | 1975 | 1976 | 1977 | 1978 | 1979 |
|---|---|---|---|---|---|---|---|---|---|---|---|---|---|
| *Latin America and Caribbean* | | | | | | | | | | | | | |
| Argentina: SEGBA | 6.7 | 12.4 | 8.2 | 5.4 | 1.8 | 1.3 | 0.6 | -1.4 | -3.7 | -1.5 | 1.6 | 5.2 | -1.9 |
| Bolivia: ENDE | n.a. | n.a. | 5.7 | 5.0 | 5.7 | 9.3 | 8.3 | 6.8 | 5.7 | 8.4 | 10.6 | n.a. | n.a. |
| Brazil | | | | | | | | | | | | | |
| CEMIG | 12.6 | 11.1 | 11.7 | 13.5 | 11.9 | 15.5 | 15.1 | 15.7 | 16.7 | 16.4 | n.a. | n.a. | n.a. |
| Light | n.a. | n.a. | n.a. | n.a. | n.a. | 14.8 | 15.1 | 13.5 | 12.0 | 13.9 | 9.1 | n.a. | n.a. |
| ELECTROSUL | n.a. | n.a. | n.a. | 11.4 | 10.2 | 10.7 | 9.7 | 11.5 | 11.6 | 15.1 | 14.3 | n.a. | n.a. |
| Furnas | n.a. | n.a. | 18.5 | 18.8 | 15.4 | 18.2 | 17.0 | 17.0 | 18.9 | 25.0 | 16.8 | 15.4 | n.a. |
| CESP | n.a. | 7.0 | 3.7 | 7.8 | 8.3 | 11.2 | 12.9 | 16.9 | 16.5 | n.a. | n.a. | n.a. | n.a. |
| Chile: ENDESA | 7.0 | 3.9 | 6.5 | 8.2 | 5.3 | 5.9 | 5.0[b] | n.a. | n.a. | n.a. | n.a. | n.a. | n.a. |
| Colombia | | | | | | | | | | | | | |
| EEEB | n.a. | 8.0 | 9.3 | 10.2 | 10.5 | 10.9 | 12.5 | 10.6 | n.a. | n.a. | n.a. | n.a. | n.a. |
| ISA | n.a. | n.a. | n.a. | n.a. | 1.7 | 1.9 | 1.3 | 1.5 | 1.7 | 12.0 | n.a. | n.a. | n.a. |
| Costa Rica: ICE | 6.3 | 7.5 | 8.8 | 10.9 | 12.0 | 13.2 | 12.7 | 10.2 | 9.4 | 12.3 | 13.9 | n.a. | n.a. |
| El Salvador: CEL | 11.1 | 10.8 | 12.0 | 11.6 | 11.0 | 12.1 | 11.0 | 9.5 | 5.2 | 20.2 | 21.3 | 16.4 | n.a. |
| Guatemala: INDE | 5.9 | 5.0 | 5.6 | 5.9 | 5.5 | 10.3 | 9.6 | 6.1 | 6.5 | 8.2 | 2.8[c] | n.a. | n.a. |
| Honduras: ENEE | 12.5 | 14.5 | 16.0 | 15.6 | 10.7 | 9.8 | 10.7 | 8.9 | 7.7 | 5.9 | 5.6 | n.a. | n.a. |
| Mexico: CEE | 9.7 | 9.8 | 9.8 | 8.8 | 8.1 | 7.5 | 8.1 | 5.7 | 3.9 | n.a. | n.a. | n.a. | n.a. |
| Nicaragua: ENALUF | 10.9 | 12.8 | 12.7 | 13.3 | 11.2 | 9.4 | 4.4 | 5.8 | 8.4 | 9.3 | 8.5 | 8.5 | n.a. |
| Panama: IRHE | n.a. | 1.0 | 4.1 | 7.3 | 7.7 | 11.3 | 11.7 | 4.5 | 7.5 | 2.8[d] | 6.9 | n.a. | n.a. |
| Peru | | | | | | | | | | | | | |
| EEA | n.a. | 9.0 | 9.3 | 9.9 | 8.8 | 8.3 | 6.5 | 6.7 | 7.3 | 7.3 | 8.8 | 8.9 | 9.3 |
| Electrolima | n.a. | n.a. | n.a. | n.a. | n.a. | n.a. | n.a. | n.a. | n.a. | n.a. | n.a. | n.a. | n.a. |
| Trinidad & Tobago: T&TEC | 8.1 | 10.0 | 12.0 | 8.1 | 9.4 | n.a. | n.a. | n.a. | n.a. | n.a. | n.a. | n.a. | n.a. |
| Uruguay: UTE | n.a. | n.a. | n.a. | n.a. | n.a. | n.a. | 3.4 | -0.3 | n.a. | 6.6 | 8.0 | n.a. | n.a. |
| Venezuela: EDELCA | n.a. | n.a. | 3.9 | 2.2 | 3.2 | 5.0 | 5.3 | 5.6 | 7.0 | n.a. | n.a. | n.a. | n.a. |

*(continued on next page)*

# Appendix Table 6 (continued)

| Borrower | 1967 | 1968 | 1969 | 1970 | 1971 | 1972 | 1973 | 1974 | 1975 | 1976 | 1977 | 1978 | 1979 |
|---|---|---|---|---|---|---|---|---|---|---|---|---|---|
| **Africa** | | | | | | | | | | | | | |
| **Ghana** | | | | | | | | | | | | | |
| ECG | n.a. | 26.3 | 14.6 | 10.9 | 7.7 | 7.1 | 7.1 | 2.6 | 3.3 | n.a. | n.a. | n.a. | n.a. |
| VRA | n.a. | n.a. | 3.8 | 4.0 | 4.1 | 4.6 | 5.1 | 6.0 | 5.5 | n.a. | n.a. | n.a. | n.a. |
| Kenya: EAPL, TRDC, and KPC | n.a. | n.a. | n.a. | n.a. | n.a. | 8.2 | 7.2 | 6.9 | 7.9 | 5.5 | 8.6 | n.a. | n.a. |
| Liberia: PCA and LEC | 4.4 | 4.2 | 5.4 | 6.6 | 6.3 | 8.2 | 4.2 | 5.1 | 6.6 | 6.9 | n.a. | n.a. | n.a. |
| Malawi: ESCOM | n.a. | n.a. | n.a. | n.a. | n.a. | n.a. | 10.3 | 8.2 | 13.2 | 12.9 | 14.5 | n.a. | n.a. |
| **Nigeria** | | | | | | | | | | | | | |
| NEPA[e] | n.a. | n.a. | n.a. | n.a. | n.a. | 6.7 | 4.6 | 4.1 | 4.4 | 3.7 | 3.3 | 3.9 | n.a. |
| NEPA[f] | n.a. | n.a. | n.a. | n.a. | n.a. | 4.4 | 3.3 | 1.7 | 0.8 | -0.4 | -0.7 | -0.5 | n.a. |
| Sierra Leone: SLEC | n.a. | n.a. | 7.1 | 12.6 | 9.9 | 3.4 | n.a. | n.a. | n.a. | n.a. | n.a. | n.a. | n.a. |
| Tanzania: TANESCO | n.a. | n.a. | n.a. | 10.3 | 10.4 | 11.7 | 13.4 | 6.3 | 2.4 | 1.2 | 4.0 | n.a. | n.a. |
| **Asia** | | | | | | | | | | | | | |
| Malaysia: NEB | 10.9 | 10.1 | 8.8 | 9.9 | 11.0 | 10.8 | 11.9 | 10.2 | 8.2 | 13.4 | 10.2 | n.a. | n.a. |
| Papua New Guinea: ELCOM | n.a. | n.a. | n.a. | 7.6 | 7.4 | 10.5 | 5.9 | 6.9 | 8.7 | 11.3 | n.a. | n.a. | n.a. |
| **Philippines** | | | | | | | | | | | | | |
| MERALCO | 8.4 | n.a. | n.a. | n.a. | n.a. | n.a. | n.a. | n.a. | n.a. | n.a. | n.a. | n.a. | n.a. |
| NPC | 10.4 | 9.3 | 4.8 | 2.7 | 4.51 | 5.7 | 4.8 | 3.4 | 6.4 | -3.5 | n.a. | 7.56 | 6.3 |
| Sector[g] | n.a. | n.a. | n.a. | 10.0 | 10.2 | 10.7 | 11.0 | 8.7 | 8.2 | 9.9 | n.a. | n.a. | n.a. |
| Singapore: PUB | 9.3 | 12.4 | 12.6 | 14.5 | 15.7 | 15.9 | n.a. | n.a. | n.a. | n.a. | n.a. | n.a. | n.a. |
| Taiwan: Taipower | n.a. | 8.3 | 10.4 | 12.5 | 11.1 | 11.7 | 11.1 | 15.2 | 13.3 | 8.5 | 11.0 | n.a. | n.a. |
| Thailand: EGAT | 6.4 | 10.3 | 6.5 | 7.9 | 10.1 | 9.3 | 9.5 | 8.3 | 7.6 | 10.4 | n.a. | n.a. | n.a. |

*Others*

| | | | | | | | | | | | | | |
|---|---|---|---|---|---|---|---|---|---|---|---|---|---|
| Cyprus: EAC | n.a. | n.a. | n.a. | 10.4 | 9.3 | 10.0 | 10.4 | 5.3 | 7.9 | 10.7 | 12.3 | 13.4 | 15.9 |
| Ireland: ESB | n.a. | n.a. | n.a. | 7.3 | 5.8 | 7.5 | 8.2 | 7.1 | n.a. | n.a. | n.a. | n.a. | n.a. |
| Tunisia: STEG | n.a. | n.a. | n.a. | n.a. | 12.7 | 9.8 | 11.6 | 12.0 | 15.8 | 13.9 | 13.8 | n.a. | n.a. |
| Turkey | | | | | | | | | | | | | |
| TEK | n.a. | n.a. | n.a. | 3.9 | 4.9 | 7.9 | 2.7 | 2.3 | 2.3 | 4.1 | 3.6 | 3.9 | n.a. |
| CEAS | n.a. | n.a. | n.a. | n.a. | 14.1 | 14.9 | 9.2 | 8.6 | n.a. | n.a. | n.a. | n.a. | n.a. |

n.a. Not available.

a. As calculated by the World Bank.

b. As calculated in accordance with Chilean law; figures for 1956–58 on basis of unrevalued assets.

c. From 1972 the return is for the whole sector; that is, INDE and EEG together.

d. Assets were revalued in 1976.

e. Return on book value of assets.

f. Return on revalued assets.

g. NPC and MERALCO together.

Appendix Table 7.  *India: Financial Rates of Return for State Electricity Boards and the Effect of Rural Electrification (RE)*

| State Electricity Board | Target date[a] | 1970 | 1976 | 1977 | 1978 | 1979 RE | 1979 Other operations | 1979 Total |
|---|---|---|---|---|---|---|---|---|
| Andhra Pradesh | 1973 | 7.4 | 7.7 | 9.0 | 9.5 | −2.5 | 12.0 | 9.5 |
| Bihar | 1975 | 2.0 | 7.0 | 8.1 | 7.5 | 1.6 | −0.2 | 1.4 |
| Gujarat | 1974 | 7.0 | 7.9 | 9.7 | 9.5 | −1.3 | 11.0 | 9.7 |
| Haryana | 1974 | 8.0 | 7.2 | 6.4 | 7.2 | −2.5 | 12.5 | 10.0 |
| Maharashtra | 1974 | 8.7 | 10.0 | 13.0 | 15.3 | −2.6 | 16.8 | 14.2 |
| Punjab | 1974 | 7.7 | 7.4 | 8.2 | 9.5 | −0.4 | 9.9 | 9.5 |
| Rajasthan | 1977 | 4.9 | 8.7 | 9.2 | 7.9 | 1.8 | 6.8 | 8.6 |
| Uttar Pradesh | 1975 | 5.1 | 4.6 | 5.8 | 3.0[b] | −6.1 | 7.9 | 1.8 |
| West Bengal | 1975 | 8.5 | 6.0 | 9.5 | 7.2[b] | −0.3 | 9.7 | 9.4 |

a.  The second transmission credit stipulated that a return of 9.5 percent should be earned by the date shown.

b.  Estimate.

## Appendix Table 8.  *Summary of Project Results*

| | |
|---|---|
| 1. Projects with results generally in line with expectations | |
| Hydro projects | 21 |
| Steam thermal | 4 |
| Gas turbines and diesels | 5 |
| Transmission and distribution | 3 |
| Subtotal | 33 |
| 2. Projects delayed but still in line with demand | 9 |
| 3. Projects completed ahead of demand | 4 |
| 4. Projects delayed with adverse consequences | 18 |
| 5. Others | 2 |
| Total | 66 |

*Note:* For identification of these projects, see appendix table 9.

## Appendix Table 9. *Project Results*

| Economy and project | Cost overrun (percent) | Time overrun |
|---|---|---|
| *1. Projects with results generally in line with expectations* | | |
| *Hydro projects* | | |
| Argentina (El Chocon) | 13[a] | None |
| Bolivia (Santa Isabel) | 4[b] | 18 months[d] |
| Brazil (Estreito) | Project extended | None |
| Brazil (Porto Colombia) | 38 | None |
| Brazil (Jaguara) | 28 | Negligible |
| Brazil (Marimbondo) | 11[b] | None |
| Brazil (Salto Osorio) | 36[b] | 2–6 months |
| Chile (El Toro) | 11 | Minor[c] |
| Colombia (Canoas and El Colegio) | 12 | None |
| El Salvador (Cerron Grande and Ahuachapan) | 9[b] | 2 months |
| Ghana (Volta extension) | 43[b] | None |
| Guatemala (Jurun-Marinala) | 14 | None |
| Honduras (Rio Lindo, Stage II) | 23 | 6 months |
| Kenya (Kamburu) | 9 | 5 months |
| Malawi (Tedzani, Stage I) | 19 | 4 months |
| Papua New Guinea (Upper Ramu) | 9.2[b] | 5–9 months |
| Taiwan (Tachien, two units) | 7 | 6 months |
| Tanzania (Kidatu, Stage I) | 33 | None |
| Thailand (Sirikit hydro) | None | None |
| *Thermal projects: Steam* | | |
| Argentina (Segba III) | 21 | 6 months |
| Cyprus (Moni III) | 6[b] | 9 months |
| Taiwan (Talin Unit No. 4) | None | 3 months early |
| Trinidad and Tobago (Port of Spain) | 10 | None |
| *Thermal projects: Gas turbines and diesels* | | |
| Bolivia (Santa Cruz gas turbine and transmission) | −16[b] | Negligible |
| Costa Rica (Gas turbines and diesels) | 5 | None |
| El Salvador (Soyapango gas turbine) | 27 | None |
| Haiti (Diesel, Port-au-Prince) | 14 | 9 months |
| Tunisia (Gas turbines, transmission and distribution) | None | 2–3 months |
| *Transmission and distribution* | | |
| Brazil (Distribution) | __e | __e |
| Ghana (Distribution) | 9[b] | 6 months |
| Honduras (Transmission and distribution) | 13 | 15–22 months |

*(continued on next page)*

## Appendix Table 9 *(continued)*

| Economy and project | Cost overrun (percent) | Time overrun |
|---|---|---|
| *2. Projects delayed but still in line with demand* | | |
| Brazil (Volta Grande hydro) | 130 | 15 months |
| Colombia (Medellin-Guatape) | None | 2 years, 9 months |
| Ireland (Tarbert I) | 30 | 11 months |
| Ireland (Tarbert II) | 17 | 11 months |
| Peru (Matucana hydro) | 6 | 10 months |
| Philippines (Bataan thermal) | n.a. | 18 months |
| Sierra Leone (Diesel units and distribution) | 19 | 14 months |
| Sudan (Roseires hydro) | −9 | 13 months |
| Turkey (Keban transmission) | 100 | 2 years |
| *3. Projects completed ahead of demand* | | |
| Ghana (Distribution) | None | 12 months |
| Thailand (South Bangkok thermal) | None | 1 month ahead |
| Ethiopia (Finchaa hydro) | 20 | 9 months |
| Philippines (Maria Cristina additional unit in hydro plant) | n.a. | 22 months |
| *4. Projects delayed with adverse consequences* [f] | | |
| Brazil (Xavantes hydro) | 660 | 3 years |
| Costa Rica (Tapanti hydro) | 84 | 16 months |
| Guatemala (Escuintla thermal) | None | 21 months |
| Taiwan (Tachien hydro) | 71 | 6 months |
| Turkey (Kadincik hydro) | 16 | 13 months |
| *Projects where delay led to some load shedding* | | |
| Colombia (ISA) | 34 | 4 years, 9 months |
| Colombia (Chivor hydro) | 54 | 15 months |
| Ecuador (Nayon hydro) | −18 | 23 months |
| Malaysia (Additions to Post Dickson thermal I) | −25 | 2 years |
| Malaysia (Additions to Post Dickson thermal II) | 15 | 24–27 months |
| Panama (Bayano hydro) | 88 | 19 months |
| Uruguay (Unit at Battl thermal plant and distribution) | 72 | 35 months |
| Venezuela (Extension of Guri hydro project) | 74 | 24 months |
| *Transmission and distribution projects* | | |
| Brazil (Subtransmission and distribution) | —[g] | 1–3 years |
| India (Transmission) | −4 | 18 months |
| Indonesia (Distribution) | 33 | 3½ years |
| Iran (Tehran distribution) | —[h] | 3 years |
| Pakistan (Transmission, distribution, and substations) | —[i] | —[i] |

## Appendix Table 9 *(continued)*

| Economy and project | Cost overrun *(percent)* | Time overrun |
|---|---|---|
| *5. Other Projects* | | |
| Ireland (Pumped storage) | 79 | 6–14 months |
| Liberia (Hydro expansion) | 20 | 4–7 months |
| Liberia (Thermal expansion) | 26 | 12–24 months |

n.a. Not available.

*Note:* Most generation projects include some associated transmission lines. The delay shown relates to the main part of the project. Cost overruns and time overruns are from World Bank data.

a. Plus or minus depending on method of calculating exchange rate.

b. In constant prices.

c. Except for Alto Polcura division, which was delayed by five years.

d. Appraisal report recognizes schedule as being optimistic.

e. These projects were parts of larger programs that were substantially enlarged in the course of execution.

f. The consequences of the delay in Costa Rica and Taiwan were earlier installation of gas turbines; in Guatemala, the use of more expensive plant; in Turkey, the use of higher-cost power; and in Brazil, uncertain.

g. Program substantially altered during execution.

h. Project doubled in scale during execution.

i. The project was delayed by the separation of Bangladesh in 1971; construction did not start until 1976 and continued until 1980.

Appendix Table 10. *Causes of Delay*

| Economy and Project | Delay | Exogenous causes | Endogenous causes |
|---|---|---|---|
| Brazil (Xavantes) | 3 years | — | Borrower taken over by another utility with consequent adjustments to project |
| Chile (Alto Polcura diversion) | 5 years | Tunneling problems | Labor problems |
| Colombia (Guatape hydro) | 2 years, 9 months | Geological and other construction problems; delay in delivery of equipment | — |
| Colombia (ISA and Chivor) | 4 years, 9 months | — | Shortage of finance |
| Costa Rica (Tapanti) | 16 months | Tunneling problems | — |
| Guatemala (Escuintla) | 21 months | Initial site found subject to flooding | — |
| Indonesia (First and second distribution) | | — | Procurement lengthy official procedures and unfamiliarity with Bank requirements for international competitive bidding. |
| Malaysia (Port Dickson) | 27 months | Delay in delivery of equipment | — |
| Panama (Bayano) | 19 months | Financial and personnel difficulties of civil works contractor | Revision of project design and additional test drilling; borrower's lacked experience with large contractor |
| Philippines (Bataan) | 18 months | Financial problems of contractor | Procurement: lengthy official procedures |
| Philippines (Maria Cristina) | 22 months | | |
| Turkey (Kadincik) | 13 months | Tunneling problems | — |
| Uruguay (Battl extension) | 35 months | Delay in delivery of equipment | Procurement: lengthy procedures |
| Venezuela (Guri extension) | 24 months | — | Procurement: only bid was very high and contract was therefore divided in two parts |

# Index

Accounting, 69, 123, 133
Administración Nacional de Usinas y
  Transmisiónes Eléctricas (UTE.
  Uruguay), 61–62
Africa, 19, 64, 149–56, 157–58
Agencies. *See* Power agencies
Agua y Energia Eléctrica (AYEE,
  Argentina), 91, 93
Ahauchapan geothermal project (El
  Salvador), 109
Anderson, Dennis, 66n, 105n
Appraisal reports, 43, 70, 125, 142,
  143; actual project and, 108–09;
  evolution of, 98–102; influence of,
  135; nature and purpose of, 7–8;
  project cycle and, 9; sector approach
  in Philippines and, 46; as World Bank
  activity, 18. *See also* Project
  evaluation
Argentina: as Bank borrower, 59–61;
  power sector in, 90–94; tariffs and, 29
Asia, 64, 145–49
Asher, Robert E., 4, 121n, 122, 146n
Auditing, 33, 106, 111, 115, 118; delay
  and, 112
Austria, 16, 98

Baum, Warren C., 7n, 9, 11n
Binga project (Philippines), 41
Bolivia, 158–59
Brazil, 19, 23, 65, 77, 86, 97, 126, 141;
  capacity to carry out project in,
  68–69; organization of power sector
  in, 45, 83–84; regulatory legislation in,
  35–38; tariff rates in, 25, 47–48

Cameron Highlands hydroelectric project
  (Malaysia), 34–35
Canaveral hydropower project
  (Honduras), 34

Cash generation, 28–29, 58, 67, 108,
  119
Cavers, David F., 25n
Centrais Elétricas Brasileiras, S.A.
  (ELETROBRAS, Brazil), 83–84, 86
Centrais Elétricas de Minas Gerais
  (CEMIG, Brazil), 36
Central America, 17
Central Electricity Authority (CEA,
  India), 85, 86, 87
Central Elétrica de Furnas (Brazil), 36
Central Hidroeléctrica del Rio
  Anchicaya Ltd. (CHIDRAL, Colombia),
  94
Ceylon Electricity Board (CEB), 72
Chile, 67, 88; regulatory legislation in,
  38–39
Chivor hydro project (Colombia), 96
CNFL power agency (Costa Rica), 45, 88
Colombia, 15, 19, 143; organization and,
  94–97, 142; rate covenant and, 26
Comisión Ejecutiva Hidroeléctrica del
  Rio Lempa (CEL, El Salvador), 43–44,
  45, 46
Comisión Federal de Electricidad (CFE,
  Mexico), 25, 29, 53–55, 80–82
Comisión Nacional de la Cuenca del
  Plata (CONCAP, Argentina), 93
Companhia Estadual de Energie
  Eléctrica (CEEE, Brazil), 68–69
Companhia Hidro-Eléctrica do São
  Francisco (CHESF, Brazil), 83
Compañia de Alumbrado Eléctrico de
  San Salvador (CAESS, El Salvador),
  43–44, 45, 46
Compañia Argentina de Electricidad
  (CADE, Argentina), 91
Compañia Italo Argentina de
  Electricidad (CIAE, Argentina), 91, 92,
  93

Compañia de Luz y Fuerza del Centro (Centro, Mexico), 80, 81, 82
Compañia Panamania de Fuerza y Luz (FyL, Panama), 89
Consultants, 10, 57, 85, 109n, 117; advisory services and, 42; in Argentina, 92; in Colombia, 94–95; dams and, 134–35; Indonesia's PLN and, 72; Liberia's LEC and, 76; in Mexico, 80; World Bank and, 77–78
Contractors, 77–78
Costa Rica, 109, 113; organizational arrangement in, 45–46, 88; rate covenants in, 46
Costs: Argentina and long-run marginal, 61; defining marginal, 31–32; effects of overrun in, 113–15, 117–18; estimated and actual, 108–10; fuel, 40; seminars for managers and, 66
Covenants. *See* Loan agreements
Cukurova Electric Company (CEAS, Turkey), 63–64, 71

Damodar Valley Corporation (DVC), 26, 49, 66
Dams, 16, 134–35, 149, 152, 153
Debt limitation, 33, 54
Debt service, 5n, 60, 64
Delay: audit reports and, 112; causes of, 182; consequences of, 115–17, 118–20; costs and, 109; importance of, 111; of loans, 137; timing overestimation and, 142–43
Demand, 119, 129, 139; developing countries and, 130–31; estimation difficulties and, 103; forecasting, 104–07; project appraisal and, 99, 100, 101
Denmark, 21
Developing countries, 3; energy and, 126–27; energy consumption and, 129; energy demand and, 130–31; power industries in, 79
Disbursement: delay and, 111–12; difficulties with, 111; for electric power, 163; investment in power and, 168–71; by region and economy, 164–67; supervision of, 135–36; World Bank commitments and, 20–23
Distribution, power, 12, 22, 157; delay in projects for, 116; in Istanbul, 63;

project selection and, 15

East Africa Power and Lighting Company (EAP&L), 151–52
Economic Commission for Latin America, 17
Ecuador, 159
Education. *See* Training
Efficiency, 6; energy losses and, 128; engineering, 133; engines and, 129; increase in fuel, 58; of SEGBA (Brazil), 92; utility prices and, 30–32, 65–66
Egypt, 155–56
El Cajon hydro project (Honduras), 17
El Chocon project (Argentina), 59, 93
Electricity Authority of Malta, 71
Electricity Corporation of Ghana (ECG), 149, 150
Electricity Corporation of Nigeria (ECN), 152, 153
Electricity Generating Authority of Thailand (EGAT), 47
Electricity (Supply) Act of 1948 (India), 50, 51, 52, 85
Electric power systems: energy sector and, 126–28; evolution of, 12–14; open-ended nature of, 143; organization of, 40–49
El Salvador, 16, 106, 109; financial problems of, 43–44; organizational structure of, 45–46, 88; rate covenant and, 46
Empresa Eléctrica de Guatemala S.A. (EEG), 44, 45, 88
Empresa Energia Eléctrica de Bogotá (EEEB, Colombia), 94, 97
Empresa Nacional de Electricidad (ENDE, Bolivia), 158–59
Empresa Nacional de Electricidad (ENDESA, Chile), 38, 39, 88
Empresa Nacional de Luz y Fuerza (Nicaragua), 71
Empresa Pública de Medellin (EPM, Colombia), 94, 96
Entidad Binacional Yacyreta-Apipe (EBY, Argentina), 59
Environmental concern, 125–26
Evaluation. *See* Project evaluation
Expansion of power systems, 5, 116, 134; least-cost and, 115; project appraisal and, 100, 101, 102; rural

electrification and, 102–04

Finance: cost and time overruns and, 113–20; efficiency pricing and, 30–32; estimated and actual costs and, 108–10; investment programs and, 66–67; Mexico and, 54–56; perspective on, 64–65; project appraisals and, 8; protective covenants and, 10; supervision and, 45; World Bank approach to rates and, 24–30; World Bank objectives and, 132–33, 144; World Bank projects and, 5–6
France, 80
Fuel: hydro projects and, 99, 102, 127; increase in efficiency and, 58; prices for, 117, 130; rise in price of, 16, 62, 63, 102, 115, 117, 124, 126, 131

General Public Utilities Corporation of New York, 41
Generation, power, 12, 108; in Argentina, 94; in Colombia, 95, 97; demand and, 103; investment programs and, 67; in Thailand, 47
Geothermal power, 16, 109
Ghana, 106, 126, 149–50
Global Guarantee Fund (Brazil), 45, 47–48, 86
Government: power agencies and, 70–73; program effectiveness and, 4; project support and, 138; rates and, 33–35; World Bank covenants and, 73
Guatemala, 44, 45; organization and, 88–89; rate covenant in, 46
Guayabo project (El Salvador), 43–44

Hidroeléctrica Norpatagonia (HIDRONOR, Argentina), 59, 93
Honduras, 17, 106; financial policies and, 34
Hydroelectric power, 13, 44, 114, 115, 117; in Argentina, 93, in Brazil, 84; in Colombia, 97; costs and, 117–18; disbursement and delay and, 111–12; environment and, 125–26; financial policies and, 34–35; in India, 84, 86; priority of, 127; project appraisal and, 98, 99, 102; project in Honduras, 17; in Turkey, 64

ICE power agency (Costa Rica), 45–46, 88, 113
India, 15, 19, 23, 107, 118, 119; as major borrowing country, 49–52; organization and, 84–87, 142; rate of return and, 178; tariffs and, 26–27
Indonesia, 19, 80, 143; as Bank borrower, 56–59; rehabilitation of PLN in, 71–72
Industria Eléctrica Mexicana, S.A. de C.V. (IEMS), 80, 81
Inflation: in Argentina, 59, 60; cost estimates and, 109, 110; cost overruns and, 115; financial policies and, 35–40; lending practices and, 20–21; rate increases and, 25; social and economic conflicts and, 65; in Turkey, 62; in Uruguay, 61, 62; World Bank loans and, 140
Institution building, 3, 6, 70, 122, 123, 132–33
Instituto Nacional de Electrificacion (INDE, Guatemala), 44, 45
Integration of systems, 13, 15, 80–97, 158
Interconexión Eléctrica, S.A. (ISA, Colombia), 95–96, 97
International Development Association (IDA), 5n, 132, 135; disbursements and, 20; education and, 74; electric power project commitment of, 18–19; India and, 49; Indonesia and, 56–57
International Monetary Fund (IMF), 63
Investment planning, 9, 128, 137; in Brazil, 68–69, 84; financial covenant and, 33; financial stringency and, 66–67; integrated networks and, 14; investment requirements and, 129–31; long-term, 118; in Mexico, 81; project appraisal and, 99; the World Bank and, 133, 168–71
Iran, 156–57
Italy, 16, 128

Japan, 19, 21; tariff rates and, 25

Karachi Electricity Supply Corporation (KESC, Pakistan), 145
Kariba dam, 16
Kenya, 16, 151–52
Kenya Power Company (KPC), 151

Kothagudem project (India), 50
Koyna hydroelectric project (India)
   26–27, 49–50

Loans (World Bank): additional
   (subsequent), 136; lending areas of,
   121–22, 124; methods and, 133–37;
   objectives and, 132–33, 137–39;
   results of, 139–44; trend in, 20–22;
   volume and distribution of, 18–20;
   withholding of, 135. *See also* World
   Bank; *names of specific agencies and
   countries*
Loan agreement, 7, 10, 136; application
   of World Bank policy and, 33–40;
   financial covenants and, 28, 32–33,
   64; industry organization and, 40–45;
   rates and, 25, 26, 29; sectoral
   organization and, 45–49
Latin America, 17, 80; loans to, 19;
   power regulation in, 25n
Legislation, 111; in Brazil, 68, 69; in
   India, 50, 51, 52, 85; inflation and
   lag in, 37–39
Liberia, 107
Liberian Electric Company (LEC), 76
Luzon grid, 46, 47

Malaysia, 34–35
Management: efficiency pricing and, 66;
   power agencies and, 71–72, 73–74,
   76; problems with, 122–23; project
   appraisals and, 8
Manila Electric Company (MERALCO,
   Philippines), 41–43, 89–90; rates and,
   46
Mason, Edward S., 4, 121n, 122, 146n
Metropolitan Electricity Authority (MEA,
   Thailand), 47
Mexican Light and Power Company
   (Mexlight), 24–25, 53, 80, 81, 82
Mexican Tariff Commission, 29
Mexico, 19, 66, 155; organization and,
   80–83; tariff rates and, 24–25, 29; as
   World Bank borrower, 53–56
Munashinghe, Mohan, 66n

Nacional Financiera (NAFINSA, Mexico),
   54
Nare project (Colombia), 94

National Department of Water and
   Electric Energy (DNAEE, Brazil), 38,
   45, 65, 83, 86
National Electric Power Authority
   (NEDA, Nigeria), 153
National Electricity Board (NEB,
   Malaysia), 65
National Hydro Power Corporation
   (NHPC, India), 86, 87
National Power Corporation (NPC,
   Philippines), 41–43, 46, 89–90
National Thermal Power Corporation
   (NTPC, India), 86, 87, 119
Nelson, James R., 25n
New Zealand, 19, 21
Nicaragua, 17, 71, 113; financial
   policies of, 34
Niger Dams Authority (NDA), 152, 153
Nigeria, 66, 119–20, 152–53
Norway, 16, 21
Nuclear power, 127–28

Organization of power industry, 13–14,
   40–49, 79–97; in Argentina, 90–94;
   authority and, 70–73; in Brazil, 69,
   84; in Colombia, 94–97; management
   and, 71–72, 73–74; procurement and,
   77–79; project appraisals and, 8;
   training and, 74–77
Office of Environmental Affairs, 125
Oil: importing of, 126–27; price rise
   in, 16, 62, 63, 102, 115, 117, 124,
   126, 131
Operations Evaluation Department (OED,
   World Bank), 4, 106, 111, 115, 134
Owens Falls project (Uganda), 16

Pakistan, 145–48
Panama, 89
Paulo Alfonso hydro project (Brazil),
   126
Peru, 159–60
Perusahaan Listrik Negara (PLN,
   Indonesia), 57–58, 71–72, 143
Philippine Electric Plant Owners
   Association, 41
Philippines, 106; financial problems of,
   40–43; power sector in, 89–90; rates
   and, 46–47
Pinedo Plan (Argentina), 91

Power agencies, 44, 45; ability to carry
out projects and, 3, 68–70, 73;
building successful, 123; formula for
running, 142; investment programs
and, 66–67; management and,
71–72, 73–74; manpower and, 74;
organization and, 13–14, 70–73;
procurement and, 77–79; training and,
73–77; World Bank and, 140–41
Power Development Council
(Philippines), 41–42
Pricing: Bank's approach to, 24–30;
Colombia's power system and, 95, 97;
efficiency, 30–32, 65–66, 140; of
energy types, 127; shadow, 103, 131;
of power, 131; public utility, 18
Procurement, 77–79
Project evaluation, 4; Indonesia's PLN
and, 57; lending for electric power
and, 5; project cycle and, 11. *See also*
Appraisal reports
Project Performance Audit Reports, 4
Project Preparation Facility, 112–13
Projects: ability to carry out, 3, 68–70,
73; analyses of, 100; bidding on, 78;
cycle of, 9–12; defining, 108;
estimated and actual costs of, 108–10;
government support of, 138;
international aspects of, 16, 17; results
of, 178, 179–81; timing of, 110–13;
World Bank policies and, 4–5
Project selection, 14–17, 99
Provincial Electricity Authority (PEA,
Thailand), 47
Public Utilities Board of Singapore
(PUB), 148

Rate of return, 140; autonomous
agencies and, 123, 125; financial
agreements and, 28, 32–33; financial
results and, 64, 65; incremental
financial, 100, 102; in India, 178; in
Mexico, 53, 54, 55, 56; in Philippines,
42–43; project appraisals and, 8,
98–102; rate base and, 25n, 28–29,
30; sectoral organization and, 45–49;
by selected borrowers, 173–77; in
Turkey, 62; in Uruguay, 62
Regional Electricity Boards (REBs,
India), 85, 87

Regulation, 13, 25n; inflation and,
37–39
Repayment, 10, 24, 44, 135
Rural electrification, 157, 178; in India,
51–52; system extension and, 102–04;
World Bank policies and, 15–16,
124–25
Rural sector, 8, 15–16. *See also* Rural
electrification

Salaries, 74, 92, 123
Servicios Eléctricos del Gran Buenos
Aires (SEGBA, Argentina), 59–60,
91–94
Singapore, 21, 148
Société Tunisienne d'Electricité et du
Gaz (STEG, Tunisia), 157
South Africa, 19
Squire, Lyn, 125n
Sri Lanka, 72, 143
State Economic Enterprise (SEE,
Turkey), 74
State Electricity Boards (SEBs, India),
50–51, 52, 85
Supervision missions, 11; loans to Brazil
and, 68; the World Bank and, 134
Swaziland Electricity Board, 71
Sweden, 16

Taiwan, 149
Tana River Development Company
(TRDC, Kenya), 151
Tanzania, 154–55
Tariffs, 14, 119, 140, 157, 159; in
Argentina, 59, 60, 61, 92; in Brazil,
69; economic efficiency and, 30–32;
governments and, 33–35; increases in,
41, 43, 53, 55, 56, 58, 59, 62, 65,
92, 150, 155; in Indonesia, 58;
lifeline, 32; in Mexico, 54, 55, 56;
rate of return and, 100, 101; in
Turkey, 62–63, 64; World Bank
approach to, 24–30
Tata Consulting Engineers (India), 76
Tata Power Company (India), 49
Tax: Argentina's power agencies and,
60; Brazil's electrification, 68;
electricity (India), 51; power
consumption (Mexico), 54, 55

Technical assistance, 10, 122, 132
Tehran Regional Electricity Company
  (TREC, Iran), 156
Tendler, Judith, 104n, 125n
Thailand, 19, 98, 126; financial policies
  and, 35
Thermal power, 13, 15, 84, 86, 89,
  115, 119, 128; costs and, 117–18
Time overruns. *See* Delay
Timing (project), 110–13; estimation of,
  142–43; overruns and, 115–17,
  118–20
Training, 6, 58, 137, 156; power
  agencies and, 74–77
Transmission, power, 12, 22, 108; in
  Argentina, 94; in Colombia, 95, 97;
  high voltage, 13; in India, 52;
  international connections and, 17;
  loans for, 15; new technology and, 77;
  rural electrification and, 16; in
  Thailand, 47; in Yugoslavia, 48
Trombay project (India), 49
Tunisia, 157–58
Tunnels, 109, 134
Turkey, 62–64, 71, 118–19
Turkish Electricity Authority (TEK),
  62–63, 64, 71, 74, 119
Turvey, Ralph, 66n

Uganda, 16
Urban sector: electric power system and,
  12, 40; World Bank policies and, 8
Uruguay, 61–62, 107
Usinas Eléctricas do Paranapanema
  (USELPA, Brazil), 36

van der Tak, Herman, 125n

Venezuela, 21, 107
Villaflores, Vilma, 105n
Volta Aluminum Company (VALCO,
  Ghana, 149, 150
Volta River Authority (VRA, Ghana),
  149–50

Warford, Jeremy, 66n
Water and Power Development
  Authority (WAPDA, Pakistan), 145–48
World Bank: achievements of, 139–44;
  borrowers and, 137–39; changing
  approach to development, 121–26;
  debt limitation and, 33; disbursement
  and, 20–23; electric power project
  commitment of, 18–20; energy studies,
  126, 129; financial policy toward
  Mexico, 54–56; governments and rates
  and, 33–35; industry organization and,
  40–45; inflation and, 20, 35; methods
  of, 133–37; objectives of, 132–33,
  137–39; power systems and, 12–14;
  project cycle of, 9–12; as project
  lender, 7–8; project selection and,
  14–17; regulatory legislation and,
  35–40; sectoral organization and,
  45–49; sector studies, 18; utility
  pricing and, 24–32. *See also* Loans;
  *names of specific agencies and
  countries*

Yacyreta project (Argentina), 59
Yanhee Project (Thailand), 35, 47, 98
Yugoslavia, 23, 48, 67

Zambia, 16
Zimbabwe, 16

The full range of World Bank publications, both free and for sale, is described in the *Catalog of Publications*; the continuing research program is outlined in *Abstracts of Current Studies*. Both booklets are updated annually; the most recent edition of each is available without charge from the Publications Sales Unit, Department B, The World Bank, 1818 H Street, N.W., Washington, D.C. 20433, U.S.A.

Hugh Collier, a staff member of the World Bank for more than thirty years, has held many positions in both operational and economic departments, including chief evaluation officer in the Operations Evaluation Department.